"FINANC
IS YOUR FIR
FINANCIAL

Gerald Ford

MONEY MATTERS

Your IDS Guide to Financial Planning

"MONEY MATTERS touches on almost every topic you need to consider whether you're just getting started or a veteran in need of a financial check-up."

Vernon Jordan, Jr.,
Akin, Gump, Strauss, Hauer & Feld

"In MONEY MATTERS you'll learn how determination and planning can make your financial goals a reality."

Debbi Fields,
Creator of Mrs. Fields' Cookies

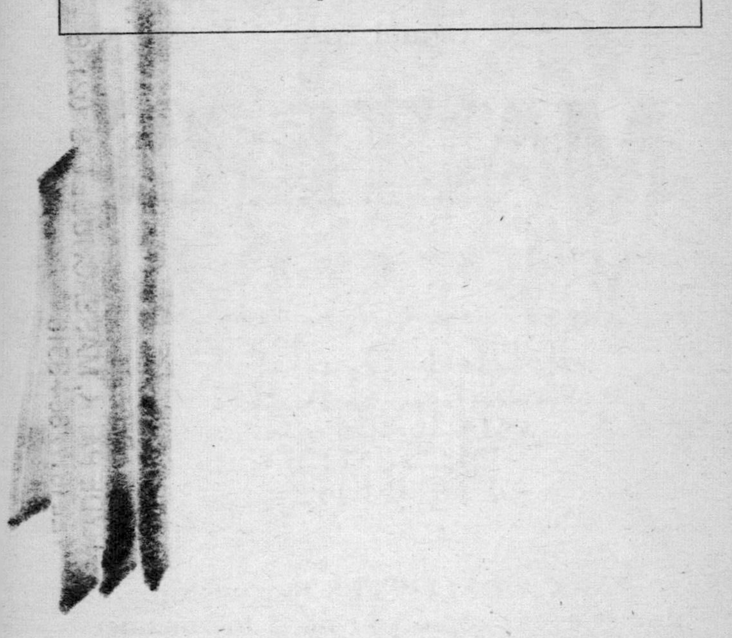

MONEY MATTERS

Your IDS Guide to Financial Planning

AVON BOOKS NEW YORK

This book went to press in February 1990 and reflects the rules and regulations in effect at that time. IDS Financial Services Inc. has worked diligently to ensure that the information contained herein is current and accurate, but rules and regulations will vary from place to place and change over time. To be sure that you have the most current and complete information possible, IDS recommends that you verify all facts and figures with a trusted adviser or another qualified professional prior to making investment or tax-related decisions.

All graphic elements in this book are from IDS Financial Services Inc. sources, unless otherwise indicated.

MONEY MATTERS: YOUR IDS GUIDE TO FINANCIAL PLANNING is an original publication of Avon Books. This work has never before appeared in book form.

AVON BOOKS
A division of
The Hearst Corporation
105 Madison Avenue
New York, New York 10016

Published by arrangement with IDS Financial Services Inc.
Library of Congress Catalog Card Number: 89-92476
ISBN: 0-380-75776-1

First Avon Books Printing: April 1990

Printed in the U.S.A.

RA 10 9 8 7 6 5 4 3 2 1

To all the IDS people who epitomize our corporate values and who, through their enthusiastic commitment to financial planning, make our company a great place to work and to do business with.

SPECIAL THANKS

To David Highfill, assistant editor and project manager extraordinaire.

The following IDS people have shared their professional and technical expertise. Without their significant contributions, this book would not have been possible:

Bevan Alvey
Bob Arndt
Tim Bechtold
Bill Bergstrom
Jane Bergstrom
Bernie Bunce
Ted Busboom
John Carney
Gaile Champ
Kerri Champion
Lynn Closway
Susan Cogger
Juanita Costa
Bob Cummings
Alan Dakay
Marie Davis
Bernie DeLaRosa
Sharon Dobbs
Mike Ducar
Bill Erager
Meredith Fernstrom
Pete Gallus
Harry Gatsch
Barb Hagen
Wendell Halvorson
John Harris
Colleen Harvey
Bob Healy
Bob Heinz
Leslie Hollister
Jan Holman
Diane Hummon
Sherry Johnson
Nancy Jones
Doug Jordal
Tom Kelly
Carol Kerner
Marian Kessler
Bob Kiefer
Jack Kispert
Mary Komornicka
Lynne Krehbiel
Lori Larson
Ryan Larson
Gary Lawrence
Rianne Leaf
Katie Libbe
Jim Litwin
Vicki Lubben
Sidney Madlock

Tim Meehan
Jim Mitchell
Christine Naylor
Lynn Nelson
Dale Norton
Frans Officer
Edith Philippi
Char Pozzini
Susan Sawyer
Glenn Seibel
Scott Scovel
Jim Solberg
Ross Stonesifer
Janet Sundeen
Catherine Taylor
Jack Thomas
Julie Trombley
Jean Uble
Lorri Vanhove
Russ Vestlie
Jerry Wade
Mike Weiner
Dan Williams
Mike Wolf
Gene Zelazny
Gary Ziemer
Laura Zimmerman

CONTENTS

PART 4
YOUR HOME

PART 5
MANAGING YOUR DEBTS

PART 6
YOUR INCOME TAXES

PART 7
YOUR RETIREMENT

PART 8
YOUR ESTATE PLAN

FOREWORD

by Harvey Golub
president and chief executive officer
of IDS Financial Services Inc.

Whether you're just starting out or are a sophisticated money manager, you know that you can do a better job of managing your finances and preparing to meet your financial goals and objectives.

In this guide, we cover a broad range of topics—from how to determine your current net worth to how to preserve your wealth by using estate planning vehicles. Our intent is not to try to make you an expert on each topic, but rather to provide an overview of the financial planning process to help you better understand how to make it work for you.

And although there's debate about what actually constitutes financial planning, we believe it's really very simple: it's a process for identifying your financial concerns and objectives, analyzing your current situation, finding realistic solutions, and implementing them over time.

IDS' business mission is "to help people achieve their financial objectives—prudently and thoughtfully—through financial planning." While I obviously believe in IDS' financial planning philosophy and process, I realize that most readers are not interested in reading IDS sales literature.

Therefore, we have written this book to educate people about financial planning basics—not to discuss IDS. In other words, we are trying to be objective. You can implement any or all of the strategies you learn about with

IDS . . . or with another competent financial services company. Of course, I hope you choose to do business with us.

This book discusses the six areas of financial planning that we believe everyone should consider: examining *your current financial situation*, looking at whether you have *adequate protection against risks*, *accumulating wealth*, managing *income taxes*, planning for *retirement*, and *preserving wealth.*

Through this book, we'd like to share with you information that can help you achieve your financial goals—whether they include planning for retirement, sending your children to college or putting enough money aside for a vacation you've always dreamed of taking but could never afford.

This is neither a do-it-yourself handbook nor does it cover all aspects of financial planning. While our financial planning philosophy and process is straightforward, the execution is sometimes complex. Our objective in writing this book is to provide you with enough information to ask appropriate questions of your financial advisers and make intelligent decisions about your financial situation.

We hope *Money Matters: Your IDS Guide to Financial Planning* will inspire you and get you started on that financial planning process you've been postponing for years. Now is the time to get control of your financial future. Achieving your financial dreams can be a reality if you begin planning now.

PART 1

YOUR FINANCIAL PLAN

- WHERE DO YOU BEGIN?

CHAPTER 1

WHERE DO YOU BEGIN?

You have dreams and plans for the future—buying a new home, going on that once-in-a-lifetime vacation, sending the children to college, enjoying a comfortable retirement.

But unless you set specific goals and objectives for yourself and take action to achieve them, your dreams and plans will remain just that.

By setting goals, you also set priorities.

When you set priorities, you make choices you might not have even thought about before—choices that are important to you and, possibly, to members of your family.

The key here is to take charge of your financial future rather than letting your future control you.

One of the first steps in your financial planning process should be to set goals. These goals will be as unusual and as individual as you are. They might include saving enough money to repaint the house or to take that dream vacation in Tahiti or even to pay off your credit card debt.

By having a plan in place, you have a much better chance of reaching your goals and of coming out ahead—rather than always trying to catch up with your day-to-day expenses.

In this book, we help you get started. If you do your own financial planning, it pays to become familiar with the financial planning techniques that follow. If you work with a trusted financial adviser, this book will give you the confidence you need to ask the right questions about your lifetime finances—putting you in the driver's seat.

By achieving an educated perspective on the money in your life, you will be on the road to financial security.

That's because, if you're like most of us, you need to acquire enough money to make your dreams come true. The good news is, you can—by planning.

In this chapter, we help you get started.

Where do you begin?

There's only one way to achieve financial security, and that is to identify your goals and objectives and set out to meet them.

Financial planning is simply the process that enables you to identify these goals and objectives and design strategies—and a timetable—to help achieve them.

By definition, goals are the big picture, the broad outline of what you want to achieve—"I want to pay for my child's college education," for example.

Objectives are more specific and tied to a timetable—"I want to accumulate $58,000 by 1996 to pay for my child's college education."

It's easier to figure out what you really want in life if you take one step at a time.

You know what you want, and when, so what's next?

The next step is to sketch out your financial picture as it exists today. After all, you can't calculate where you're going unless you know where you stand now. You'll need to take a look at your income and expenses—that is, your cash flow—and your net worth, that is, your assets minus your liabilities.

Take a look at exactly how much is available to you in case of an emergency. How much discretionary income do you have after you meet your fixed expenses? And how much of that can you comfortably save or invest?

To find answers to these questions, most financial planners will look at your cash flow and suggest drawing up a budget. A budget lets you see how you're actually spending your money today compared to how you *think*

FIGURING YOUR NET CASH FLOW

MONTHLY EXPENSES

$	Mortgage payment
$	Vacation home mortgage
$	Automobile loan
$	Personal loans
$	Charge accounts
$	Federal income taxes
$	State income taxes
$	FICA (Social Security)
$	Real estate taxes
$	Other taxes
$	Utilities (electricity, heat, water, telephone, etc.)
$	Household repairs and maintenance
$	Food
$	Clothing/laundry
$	Education expenses
$	Child care
$	Automobile expenses (gas, repairs, etc.)
$	Other transportation
$	Life insurance
$	Homeowner's insurance
$	Automobile insurance
$	Medical, dental, disability insurance
$	Unreimbursed medical, dental expenses
$	Entertaining/dining
$	Recreation/travel
$	Club dues
$	Hobbies
$	Gifts
$	Major home improvements & furnishings
$	Other expenses
$	Total monthly expenses

FIGURING YOUR NET CASH FLOW

MONTHLY INCOME	
$	Wages, salary, tips
$	Alimony, child support
$	Dividends from stocks, mutual funds, etc.
$	Interest on savings accounts, bonds, CDs, etc.
$	Social Security benefits
$	Pensions
$	Other income
$	Total monthly income

NET CASH FLOW	
$	Total monthly income
$	Total monthly expense
$	Discretionary monthly income (Subtract your expenses from your income)

you're spending it. You can use your budget to help you change your spending patterns.

Budgeting is simple—or rather, should be. Your family budget can be as uncomplicated as you want to make it. In fact, we urge that you do keep it simple.

If recording monthly spending eats up a lot of time, most of us won't do it. And if the budget imposes unreasonable restrictions on you or other family members, you will most likely ignore it. Think of your family budget as a financial planning and management tool.

The preceding page contains a sample budget worksheet with spending categories already listed. You can use that budget worksheet, you can modify it, or you can draft your own. And you can have as many or as few categories in your budget as you like.

What's important is that you do it.

The next step is to examine your financial position and calculate your net worth. Net worth is what's left after you subtract what you owe (your liabilities) from what you own (your assets). It's a snapshot of your current financial situation.

If you have more assets than liabilities, you have a positive net worth; in other words, you're in good financial shape.

If you have a negative net worth—you owe more than you own—you have a little more work in store for you.

Comparing your current net worth to previous years' may tip you off to problems in the way you're conducting your day-to-day financial affairs. The results can also make you feel good about the efforts you've made to take control of your financial life.

Financial planners use net worth statements to identify trends in their clients' financial well-being. A sample net worth statement is shown on the next two pages.

What is a financial planner?

A financial planner is simply a person who works with you to establish and achieve your financial needs and objectives. People who belong to just about any income level may benefit from a planner's services.

A planner will provide information for saving on your taxes, buying adequate insurance coverage, and drawing up an investment plan. Planners have a working knowledge of retirement and estate planning, investments, insurance, and family budgeting—including strategies for planning for a child's education. Planners also refer their clients to other professionals, for complicated tax or legal matters, for example.

Whether a planner can be helpful to you—consumer groups say—depends not so much on your net worth as on the time you're willing to devote to analyzing your own situation, your financial circumstances, and your knowledge of finances.

FIGURING YOUR NET WORTH

PROPERTY ASSETS

$	Residence
$	Vacation Home
$	Furnishings
$	Automobiles
$	Art, jewelry or other valuables

EQUITY ASSETS

$	Stocks
$	Equity mutual funds
$	Variable annuities
$	Limited partnerships
$	Rental real estate
$	Business interests

FIXED ASSETS

$	U.S. government bonds and agency securities
$	Municipal bonds
$	Corporate bonds
$	Face amount certificates
$	Fixed-dollar annuities
$	Other fixed assets

CASH RESERVE ASSETS

$	Checking accounts
$	Savings accounts
$	Money-market funds
$	Certificates of deposit
$	Other cash reserve accounts
$	Total assets

FIGURING YOUR NET WORTH

LIABILITIES

$	Home mortgage
$	Other mortgage
$	Automobile loans
$	Bank loans
$	Personal loans
$	Charge account debt
$	Other debts
$	Total liabilities

NET WORTH

$	Total assets
$	Total liabilities
$	Net worth (subtract your liabilities from your assets)

Set a goal for yourself

What would you like your net worth to be

$ ________ in 5 years?

$ ________ in 10 years?

Where do you turn if you would like help from a financial planner?

There's no secret about finding a good planner. You go about choosing a planner in the same way as any professional, such as a doctor or lawyer. Ask your friends, relatives, and business associates to recommend a planner that they're happy with.

Planners come in a variety of types.

Some are self-employed while others are agents or employees of financial planning companies.

The planner you select may have a number of licenses—for example, a license for selling insurance or securities. Many planners have extensive professional and educational experience. Some planners have professional designations—such as CFP, CLU, ChFC, and CFA.

While these designations don't guarantee quality, they may indicate a greater interest on the planner's part in providing competent and ethical service. They also may ensure that the planner participates regularly in continuing-education programs.

Here are some additional tips to follow:

- Make sure your planner tailors his or her investment recommendations according to your risk tolerance. For example, if you're a conservative investor, you'll want a planner with a conservative investment strategy.
- A good planner will listen carefully to your opinions and goals and help you devise clear strategies to meet your objectives. He or she should also present you with an understandable written analysis, as well as recommendations of your needs, your goals, and your present financial situation—a financial plan.
- A planner should indicate that he or she will regularly review your progress in meeting your goals.
- Find out if the planner sells products as well as advice and whether he or she is limited to recommending products offered by one company.
- Be sure you understand a planner's fee schedule. You

should receive a written summary of his or her services and fees.

- Find out how much involvement you'll have with managing your investments.
- A planner should also be able to refer you to other financial planning experts, as well as to reliable sources of information.
- Consider interviewing a financial planner before making a choice, and prepare for the interview by writing down your specific goals, your expectations of the planner, and your attitudes toward investing. Do you want someone who can help you with your investment strategies, or someone who can help you plan your entire financial future?
- Organize your financial records to help you present your financial situation to the planner clearly.

How much does financial planning cost?

Financial planners get their compensation in several different ways. Basically, there are three broad types of planners: fee only, fee plus commission, or commission only.

These categories can be broken down still further. For example, some planners charge an hourly fee, others charge an agreed-upon flat fee for specific services, and still others take a percentage of your annual income or total assets. Some planners get a commission on financial products you purchase and others charge a fee that is offset by commissions on investments they make for you.

What kind of information is needed to prepare a plan?

While you'll want to thoroughly check out any potential financial planner, you should be aware that financial planners also need information from you.

In order to prepare a detailed and thorough plan for you, your planner will ask you for lots of information.

Expect to be asked the names, addresses, birthdays, and so forth of all persons who will be affected by your financial plan; the names and phone numbers of your attorney, accountant, and banker; lists of all bank accounts, stocks, bonds, and other assets with the purchase date and current value of each; descriptions of all your financial commitments (how much, how long, the reasons, and so forth); the current value of real and personal property; your current income (including salary records and recent tax returns) and your expectations for your family's future earnings; your family budget, including fixed and variable expenses; your retirement plans, regardless of your current age; and a statement of your long- and short-term goals and priorities, including how much money you'll need to achieve them and for how long, how much you want to invest, and how much risk you can afford.

Where can you write for more information on financial planners?
You may write or telephone these organizations:

International Association for Financial Planning
Two Concourse Pkw., Suite 800
Atlanta, GA 30328
(404) 396-1605

Institute of Certified Financial Planners
10065 E. Harvard Ave., Suite 320
Denver, CO 80231-3942
(303) 751-7600

Securities and Exchange Commission (SEC)
Office of Consumer Affairs and Information Services
450 Fifth St., NW
Washington, DC 20549
(202) 272-7440

What kind of investments should you look at in order to achieve your goals?
That's the subject of Part 2—Accumulating Wealth. In the next chapters, we'll tell you in detail about the kinds of investments available to you.

PART 2

ACCUMULATING WEALTH

- WHAT YOU NEED TO KNOW BEFORE YOU INVEST
- CASH EQUIVALENTS
- FIXED-INCOME INVESTMENTS
- EQUITY INVESTMENTS
- REAL ESTATE INVESTMENTS
- HARD ASSET INVESTMENTS
- MANAGED INVESTMENTS

CHAPTER 2

WHAT YOU NEED TO KNOW BEFORE YOU INVEST

You know your goals and objectives, and now you're ready to move toward them. How do you get started? The way to achieve your dreams and plans is by saving and investing, and that's what this chapter is all about. We start at the beginning—with saving.

What's the best way to accumulate money?
You've heard it before, but it bears repeating. Tucking away dollars on a monthly basis is an easy, almost effortless way to save money.

What should you do with the money you save?
As any financial planner will tell you, you should establish an emergency fund before you begin to think about working toward your goals.

What's most difficult about maintaining an emergency fund is keeping your hands off it until a real emergency comes along.

So, see to it that your money is accessible—but not immediately so. That way, you won't be tempted to dip into it for something other than an emergency. Here are some other rules of thumb to follow when it comes to setting up and maintaining your emergency fund.

Don't invest your emergency fund dollars in stocks or other financial instruments that fluctuate in value. If an emergency arose when the price of your investments was depressed, you'd have to take a loss to get your cash out—not a pleasant thought.

Also, don't sock away emergency fund dollars in certificates of deposit. Early withdrawal—as the fine print warns—may result in substantial penalties.

Instead, maintain your emergency funds in liquid passbook savings accounts, bank money-market deposit accounts, or money-market mutual funds. Here, they'll earn a competitive rate of interest, but it costs you nothing if you withdraw them in a hurry.

How much should you set aside in your fund?

Three to six months' income is the amount we recommend. If you think the chances are great that you'll need more than that amount—you're contemplating a job change, for instance—then increase the amount you're setting aside.

In deciding how much you need to stash away in the emergency fund, consider the other money you can draw on in a genuine emergency: unemployment compensation, for example, or disability benefits from Social Security or your employer.

How can you build up your fund?

If you have the cash available now in an account where it's accessible, designate that amount, or some portion of it, as your emergency fund. After you have done so, create your own rules about what constitutes an emergency—and what doesn't—and stick to them.

We find that it's almost always better to segregate your emergency funds into a separate account and not mix them with other monies. That way you reduce the temptation to borrow from the emergency kitty in nonemergency situations.

If you don't have enough money now to create an emergency fund, decide how much more you need and set about putting that money aside.

One way to save is to enlist the help of others. How? Most banks will automatically deduct from your checking account a contribution to a savings account.

Let the savings account serve as your emergency fund. When the amount it contains is small, the bank may not pay a high rate of interest on those funds.

But as the amount grows, it will probably meet the minimum balance requirements of a money-market or other higher-interest-paying account.

Most employers can arrange to have your regular paycheck allocated over several different accounts. You can create your emergency account in a bank separate from the one where you keep your checking account, then add to this new account through regular, painless payroll deductions.

If you must handle the monthly contribution yourself, make a rule. Decide, for instance, that the emergency fund is the first check you'll write after each payday.

Without this "pay-yourself-first" rule, you may find that you have spent your entire paycheck and have nothing left over for that rainy-day account.

And here's one last suggestion. Let's say that you've been building your emergency fund by earmarking for it half of the 10 percent that constitutes your customary savings program. When the fund reaches its desired level, don't reduce your savings.

You've already built up the savings habit, so hold onto it. Simply shift the money that you've been putting into the emergency fund into some other form of investment.

After you establish an emergency fund, then what?
You begin an investment program.

Is investing risky?
There's no escaping it. Everything we do is at least a little risky—whether it's commuting to work, buying a new house, or falling in love.

But we're willing to take risks, because they return to

us something we want or need. We are all experts at sizing up the tradeoffs between risk and return in our everyday lives. When it comes to money, however, this proficiency sometimes disappears.

Many of us hope to avoid risk entirely. Or we toss our entire life savings into a very risky investment we know almost nothing about.

Even without the benefit of hindsight, it's possible to make some judgment about the relative risk of various types of investments.

As a rule, the more an investment's price fluctuates in value, and the larger the number of factors that can affect its price, the riskier it is.

You should know that although risk taking carries with it the potential for higher returns, wide price fluctuations make it impossible to count on achieving any specific return and increase the chances that you'll lose your principal.

Is there a way to reduce investment risk?

One way is to diversify—that is, spread your dollars over a variety of investments. That way, if one declines in value, you won't be wiped out.

You can diversify by investing in a variety of areas—from cash and cash equivalents to fixed-income instruments, equities, and hard assets.

Investors with smaller net worths may not find it feasible to spread money over different investments to reduce risk sufficiently.

There's another way to achieve diversification on your own, through mutual funds. That's one reason 21 million families have put more than $400 billion into these investment vehicles.

When you invest in a mutual fund, you usually get instant diversification. You purchase shares from an investment company that holds a portfolio that is composed of securities, say—not just a single stock.

With diversification comes decreased risk.

Mutual funds come in all shapes and sizes. There are mutual funds that specialize in everything from international stocks to ecologically sound stocks.

Another way to manage market risk is to *dollar-cost average*. With dollar-cost averaging, you can invest systematically in the stock market without responding to ups and downs.

Dollar-cost averaging can turn volatile stock market conditions into a long-term investment advantage. Whether you want to invest large amounts of money or tuck away small amounts on a regular basis, the concept is the same.

You invest a consistent amount month after month—to help smooth out the peaks and valleys of share prices over time. So, you buy smart by buying more shares when the price is low and fewer shares when the price is high.

Unlike many other touted investment formulas, dollar-cost averaging is a snap to execute. Select a stock or mutual fund that you want to accumulate over a long period of time, and buy a predetermined dollar amount of shares on selected dates—$200 every month, say.

The success of dollar-cost averaging depends on investing regularly over a long period of time, which allows the law of averages to work in your favor.

Here's a hypothetical example, which is illustrated in the chart on the next page. Say that you invest $100 a month for five months in an equity mutual fund.

Your average market price per share is $5.20—that is, $26 divided by 5 months. Your average cost per share is $4.65—that is, $500 divided by 107.50.

And the market value of the $500 you invested adds up to $537.50—that is, the current market price of $5.00 per share times 107.50 total shares.

Here's another way to use this method of investing. Say you have a large sum of money to invest—$10,000. What should you do? Opt for safety in the form of a Treasury bill, for instance, or look for a more aggressive investment with higher potential returns?

HOW DOLLAR-COST AVERAGING WORKS

	Regular investment	Price per share	Shares purchased
Month 1	$100	$6.00	16.7
Month 2	$100	3.00	33.3
	Buys more shares when price is down		
Month 3	$100	4.00	25.0
Month 4	$100	8.00	12.5
	Buys fewer shares when price is up		
Month 5	$100	5.00	20.0
Total	$500	$26.00	107.5
Average price	$5.20	(26 ÷ 5)	
Average cost	$4.65	($500 ÷ 107.5)	

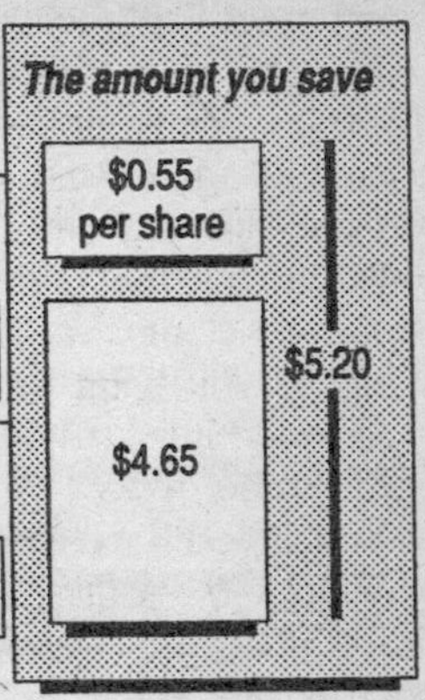

The amount you save

$0.55 per share

$4.65

$5.20

Amount saved $.55 per share or $59.13 total

By using diversification and dollar-cost averaging you can come close to having both.

For example, you could put your money into a money-market fund that you designate as a temporary holding fund. Then use dollar-cost averaging to buy shares in stocks or a mutual fund. Your money could earn attractive returns while you ease into the market on a regular basis.

Dollar-cost averaging cannot guarantee a profit or protect you against loss, but you'll have a better chance of beating the market than if you tried timing it.

And if you remain true to the strategy—if you invest consistently for the long term, even when prices are down—you'll probably come out ahead in the long run.

Tip: You can apply dollar-cost averaging to individual stocks, but the technique works particularly well with mutual funds. The reason is simple. It's easier to regularly invest rounded dollar amounts in a mutual fund than in shares of an individual company.

What investments should you select?

To develop an investment portfolio, you must ask yourself a series of questions to determine which investments would best suit your situation.

And, you should pay special attention to two key factors: your goals and your risk tolerance. Your financial planner will help you with this process. He or she will help you determine your goals and objectives along with a projected time line for each. Then, you can select the investments that will help you realize each of your aims.

For example, if you must reach a particular goal within one or two years—say your son or daughter will start college—you may be tempted to select an investment with a high potential return. But you must keep in mind that a greater return generally means greater risk.

Determining risk tolerance is sometimes more difficult than stating your goals and objectives and time frames for achieving them. Here are a few questions a financial planner might ask you to help you establish your tolerance for risk.

What are your current investments? Are you happy with them and with their performance? How do you feel when your investment falls in value? When it comes to investing, which are you most concerned about: growth, or the safety of your principal and income?

Take time to analyze your situation and your feelings when investing. Set up hypothetical situations, too, so you can project your reactions under different circumstances.

After defining how long you have to reach your goals

and your risk tolerance, review the characteristics of different investments.

See how little—or how much—risk they carry. Check if they offer growth opportunities or current income. Estimate how long you may need to hold a specific investment to reach your goals. Evaluate their performance records. And ask your financial planner for recommendations and advice. The chart at right matches common investment objectives with appropriate investment vehicles.

By matching your own personality and financial goals with the appropriate types of investments, you can design an investment portfolio that can help you reap the profits you need to meet your goals and objectives—without losing any sleep.

How do you make your dollars grow faster?
Cash in on the benefits of tax deferral by socking dollars away in a tax-deferred savings account or plan. What, you ask, is a tax-deferred account?

It's an account or plan on which the earnings—the interest and dividends—accumulate tax-deferred until they are withdrawn. Examples of tax-deferred accounts are annuities and qualified retirement plans, such as Keoghs and Individual Retirement Accounts (IRAs).

The advantages of tax deferral are clear. For every dollar not taken out of your investment earnings in taxes, your tax-deferred account accumulates even more for you.

Say, for example, that you're saving for a trip around the world after you retire. You invest in an annuity that matures when you reach retirement age.

Your earnings on the amount you deposited in the annuity accumulate tax-deferred. You pay no taxes on the interest and dividends until they are withdrawn.

Or, say that you invest $2,000 in an IRA on the first day of each year. You're in the 28 percent tax bracket, and your effective annual yield on your investment is 10 percent.

INVESTMENT OBJECTIVE MATRIX

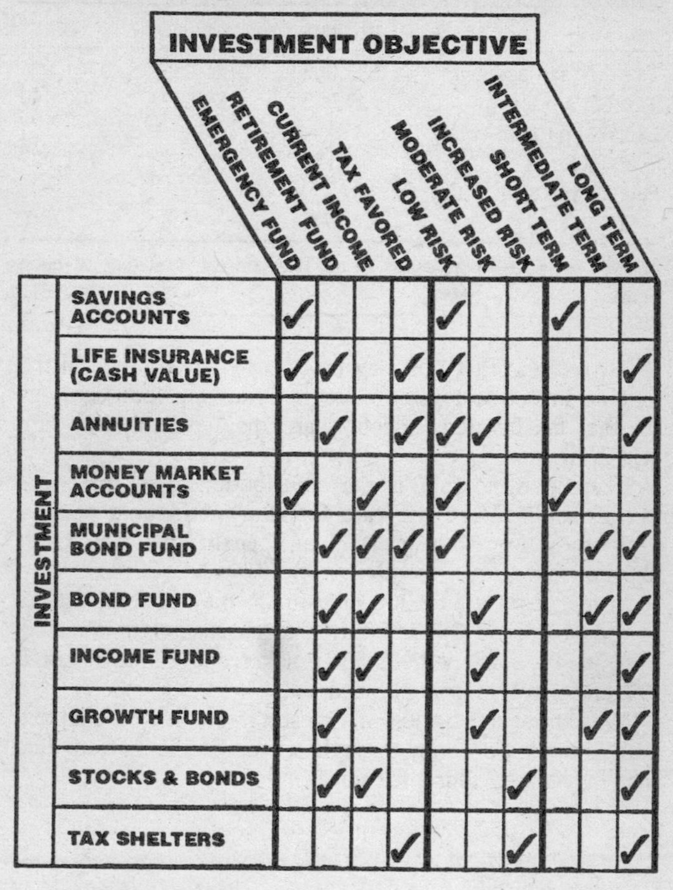

INVESTMENT	EMERGENCY FUND	RETIREMENT FUND	CURRENT INCOME	TAX FAVORED	LOW RISK	MODERATE RISK	INCREASED RISK	SHORT TERM	INTERMEDIATE TERM	LONG TERM
SAVINGS ACCOUNTS	✓				✓			✓		
LIFE INSURANCE (CASH VALUE)	✓	✓		✓	✓					✓
ANNUITIES		✓		✓	✓	✓				✓
MONEY MARKET ACCOUNTS	✓		✓		✓			✓		
MUNICIPAL BOND FUND		✓	✓	✓	✓				✓	✓
BOND FUND		✓	✓			✓			✓	✓
INCOME FUND		✓	✓			✓				✓
GROWTH FUND		✓				✓			✓	✓
STOCKS & BONDS		✓	✓				✓			✓
TAX SHELTERS				✓			✓			✓

The chart on the next pages compares the potential growth of your investment where the earnings accumulate tax-deferred to one where all earnings are taxed.

Power of Tax Deferral—$2,000 Annual IRA Contribution

	10 years	20	30
Tax-deferred account*	$35,062	$126,005	$361,886
Taxable account	29,903	89,837	209,959
Dollars you gain with tax deferral	5,159	36,168	151,927
Percent you gain with tax deferral	17%	40%	72%

*Based on $2,000 invested in an IRA on the first day of each year.

We assume that you pay taxes on your earnings in the taxable investment year to year. Taxes on your earnings in the tax-favored account are paid when they are withdrawn.

Keep in mind that if the contributions you make are tax-deductible—and they are for many retirement plans—you enjoy an even greater tax benefit than the chart shows.

In ten years a $10,000 investment may double, thanks to the power of tax deferral. The chart at right assumes you are in a 28 percent tax bracket and can earn an 8 percent effective annual yield.

You know the basics of investing. So, in the chapters that follow, we'll run through some specific investments that may make sense for you.

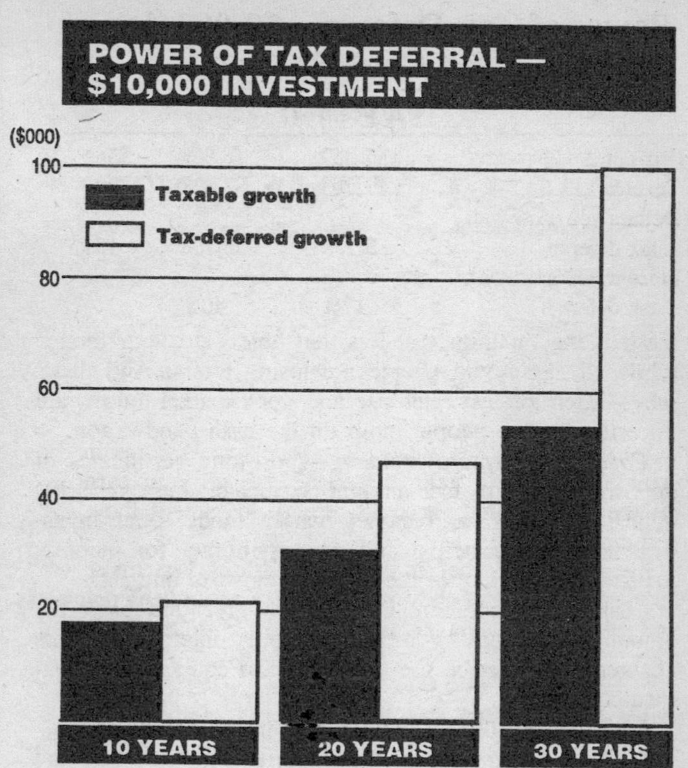
POWER OF TAX DEFERRAL —
$10,000 INVESTMENT
($000)
100
80
60
40
20
Taxable growth
Tax-deferred growth
10 YEARS
20 YEARS
30 YEARS

CHAPTER 3

CASH EQUIVALENTS

Cash is the medium that lets you hold onto your money while all about you people are losing theirs. And that's why—when interest rates rise and stock market returns are uncertain—more people jump on the cash bandwagon.

Cash equivalent investments—short-term certificates of deposit, short-term face-amount certificates, money-market deposit accounts, and money-market funds—offer investors safety of principal and an opportunity for income, depending on whether the vehicle reinvests interest.

Cash equivalents are designed to give you back the amount of money you put in, plus interest. In this chapter, we describe the array of cash equivalent investments.

Let's begin, though, with a few words about safety.

It's true that more banks and thrifts failed in 1988 and 1989 than at any time since the Great Depression. But you can rest assured that the money you deposit in federally insured institutions is still safe up to a $100,000 limit. At no time has a depositor lost one cent of his or her insured dollars.

Banks, thrift institutions, and credit unions that are members of the Federal Deposit Insurance Corporation (FDIC), the Federal Savings and Loan Insurance Corporation (FSLIC), or the National Credit Union Administration (NCUA) offer insured deposits up to $100,000 per depository.

That is, the dollars deposited in accounts in your name

at an institution are added together, and the total—including any interest due you—is insured by the appropriate federal agency for up to $100,000. An exception to this rule: Dollars deposited in an Individual Retirement Account (IRA) offered by one of the types of institutions we just discussed are insured separately up to $100,000.

Tip: You're at risk only if you stash away more than $100,000 at any single institution. But here's a way to extend the $100,000 limit to $300,000.

If you're married, you can maintain $100,000 in accounts in your name, $100,000 in accounts in your spouse's name, and $100,000 in joint accounts—that is, accounts in both your names. Federal insurance covers only the first $100,000 deposited in accounts in any single name. But joint accounts and accounts with a spouse are insured separately. If you aren't married, you can accomplish the same objective by using a joint ownership account and a trust.

You should know that the safety net of federal insurance extends *only* to banks, thrifts, and credit unions that are members of the FDIC, FSLIC, or NCUA.

However, other institutions that offer face-amount certificates provide safety for investors by backing the investment 100 percent by assets owned by the institution, rather than by federal insurance. These certificate companies are regulated by rules of the Securities and Exchange Commission (SEC) and must adhere to the Investment Company Act of 1940. Investments offered by face-amount certificate companies are securities, not deposits. So investment assets back face-amount certificates dollar for dollar.

Some institutions that offer certificates of deposit are state-insured, which means their deposits are covered by a state insurance fund. As those who followed the 1985 Ohio savings and loan crisis remember, some state insurance funds have been caught without sufficient resources to protect investors.

It's easy to find out whether an institution is a member

of the FDIC, FSLIC, NCUA, or is state-insured. All you need do is ask.

The interest rate you receive at thrift institutions is sometimes slightly higher than the rate banks pay. And many institutions reward you for saving more. Investors with $10,000 to $25,000 or more to deposit often receive a higher rate of interest.

Of course, as we said earlier, your principal and interest are guaranteed up to $100,000. But if an institution fails, you have the problem of reinvesting your money—often at a lower rate if interest rates have fallen since you initially invested. And you cannot earn interest, because you cannot get at your money. A financial adviser can provide direction on how to find the right combination of high rates and safety.

Passbook Savings Accounts

WHO: Passbook accounts offer liquidity. However, if you have a lot of extra cash, it makes little sense for you to put away much of your savings in passbook accounts. These accounts are good for accumulating moderate amounts of money, though.

WHAT: If you have money in a passbook savings account, you aren't alone. To this day, billions of dollars are still squirreled away in these accounts.

Yet, they earn their owners little interest. In fact, most passbook accounts at banks pay only 5.25 percent annually and at thrift institutions 5.50 percent.

You may earn as much as three to four percentage points more simply by switching your dollars to a CD or money-market account at the same institution.

As you probably know, passbook accounts get their names from the little books most banks issued customers with savings accounts. Deposits and interest were stamped in the book.

However, in today's technological age, you usually no longer get a passbook when you open one of these accounts. Some banks and thrifts give you a plastic card, others just provide regular statements.

WHY: Passbook accounts offer liquidity, simplicity, and safety—but little else.

WHY NOT: A low rate of interest is reason enough to steer clear of these accounts.

WHERE: Once the staple of the savings industry, passbook accounts are available at virtually all bank and thrift institutions.

WHEN: If you don't have a large amount of money to invest in something else—usually less than $1,000—and if you have money in transition, these accounts make sense. It's seldom a good time to deposit a lot of money in passbook accounts, unless there are times when 5 percent is all you can get on CDs.

Money-Market Deposit Accounts

WHO: Safety-minded investors who need liquidity and are unable or unwilling to tie up their money for a month or more in CDs often opt for money-market deposit accounts.

Likewise, investors with savings in passbook accounts frequently shift them to higher-yielding money-market deposit accounts at the same bank or thrift.

WHAT: It's difficult for most of us to remember what it was like before the introduction of money-market deposit accounts. But think about what it's like now. Money you deposit in 100-percent-safe money-market deposit accounts earns you competitive rates of interest.

Let's review the basics about these accounts.

Money-market deposit accounts (as opposed to money-market funds, which we discuss later in this chapter) are offered by banks and thrifts.

The amount you earn on money-market deposits will fluctuate with interest rates. And federal regulations restrict to three the number of checks you may write each month on your money-market deposit account to anyone but yourself.

You should know, too, that most banks and thrifts require you to maintain a minimum balance in your account—typically, $500 to $2,500.

Investors will benefit in the long run if they examine exactly what various institutions offer, especially when it comes to yield.

In shopping for a money-market deposit account, you should look for an institution that offers a competitive rate of return and compounds interest frequently. You shouldn't assume that the bank will tie the rate it offers to changes in the market. Ask your bank if it ties its rate to an index. If not, you should track the rate to make sure it continues to be competitive. There are often wide variations in the market.

Daily compounding is more advantageous to you than annual or quarterly compounding. How much more? Say you deposit $15,000 into a money-market deposit account at a 9 percent interest rate.

Compounded daily, your money is worth $16,412.29 at the end of one year (a 9.42 percent yield). Compounded quarterly, it's worth $16,396.25 (a 9.31 percent yield).

The interest on money-market deposit accounts is taxed as ordinary income on your personal tax return.

Finally, don't make the mistake some investors do and confuse money-market and Super NOW checking accounts with money-market deposit accounts. They aren't the same. The rate of interest you earn on money-market deposit accounts can be two or more percentage points higher than on a money-market checking or Super NOW account. However, with these latter accounts, you can make unlimited transactions, whereas with money-market deposit accounts your transactions are limited by law.

WHY: Money-market deposit accounts offer liquidity and convenience. Most banks and thrift institutions allow you to write checks for any amount on your money-market deposit account. However, transfers on money-market deposit accounts are limited to six per month, only three of which may be by draft. Most money-market funds—by comparison—restrict you to writing checks of $500 or more, and some limit the number of checks per month.

Money-market deposit accounts also offer safety. Money you deposit in accounts at banks, thrift institutions, or credit unions that are members of the FDIC, FSLIC, or NCUA is federally insured up to the $100,000 limit.

Finally, like variable-rate CDs, money-market deposit accounts may offer you some inflation protection, since interest rates rise with inflation. The amount you earn goes up as interest rates rise.

WHY NOT: Money-market deposit accounts usually earn less than money-market funds. And you wouldn't want a money-market deposit account if you were looking for nontaxable earnings.

WHERE: Virtually every bank and thrift institution offers money-market deposit accounts.

WHEN: A money-market deposit account is an all-weather investment and a good place to maintain your emergency fund.

Money-Market Mutual Funds

WHO: People who find the liquidity of money-market deposit accounts attractive but want to earn a higher rate of interest and have professional investment management may want to turn to money-market mutual funds.

WHAT: Money-market mutual funds offered by mutual-fund companies and brokerage firms are a boon for small investors. By using their investors' deposits, these funds, in effect, make short-term loans to federal, state, and local governments and to corporations and banks.

Some safety-minded investors stick to funds that buy only government securities—and pay a lower rate of return than other funds. But you should feel comfortable putting your money into an ordinary fund that's operated by any well-established mutual-fund company or brokerage firm.

When you invest in a money-market mutual fund, you purchase shares in the fund. Each fund attempts to maintain a net asset value of $1 per share, so $1,000 buys 1,000 shares.

Your dividends are generally paid in shares.

For example, if your money-market mutual fund earns 9 percent annually, at the end of the year, your 1,000 shares, which is equivalent to a $1,000 investment, have grown to 1,090 shares, or your $1,000 is now worth $1,090.

You should study the fund prospectus to see what types of investment instruments it holds—Treasury securities, corporate debt, and so on.

You should know that, as a rule, the shorter the maturities, the lower the risk if interest rates go up—and vice versa if rates go down.

This risk, however, doesn't relate to a loss of principal, since nearly all funds maintain a constant $1 per share value.

Money-market funds resemble money-market deposit accounts in that you can make deposits or withdrawals from your account. But unlike many money-market deposit accounts, there's usually a minimum—typically $500—on the size of checks you can write on a money-market mutual fund. You can always receive any amount of money in your money-market fund account by redeeming shares.

Opening an account in a money-market mutual fund is easy.

Your financial adviser can get you started in the right direction or call the fund for information and a prospectus.

When you want to make a withdrawal, in most cases you may write a check. You can also transfer money by wire to your bank checking account. (Generally, wire transfers cost from $5 to $15 each. Also, funds may have minimum amounts that are available for transfer.)

You can open a money-market mutual fund account for as little as $500. However, a more common amount would be $1,000. And most funds charge no direct fees to shareholders except for wire-transfer expenses.

The fund, however, pays fees for many services.

The fund uses some of its assets to pay fees for various services, such as management fees to the company that advises the fund on its investments. These fees usually amount to a small portion of the earnings from a fund—somewhere in the 0.50 percent to 0.75 percent range of daily net assets.

Such fees, which are paid by the fund, not directly by the individual shareholders, are part of a fund's operating expenses.

Most funds require you to maintain a minimum balance, typically $500 to $1,000. The interest you earn is technically a dividend, since you're receiving it in your capacity as a shareholder rather than as a creditor. So, you may have to report it as a dividend on Schedule B, Form 1040, and it's taxed at ordinary income tax rates.

Most brokerage firms and other financial institutions offer tax-exempt money-market mutual funds. Interest you earn—again, this interest is technically dividends—is exempt from federal taxes, because these funds invest substantially in short-term, tax-exempt obligations of state and local governments. The interest from some of these funds is also exempt from state and local taxes.

However, you should compare yields between a tax-exempt fund and a regular money-market mutual fund. You might find you still come out ahead by opting for the taxable fund.

Here's an easy way to do this calculation. Simply divide the tax-exempt yield by 1 minus your tax bracket (expressed as a decimal).

Say your tax-exempt yield is 5 percent, and you're in

the 28 percent bracket. You divide 5 by (1 minus 0.28) or 0.72, and get 6.94, your equivalent taxable yield.

WHY: The biggest advantage of money-market mutual funds is that they usually pay a higher rate of interest than do money-market deposit accounts offered by banks and thrift institutions—but without the federal insurance of bank or thrift money-market deposit accounts. In fact, they sometimes pay as much as two to three percentage points more.

And money-market mutual funds—like money-market deposit accounts—offer liquidity and convenience.

Withdrawing money from a money-market mutual fund is easy. Most institutions where you maintain an account will cash money-market mutual-fund checks for $500 or more immediately. Or you can deposit the money-market check in your bank checking account and withdraw funds in cash.

Like money-market deposit accounts, money-market mutual funds offer some protection from inflation, since short-term interest rates rise with inflation. The primary selling point of tax-exempt funds, of course, is that the earnings they generate are usually federal-tax-free to you. Also, if you invest in a state-specific, tax-free fund for your state, your earnings are generally exempt from state taxes as well. There are even funds that are "triple-tax-free"—that is, the earnings they generate are free from city, state, and federal taxes.

WHY NOT: Some safety-minded investors steer clear of money-market mutual funds, since they aren't federally insured, and there's no guarantee against loss of principal. But you should know that just one "money-market mutual fund" ever failed to reimburse its investors in full. Even with that fund, investors got back 93 cents on the dollar.

Some money-market mutual funds are covered by private insurance policies. Another important point: A poorly managed money-market mutual fund may earn less than a typical money-market deposit account. So, look for a fund from a reputable company.

WHERE: Mutual-fund companies and brokerage firms offer money-market mutual funds. How do you find the ones with higher yields and low risk?

A number of newsletters track the performance of money-market mutual funds and money-market accounts, and you may find a subscription to one of them useful.

Among these publications are *Income & Safety* (3471 North Federal Highway, Fort Lauderdale, FL 33306); *100 Highest Yields* (P.O. Box 088888, Palm Beach, FL 33408); and *Donoghue's MoneyLetter* (P.O. Box 6640, Holliston, MA 01746).

WHEN: Money-market mutual funds pay best during times of high interest rates. But they are always a good place to keep your emergency cash fund.

United States Treasury Securities

WHO: If you live in a state with high personal income taxes—California, New York, or Massachusetts, say—and don't mind tying up your money for a time, short-term United States Treasury securities make excellent investments, because they aren't subject to state and local tax.

WHAT: Treasury bills—or T-bills, as they are commonly called—are short-term obligations of the United States government.

They are issued with maturities of 13 weeks, 26 weeks, and 52 weeks, and they are the next best thing to keeping your money in a vault ten feet underground. In fact, they are considerably better, because your money earns competitive rates of interest.

T-bills are issued by the federal government in minimum denominations of $10,000 ($5,000 for subsequent investments) and are available through a Federal Reserve Bank or—for a commission of $2 to $10 per $1,000—from a brokerage firm or bank.

Purchasing T-bills from a brokerage firm or bank eliminates the small bother of setting up a direct-deposit account with the Treasury or going in person to a Federal

Reserve Bank. But you should also know that there are fees involved that effectively eliminate a portion of your return. How much of your return?

Say, for example, that you invest $10,000 in a T-bill with an annualized yield of 9 percent. And you purchase your T-bill through your broker—for a $50 commission. That commission reduces your annualized yield from a handsome 9 percent to 8.5 percent.

You buy these T-bills at a discount to their face value. For example, you buy a one-year $10,000 Treasury bill yielding 9 percent. A week or so after you pay the $10,000, you receive a check for $900, which is your discount. At the end of the year, you receive your full $10,000 back.

If for some reason you need to liquidate before the year is over, you can do so through a bank or broker. There's no penalty attached—at least not in the form of reduced interest. And these securities trade on the secondary market.

Remember that the yield quoted you at the time the T-bill was issued is the yield if held to maturity. If you liquidate early and interest rates have risen, the value may drop and you may experience a loss on the sale. You have to pay a second brokerage commission, too.

If you purchase T-bills, it makes sense to buy them and hold them to maturity. So, if you think you'll need your cash early, opt for a more liquid investment.

You must pay federal taxes on your earnings either when the T-bill matures or if sold early. However, your earnings aren't subject to state and local income taxes.

WHY: Treasuries offer investors safety.

In fact, Treasury securities are perhaps the safest place in the world to invest your money, because your investment is as secure as the country itself.

Interest on T-bills is exempt from state and local taxes—a real boon for individual investors in high-tax states and cities. Here's an example.

Say you live in Boston and invest $10,000 in a one-year T-bill with a yield of 9.5 percent. You save $95 by earning interest that's exempt from Massachusetts's 10 percent state income tax. (If you had made an investment at a Massachusetts bank or credit union, you would have paid only 5 percent state income tax on your earnings. So, with this comparison, your savings on a T-bill comes to $47.50.)

WHY NOT: Treasury bills offer investors safety and a steady income. But the minimum investment in a T-bill is $10,000, putting them out of reach for many investors.

WHERE: You can write to your nearest Federal Reserve Bank and ask to set up a "Treasury Direct" account. Once you fill out the forms, the Federal Reserve will automatically deposit your earnings in the bank account you specify.

For a free brochure, telephone your local Federal Reserve Bank or write the Bureau of Public Debt, Department F, Washington, DC 20239-1200.

You can also buy T-bills through a bank or broker. But—as we noted earlier—you'll pay a small commission.

WHEN: These investments make sense at any time, as long as you have enough money for the initial investment and are prepared to keep your money locked up until the maturity date.

Fixed-Rate CDs

WHO: If capital preservation and income are your main goals, *fixed-rate certificates of deposit* (CDs) may be right for you.

WHAT: CDs are actually loans from an investor to a bank, thrift, or other financial institution. An investor agrees to let an institution use his or her cash for a specified amount of time and, in exchange, receives a specified rate of interest.

You should look for the CD that offers the highest *yield*—that is, the actual amount your money earns—and safety.

And pay attention to *compounding*—how often interest is paid on your interest. The yield on your CD depends on the interest rate the issuer is paying, how frequently the issuer compounds this interest, and how many days the issuer calculates are in a year.

The more frequently your interest is compounded, the higher your yield for a given rate. The yield also depends on whether the issuer pays interest on a year of 360 days or 365 days.

If the institution uses the 365 figure—called "compounding on a 365/360 basis"—your yield is slightly higher, because your interest compounds for five more days.

You can buy and redeem CDs by mail, which means that you don't need to restrict your shopping to local institutions.

Study the rates offered on CDs by institutions in a variety of locations. Then pick the one that's right for your particular needs.

CDs are offered for a variety of maturities. Some mature in as little as seven days; others take as long as ten years to reach maturity. The most common CDs come due in six months to one year and pay an interest rate that's tied to the rate of interest paid on thirteen-week Treasury bills. In the last few years, because of interest-rate fluctuations and minimal differences between short- and long-term rates, consumers have preferred these six- and twelve-month terms, so they could maintain flexibility.

Some institutions offer ordinary fixed-rate CDs for as little as $100 to $1,000, but initial deposits vary widely among institutions. The interest you earn on these CDs is taxed as ordinary income on your federal income tax return.

So-called *jumbo CDs* are those that come in denominations of $90,000 to $100,000 or more. Some banks have begun offering these certificates in denominations of less than $100,000, so the interest you earn will still be covered by federal insurance, which is capped at $100,000. (If you invest in a jumbo of $100,000 or more, the interest won't be covered if the issuing institution defaults.)

WHY: The primary advantage of CDs is that you're guaranteed a certain rate, and you know you're going to get your money out at maturity.

WHY NOT: The primary disadvantage of CDs is that you may pay a substantial penalty—usually one to three months of simple interest—if you withdraw your money before maturity. So, if there's a possibility that you'll need your cash early, you should choose a more liquid investment. Some banks won't allow you to withdraw part of your CD. You must withdraw all or nothing.

To avoid the penalty, you could borrow money and use your certificate of deposit as collateral. If your CD is near maturity, you may come out better this way than by withdrawing your money and incurring a penalty.

WHERE: CDs are available not only from banks and thrifts but through other financial institutions as well, such as brokerage houses. CDs purchased through brokerage firms come from banks and savings and loans around the country and sometimes pay a higher rate of interest than CDs bought from your local banks and thrifts.

In most cases, brokerages do not impose a penalty on early withdrawal—an advantage over CDs purchased at a bank. Because some brokerages make a secondary market in the CDs they offer, they will help you sell your CD.

However, don't assume that you'll always receive full face value. As with bonds, the market value of CDs fluctuates. Depending on interest rates, you may sell at a loss. Of course, you may occasionally sell at a profit, too.

A brokerage firm, which makes a secondary market, will attempt to sell your CD to someone else. However, sometimes this may not be possible—particularly if rates have increased since you bought the CD—and you may not recover your full principal amount plus any interest that has accrued.

You should know that some brokerage firms pool dollars to invest in CDs from institutions across the country. These pools sometimes invest in jumbo CDs, which means that some of their deposits may not be covered by federal insurance. So ask before you invest.

WHEN: If you think interest rates are going up, invest only in shorter-term CDs. If you think rates are heading down, opt for longer-term vehicles. Stagger maturities, so you're protected against rising and falling interest rates.

Variable-Rate CDs

WHO: If your goals include preservation of principal, a steady stream of income, and the chance of an increasing rate of return, *variable-rate certificates of deposit* may make sense for you.

WHAT: Variable-rate CDs come in many types. Some are tied to the performance of a stock market index (such as the Standard & Poor's 500); or to the performance of another common index, such as the yield on United States Treasury bills.

Banks introduced market index CDs—as they came to be known—in the days before the 1987 stock market crash. Some examples of market index CDs are those that come in two varieties: those that pay a minimum interest rate of 4 percent (but pay a smaller percentage in the market), and those that pay a minimum of zero percent but offer a larger percent of the market rise.

At maturity, an investor receives the higher of two amounts—the minimum amount guaranteed or a percentage of the rise in the Standard & Poor 500. Remember, no matter what happens to the stock market, you'll always get your principal back up to $100,000.

Investors who opt for a zero minimum rate of return stand to gain more if the market rises than investors who opt for a 4 percent minimum rate of return.

For example, an investor who chose the 4 percent

guarantee might receive 40 percent of any rise in the market for a one-year deposit. An investor with a zero guarantee might receive as much as 75 percent of any increase in the market.

With other variable-rate CDs, institutions sometimes offer a higher introductory return for a month or two. Then, after that period, your return fluctuates with the performance of a common index, such as the Donoghue money-fund thirty-day-average yield or the United States Treasury bill yield.

One drawback is, that should interest rates decline, you may receive a lesser return with variable-rate CDs.

For example, your bank may offer you an annualized rate of 19.89 percent for the first month your money is on deposit and then the interest rate could be changed to an annualized 8.35 percent until your CD matures.

On a $10,000 investment, your interest income over the three-year life of the CD comes to $2,601.20. Sounds good? Not exactly. If you had invested your $10,000 in a fixed-rate CD with an annualized yield of 9.25 percent, your interest income would have come to $3,040.90—or $439.70 more.

The minimum investment in variable-rate CDs is typically $1,000. As with fixed-rate CDs, the interest you earn on these CDs is taxed as ordinary income.

WHY: The advantage of a variable-rate CD is that it allows your return to increase with rising market rates—that is, either stock market prices or interest rates. Some may offer a minimum rate of interest so if the market declines, you can at least count on that return.

Variable-rate CDs tied to a government or money-fund index often give you the advantage of high initial rates. However, after the introductory period—depending on the index to which the rate is tied—you'll know that you're at least getting a return that's as high as some commonly accepted average.

WHY NOT: There are times when you shouldn't invest in variable-rate CDs. When you invest in variable-rate market CDs, you're hoping that the stock market or interest rates will rise.

When you invest in other types of variable-rate CDs, you may miss out on locking in a higher rate of return for a longer period of time. If rates fall, you're getting less for your money than you could have otherwise.

WHERE: Like fixed-rate CDs, variable-rate CDs are available from banks and thrifts, as well as a variety of other financial institutions.

WHEN: The best time to invest in variable-rate CDs that are tied to the stock market is, of course, just before the market starts surging. The best time to invest in other variable-rate CDs is when you think interest rates will rise. You can diversify your CDs by staggering maturities to protect yourself against rising and falling interest rates.

Questions and Answers

I maintain accounts at a bank and at one of its branch offices. Are these accounts insured separately?
The answer is no. Deposits at branch banks are considered deposits at a single bank for purposes of federal insurance.

Money-market mutual funds invest only in United States short-term securities of domestic assets, right?
Virtually all money-market mutual funds offered in this country invest in domestic short-term assets, but there are exceptions.

Some domestic funds have a small foreign component. And we know of at least several money-market mutual funds that invest largely in foreign CDs, commercial paper, and so on. And there may be others. As a rule, the return on these global money-market mutual funds is likely to be high when the dollar is weak and low when the dollar is strong.

When I was a child, my aunt set up a savings account for me. When she passed away, the bank book was nowhere to be found. How can I trace the account?

Our advice is to write the office of the state treasurer in the state where the account was set up. States keep records and will make an effort to find the account.

In your letter, include your name, the name and address of your late aunt, and specify the year in which you think the account was opened.

You should know, though, that once a bank or thrift institution declares an account "dead" and turns it over to the state, interest no longer accrues.

CHAPTER 4

FIXED-INCOME INVESTMENTS

It used to be that safety-minded investors favored *bonds* over stocks. Bonds were a bit boring, perhaps, but they were less risky.

Bondholders knew, for instance, that their annual income from their investments wouldn't vary. And their earnings didn't depend on the vagaries of profits or the unpredictable actions of corporate directors making dividend decisions.

Moreover, while stock prices might dip and soar, the value of bonds on the secondary market changed—but only slowly and then not by much.

Alas, those were the good old days.

Now, there's almost as much excitement in managing a bond portfolio as there is in trading stocks. Most—but not quite all—of the certainties have disappeared. And bonds, in the current environment, are no longer the favorite vehicle of the faint of heart.

In fact, before the stock market took its spectacular plunge in October 1987, the bond market took its own nose dive. From April to September of 1987, bonds—depending on their type—lost from 10 to 25 percent of their value.

However, bonds are still worthwhile investments. And financial advisers recommend that most investors make bonds part of their portfolios.

But investing wisely in the bond market now demands the same kinds of evaluative skills and attention to timing as does investing in the equity market.

That's because what happens to the bond market depends on what happens to interest rates. And we all know that interest rates are anything but stable.

When interest rates rise, bondholders can expect a reduction in the value of their portfolios. When rates fall, the value of their bonds rises.

In this chapter, we examine the ins and outs of investing in the bond market. Before we start, though, here are a few terms and facts that you need to know.

A bond—by definition—is a contract between an issuer, meaning a borrower, and a bondholder, meaning you, the lender.

The riskier a bond, the higher the interest rate it pays. The issuer agrees to pay interest at a fixed rate, or *coupon rate*, at specified times, usually twice a year.

The issuer must pay back to the bondholder—you—the *face value* of the bond—meaning the value listed on the bond itself—when it matures. You can always sell the bond before it comes due—provided there's a market for it.

A *note* is a type of bond that matures in ten years or less. Bonds, on the other hand, come due anywhere from one to forty years.

The *par value* of a bond is its face value. *Current yield* is the annual return a bond pays its holder. It's figured as a percentage. You calculate this amount by dividing the income (in dollars) that you receive from a bond in a year by the current price of the bond.

Anyone who is serious about investing in bonds should become familiar with the two best known bond-rating agencies—Moody's Investor Services and Standard & Poor's.

Moody's, which is owned by Dun & Bradstreet, rates bonds on a scale from Aaa to D. Standard & Poor's, a subsidiary of McGraw-Hill, rates bonds from AAA to D. Aaa is Moody's top rating; AAA is Standard & Poor's.

The higher the rating, the better a bond issuer's ability

to make the required annual interest payments and repay the principal when due.

Examples of companies whose bonds earned high ratings in 1989: American Express, Coca-Cola, Ford Motor, General Electric, International Business Machines, Procter & Gamble, and Minnesota Mining & Manufacturing.

If you don't like much risk, you should invest only in top-of-the-line bonds. But understand that you earn less on bonds with high ratings than you do on bonds with low ratings. That's because organizations with low ratings must pay a high return to attract investors.

What happens if you invest in a bond and its rating later changes? The answer is often nothing—provided you hold the bond until maturity. But if you sell the bond before it matures, its price will rise or fall with its rating.

Say that you buy a bond and its rating is upgraded by Standard & Poor's from A to AA. What that means is the bond is now considered a less risky investment.

So the issuer may—on its new bonds—offer a lower current yield. (The issuer cannot, however, pay a lower yield on bonds that it has already sold.)

If you want to sell your bond, it should be relatively easy to find a buyer willing to pay more for the bond than you did. After all, the bond is now judged a lower risk investment than it was when you bought it. For the new buyer, it's a tradeoff—he or she accepts a lower current yield in return for less risk.

What if the rating on your bond had dropped? Its value would drop, too. If you were to sell it, you may receive less than your purchase price, and the buyer would inherit a higher current yield, along with a higher degree of risk. A financial adviser will be able to help you buy and sell your bonds.

The value of a bond moves not only with changes in its ratings but also with changes in interest rates. Here's an example.

Say that investments across the board are offering higher rates of return than they were six months ago. That means that bond issuers must also start paying higher rates on new issues to stay competitive. What does this mean for the price of the bond you currently hold?

Again, if you hold the bond until maturity, it means nothing. But if you sell, you'll receive less for your investment than you paid for it.

Say that you bought a $10,000 bond with a 9 percent coupon rate. Within a year, interest rates rise to 11 percent. Your bond continues to pay 9 percent a year, or $900. But investors can now purchase bonds paying 11 percent. So the price of your bond falls.

As a general rule, the value of a bond at any given time is affected by the date at which the bond is scheduled to mature. The price of bonds that don't mature for many years is more influenced by interest-rate fluctuations than the price of bonds that come due sooner.

The word *volatility* takes on new meaning when it comes to bonds. It describes the market that confronts long-term bond investors who have to sell before maturity. That's why it's best to buy and hold your bonds over the long term.

You should also keep in mind the term *yield to maturity*. This is the compound rate of return you'll get on your bond if you hold it until it matures.

That yield takes into account your interest payments as well as the net rise or fall in the price of the bond as it nears its maturity value.

Long-term bonds are riskier investments than short-term ones, since there's a greater chance for the economy to act in unpredictable ways. Consequently, bonds with longer maturities usually offer a higher current yield in order to attract buyers.

Two important factors to consider: *call provision* and *real rate of return*. A call provision allows an issuer of a bond to redeem it before maturity. Bonds are usually called when interest rates fall, because issuers can then refinance a debt issue at the lower rate.

Real rate of return is the current yield minus the current

inflation rate and any taxes you pay on your income from the bond. What you come up with is the most accurate measure possible for judging the success of your bond investment.

You should know that bonds—as a group—have produced about a 2 percent real rate of return over the last thirty years.

We have seen that bonds today are both unpredictable and risky. But at your disposal are two methods for blunting any unpleasant surprises that may be in store for you.

First, don't invest all your money in bonds, or even in one issue. Hedge your bets by relying on a diversified portfolio.

Second, consider a bond mutual fund, especially if you have limited money to invest. The fund can relieve you of the need to constantly monitor your money. (We'll tell you more about bond mutual funds in Chapter 8.)

Now, with bond basics behind us, let's take a look at the types of bonds available today.

Convertible Bonds

WHO: You say you're an experienced investor who is looking for income but doesn't want to forfeit the chance for capital appreciation?

Then *convertible bonds* may be right for you.

WHAT: Convertible bonds are hybrids. They are part bond and part stock. Companies use convertibility as a sweetener to enhance the marketability of these bonds.

With convertible bonds, you hold the right to swap your bonds for shares of common stock—if and when the stock rises to a trigger price. This trigger price is usually 15 to 30 percent more than the price of the stock when the bond was first issued.

So, with convertibles, you get the best of both worlds. You pocket interest income now—and perhaps handsome profits later by exchanging your bonds for stock.

The catch?

Actually, there are two. Companies pay as much as three to four percentage points less in interest on their convertibles than they do on their other bonds. And you pay more for convertible bonds than you would for the amount of stock you may exchange them for.

Here's something else you should know about convertibles. *Conversion basis* is the number of common shares you'll receive for each convertible bond.

Conversion value is the number of shares you can acquire times the price of the stock. In other words, it's the value of your investment after you convert it.

How do you calculate the conversion value of your bond? You multiply the conversion basis—twenty-five shares for each bond, say—times the current market price of the common stock—$30, for example. The result—$750—is your conversion value.

The *conversion premium* is simply the amount by which the bond exceeds the conversion value. If a stock is trading at $50 and the bond convertible at $45 is trading at $50, the premium is $5.

With convertible bonds, the big question for investors is when to convert to common stock. The answer is, you should stay with the bond only as long as it pays you higher current income than you would receive if you swapped it for stock.

WHY: Convertibles offer investors higher income than is available from stock and higher capital appreciation than is available from bonds.

When the price of a company's stock falls, the value of your bond falls, too, but not by as much as the stock. And you collect income no matter what happens to the stock (unless, of course, the company goes belly up).

WHY NOT: Convertible bonds aren't for safety-minded investors. They are riskier than other bonds, since their price fluctuates with both interest rates and the stock market. Another drawback of convertible bonds is that they don't pay as high a rate of interest as other types of bonds.

WHERE: You may purchase convertible bonds through a financial adviser or stockbroker. Convertible bond prices are listed each day in the bond tables of *The Wall Street Journal* and most daily newspapers. You'll find convertible bonds marked with a "cv."

WHEN: Convertible bonds make the most sense in a bull market, when your chances of capital appreciation are higher.

Corporate Bonds

WHO: Suppose you feel like venturing beyond the security of government-issued bonds. You may want to consider bonds issued by corporations if a steady stream of income is among your goals, and you're investing for the long haul.

WHAT: A corporate bond is another name for a corporate IOU. You lend money to a corporation in exchange for its promise to repay you that amount plus interest.

Corporate bonds come in a number of varieties, but most investors need to concern themselves with only two: *debentures* and *mortgage bonds*.

Debentures are debt instruments that are backed only by the integrity of the corporation. Many of the country's largest corporations issue debentures.

Income debentures and *subordinated debentures* both fall into the category of debentures. With income debentures, you're entitled to interest only as it's earned. A subordinated debenture is a debt that's payable only after other debts with a higher claim to a company's assets are satisfied. A *junior subordinated debenture* ranks even lower than a subordinated one. Of course, these terms become meaningful only if a corporation goes bankrupt.

A mortgage bond is secured by a mortgage on the issuer's property, and a lien is conveyed to the bondholders by a deed of trust.

Corporate bonds are higher-risk investments than government bonds. But the yields are almost always substantially greater than the yields of government bonds.

The value of corporate bonds—like the value of all bonds—falls as interest rates rise. As a hedge against the possibility of higher interest rates, you may want to consider investing in either *floating-rate bonds* or *put bonds*.

With floating-rate bonds, rates are regularly adjusted to prevailing interest levels. Put bonds can be sold back to the issuer at face value before they mature. These two bonds offer lower risk associated with short-term securities, but the tradeoff is lower yields.

Our advice—before you make any decisions about which corporate bonds to buy—is to do your homework. Talk to a financial adviser about the particular issue you're considering buying. For example, check its rating in Moody's and Standard & Poor's. And make sure to talk with a professional financial adviser before making a purchase.

You also should make sure you know whether or not the bond you're buying is *callable*. (You'll find this information in the bond's prospectus.)

Most corporate bonds are issued in denominations of $1,000 and sold in lots of five. Income that you receive from corporate bonds is taxed at ordinary rates. The 1986 tax law eliminated preferential treatment for capital gains.

WHY: When you invest in corporate bonds, you receive a higher rate of return than you would from a government bond. And—in the right environment—you also stand to pocket capital gains, since bond prices rise when interest rates fall.

In addition, corporate bonds offer you liquidity. Generally, the higher the quality rating, the greater the liquidity.

WHY NOT: One drawback of these investment vehicles is their risk. Corporate bonds are backed only by the full faith and credit of the corporation that issues them.

What if the corporation goes belly up? Bondholders

usually take priority over common stockholders when the assets are distributed.

The order in which creditors and owners are paid usually goes like this: the IRS; creditors; bondholders; preferred stockholders; and common stockholders.

But this advantage isn't much of an advantage at all. In many cases of bankruptcy, few people below the level of creditor receive any amount of compensation.

Another drawback of corporate bonds is that many of them are callable. So your ability to collect high interest rates in a low-interest-rate environment is often limited.

And the price of corporate bonds is volatile. Values rise and fall with interest rates. If you plan to sell a bond before maturity, be cautious.

WHERE: Corporate bonds are issued by a variety of companies. You purchase them through a financial adviser or stockbroker.

Although you typically pay no commission when purchasing a bond, you will probably pay a mark-up based on the bond's price when you buy a brand new issue. It's worth asking a financial adviser or broker about these fees, because they are sometimes not included on your confirmation or monthly brokerage statement.

WHEN: Corporate bonds are particularly good investments during periods of moderate economic growth accompanied by stable to declining inflation.

Junk Bonds

WHO: If your goals include a steady stream of income and the opportunity for capital appreciation, *junk bonds* may make sense for you.

WHAT: Junk bonds have fallen out of favor with safety-minded investors—thanks, in large measure, to the number of defaults.

In the last ten years, defaults on these low-grade corporate bonds—also known as *high-yielding* bonds—came to about 1.5 percent of the total dollar amount of these bonds that were outstanding. The default rate on all corporate bonds, meanwhile, was less than 0.10 percent. (In fact, these figures probably understate the problem because of the large increase in new issues of these junk bonds in recent years.)

Junk bonds are debentures—that is, corporate IOUs. And, like other debentures, they are backed only by the corporation that issues them. So, if the company declares bankruptcy, you stand to lose the entire amount you invested.

What makes junk bonds riskier than high-grade corporate bonds is that the companies that issue them are financially less than rock solid. For example, junk bonds are a favorite in corporate takeovers and leveraged buyouts and are issued to raise cash for these transactions.

By definition, junk bonds are corporate bonds that are rated below BBB or Baa or lower by Standard & Poor's or Moody's. The appeal of these bonds is that they pay significantly higher rates of interest—often as much as three percentage points—than other bonds.

Junk bonds—like other corporate bonds—are issued in denominations of $1,000 and usually sold in five lots, that is, in groups of five.

There's no doubt that these bonds attract a certain type of investor—those willing to risk big losses in exchange for the chance to earn a higher return.

You should know, though, that a bond that's rated C is paying no current interest, and one that's rated D is in arrears on interest and principal payments.

Most investors should be cautious about investing in these issues.

It's obvious that not everyone's nerves—or bank account—is suited to junk bonds. So, before you jump on the junk bondwagon, consider not only what you're likely to earn from these investment vehicles but also what you could lose.

Income from junk bonds—be it from interest payments

or capital gains—is taxed at ordinary rates on your tax return.

WHY: The biggest boon of junk bond ownership is the opportunity for high income. These bonds often pay investors as much as three percentage points more than their A-rated counterparts. Junks bonds also offer investors the opportunity for capital gains when interest rates fall or the issuer's financial position improves.

WHY NOT: Investing in junk bonds is risky business. In fact, many financial advisers consider them too speculative for most investors, unless they are a small part of a diversified portfolio.

Some junk bonds are liquid, others aren't. The market for these bonds varies by the individual issue. For example, you may have difficulty selling bonds of a company that's knee-deep in red ink. The market for junk bonds also diminishes in a recession.

WHERE: You may purchase junk bonds through your financial adviser or stockbroker. He or she will charge you a commission on the transaction.

WHEN: Like higher rated corporate bonds, junk bonds perform best in an environment of moderate economic expansion accompanied by a stable to declining rate of inflation.

Mortgage-Backed Securities

WHO: If you're safety-minded, investing for the long term, but want a higher current yield than you'll earn on Treasury issues, consider mortgage securities.

WHAT: If you're familiar with the terms *Ginnie Maes*, *Fannie Maes*, and *Freddie Macs*, you may know that they refer to pools of home mortgages.

How do these pools work?

The Government National Mortgage Association (GNMA or Ginnie Mae), Federal National Mortgage Association (FNMA or Fannie Mae), and the Federal Home Loan Mortgage Corporation (FHLMC or Freddie

Mac) purchase mortgages from banks and thrift institutions, pool them, and resell units of the pools to investors.

What do you need to know about these investments?

Let's start with Ginnie Maes.

When you invest in Ginnie Maes, you buy a portion of the thirty-year mortgages insured by the U.S. Federal Housing Administration (FHA) and the Veterans Administration (VA).

Ginnie Maes are known as *pass-through securities*, and are also sometimes referral to a mortgage-backed securities.

With pass-through securities, an institution—in this case, the Government National Mortgage Association—collects monthly interest and principal payments made on mortgagees, subtracts a small administrative fee, then passes the payments on to its investors.

Because homeowners make their mortgage payments monthly, and those payments include both principal and interest, the Government National Mortgage Association mails investors a check each month that includes both interest income and some principal.

One problem with Ginnie Maes is that you cannot predict how much you'll receive each month. The reason is that the amount the Government National Mortgage Association collects in mortgage payments fluctuates as people sell their homes and pay off their mortgages in advance.

But investors are compensated for this uncertainty with higher yields. Ginnie Maes often pay as much as one and a half to two percentage points more than U.S. Treasury bonds.

And they are just as safe as Treasury bonds because, they, too, are backed by the full faith and credit of a United States government agency. The Government National Mortgage Association is part of the U.S. Department of Housing and Urban Development.

A problem with Ginnie Maes is their cost—$25,000

each. But you can get around this problem by investing in mutual funds or *unit investment trusts* (UIT) that buy Ginnie Maes. You can purchase shares in these funds for as little as $500 to $1,000. (For more on bond funds and unit trusts, see Chapter 8.)

As with any investment vehicle, you should discuss the risks and advantages of Ginnie Mae securities with a financial adviser before you buy. Now, on to Fannie Maes and Freddie Macs.

Like Ginnie Maes, Fannie Maes and Freddie Macs are what is known as pass-through or *mortgage-backed securities*.

However, Fannie Maes and Freddie Macs invest in conventional mortgages These mortgages—unlike Ginnie Mae mortgages—aren't guaranteed by the Federal Housing Adminstration or the Veterans Administration.

So they are riskier than Ginnie Maes. But you should know that the Federal National Mortgage Association (Fannie Mae) and the Federal Home Loan Mortgage Corporation (Freddie Mac) do guarantee that you'll receive your interest payments, although the mortgage itself isn't guaranteed.

Fannie Maes and Freddie Macs pay about one half of a percentage point more in interest than does their sister, Ginnie Mae.

The Federal National Mortgage Association and the Federal Home Loan Mortgage Corporation are private corporations chartered by Congress.

Like Ginnie Maes, Fannie Maes and Freddie Macs are—at $25,000 each—pricey. But, also like Ginnie Maes, you can invest in mutual funds that purchase Fannie Maes and Freddie Macs for a small initial amount—typically $500 to $1,000.

One last type of mortgage security that you may not know about but should are those issued by state housing agencies. These agencies raise money for low-interest loans for low-income and first-time homebuyers by selling bonds to investors.

The appeal of these bonds is that they are exempt from federal taxes. They are also exempt from state taxes in the issuing state.

For example, investors in bonds issued by the New York Mortgage Agency—nicknamed Sonny Mae—pay no federal or New York taxes on the interest they earn.

Mortgage securities issued by state housing authorities are the only ones that enjoy preferential tax treatment. You pay taxes on your income and capital gains from Ginnie Maes, Fannie Maes, and Freddie Macs at ordinary rates.

WHY: Ginnie Maes, Fannie Maes, and Freddie Macs pay you a higher rate of return than you'll earn on Treasury bonds of similar maturities.

And they are reasonably safe. These securities not only enjoy government backing but they have as collateral the real estate they finance. Ginnie Maes, Fannie Maes, and Freddie Macs are also liquid. A large market exists for these securities.

WHY NOT: Typically, mortgage pass-through securities are repaid more rapidly when interest rates decline. This means you incur the risk of having to reinvest at lower interest rates. You may also lose a portion of your principal if you sell your securities before maturity—but only if you sell when interest rates are rising.

And mortgage securities provide little protection from inflation, since their value declines as interest rates increase.

WHERE: You may purchase individual mortgage-backed securities through your stockbroker, who will charge you a fee for the transaction.

WHEN: One of the best times to invest in mortgage securities—or any type of bond, for that matter—is when inflation is stable or declining.

Why? You receive a high yield relative to the quality of the security.

Something else you should know: The value of many mortgage securities climbs as interest rates decline. And what that means is this: During an environment of declining interest rates, mortgage securities offer investors the potential of capital gains.

The worst time to invest in mortgage securities is during times of rising inflation and interest rates, because the value of your securities will fall.

Municipal Bonds

WHO: You say a steady stream of income is among your goals, and you're a high-bracket taxpayer? Municipal bonds may be right for you.

WHAT: It used to be that the income you earned from *all* municipal bonds was free from federal income taxes. But not any more—thanks to the 1986 Tax Reform Act. Nowadays, income from *public-purpose* municipal bonds is tax free, while income from *private-purpose* bonds isn't.

What is the difference between the two types of bonds?

Both are issued by state and local governments. But less than 10 percent of the proceeds from public-purpose bonds goes to benefit private parties, such as corporations. By contrast, more than 10 percent of the revenues from private-purpose bonds issued benefits private parties.

This distinction applies only to bonds issued after August 7, 1986. Income from bonds issued before that date is tax-free regardless of how the proceeds are used.

But say you're in the market for municipal bonds today. And you want to know which are best for you, tax-free or taxable issues?

In general, tax-exempt bonds are a better bet if you're in a higher marginal tax bracket. But the only way to know for sure is to run the numbers.

What you want to do is compare the yields of taxable and tax-exempt bonds. And that means you must convert the yield on the tax-free bonds to an *equivalent taxable yield*.

To calculate an equivalent taxable yield, simply divide

the tax-exempt yield by 1 minus your tax bracket (expressed as a decimal).

Say, for example, that you're in the 28 percent tax bracket, and you're considering purchasing a tax-exempt bond with a 5 percent yield.

You divide that yield (5 percent) by 1 minus your tax bracket (28 percent)—or 0.72. The result—6.94—is the equivalent taxable yield of the bond. If you can find a taxable bond that pays more than 6.94 percent, you're better off with it. If not, opt for a tax-exempt bond.

What else should you know about municipal bonds? For starters, public-purpose municipal bonds offer another big advantage over private-purpose bonds.

Public-purpose bonds aren't only exempt from federal taxes but—if they are issued by your home state—from state and local taxes as well. (Only Illinois, Iowa, Kansas, Nebraska, Oklahoma, Pennsylvania, and Wisconsin are exceptions to this rule.)

And some states—fourteen to be exact—also exempt out-of-state public-purpose bonds from taxation. These states are Alaska, Florida, Indiana, Kentucky, Nevada, New Hampshire, New Mexico, North Dakota, Pennsylvania, South Dakota, Texas, Utah, Washington, and Wyoming.

You should look for bonds that are advertised as *double-tax-free*—meaning they are exempt from federal and state taxes—or *triple-tax-free*—meaning they are exempt from federal, state, and local taxes.

Public-purpose municipal bonds also offer investors liquidity and lower risk. Most municipal bonds may be bought and sold easily and quickly (though some are very illiquid). Defaults on these bonds amounted to less than 1 percent of the face value of all municipal bonds issued in the last ten years.

You should know, though, that within the municipal bond universe different types of issues exist with different degrees of risk.

General obligation bonds, for example, are backed by

the full faith and credit of the issuer. *Revenue bonds*, on the other hand, are backed only by the income from the project they are set up to finance—such as a local water or sewer project or hospital.

If the project goes belly up, you could lose your investment. Our advice to our safety-minded clients is to stick with general obligation bonds or buy insured bonds.

Insured bonds cost you nothing extra—the issuer pays the premium—but your yield is one tenth to one third of a percentage point less than on uninsured bonds.

WHY: Public-purpose municipal bonds offer investors tax-free income. They also offer lower risk and—in the case of top-rated bonds—liquidity.

WHY NOT: The value of municipal bonds fluctuates with interest rates and inflation. As interest rates and inflation rise, the value of municipal bonds falls. So municipal bonds aren't for investors who are risk-averse or who have a short time horizon.

Another drawback of municipal bonds is that they are expensive. These bonds sell in units of $5,000. But this stumbling block isn't a large one. As you will see in Chapter 8, investors can—for as little as $500—purchase shares in a mutual fund that invests in municipal bonds.

WHERE: Municipal bonds are almost always traded "over-the-counter." Therefore, the commission is in the spread between the bid and the ask price. On small blocks of bonds, the spread is generally quite wide to enable the broker to make a profit.

WHEN: You know that bonds perform best when inflation is stable or declining.

United States Treasury Securities

WHO: If you're a security-minded investor and a steady stream of income is among your goals, Treasury securities may be right for you.

WHAT: Treasury securities are the safest investments in the world, and for good reason. The idea that the United States would default on its obligations is unthinkable.

Even during the Revolutionary War, the Federal government redeemed its securities—thanks, in large measure, to lobbying by Alexander Hamilton.

Treasury securities, which are debt instruments issued by the federal government, are backed by the full faith and credit of the United States.

Americans buy them and so do foreign investors. In fact, as much as 30 percent of new debt issues now goes to Japanese investors.

Treasury notes are—by definition—obligations that mature in one to seven years. Treasury bonds mature in seven to thirty years.

You may purchase Treasury notes and bonds directly from the Federal Reserve or from a financial adviser, bank, or broker. Income from Treasury securities is taxed as ordinary income on your federal tax return. But it's generally exempt from state and local taxes.

WHY: Treasury obligations offer investors liquidity, little risk, and a steady stream of income. Some more reasons for buying Treasury obligations: they are universally accepted as collateral for loans; transaction fees are nominal; and pricing information is widely available.

WHY NOT: With Treasury obligations, you generally pay no state or local taxes on the interest you earn. That's the good news. The not-so-good news is that the yield on these Treasury bonds is about 0.75 to 1.50 percentage points lower than that of many corporate bonds.

In addition, Treasury bonds are costly. They typically are issued in minimum lots of $5,000, although they are occasionally available in $1,000 pieces.

WHERE: You may purchase U.S. Treasury bonds through your stockbroker, but, if you do so, you should be prepared to pay a small fee.

You may also buy Treasury bonds from your nearest

Federal Reserve Bank. All you need to do is ask the bank to set up a "Treasury Direct" account.

For a free brochure on this topic, telephone your local Federal Reserve Bank or write the Bureau of Public Debt, Department F, Washington, DC 20239-1200.

WHEN: Bonds prices fall when interest rates rise, and vice versa. Bonds usually perform best when interest rates and inflation are low.

Zero-Coupon Bonds

WHO: If you want to lock in a fixed rate of return and are investing for the long term, *zero-coupon bonds* may be right for you.

WHAT: You have probably heard about zero-coupon bonds from people who buy them to help finance a young child's future college education or to create a nest egg for retirement. Or, you may know investors who buy zero-coupon bonds as a way to diversify their portfolio.

First, what are these bonds?

Zero-coupon bonds are—as their name suggests—bonds without a coupon rate. You receive no periodic interest payments from these bonds.

Instead, they are sold at a deep discount from face value like a T-bill. For example, you would pay $100 for a $1,000 bond that yields 12 percent and matures in twenty years.

In other words, you get a fixed rate of return through the gradual appreciation of the security, which you redeem at face value at maturity.

Here's something you may not know.

Uncle Sam requires you to pay taxes on the interest you would earn each year on zero-coupon bonds, even though you don't actually receive any cash until the bond matures. The exception to this rule are zeros issued by a municipality since, as we have seen, that interest is tax-exempt.

You avoid paying taxes on your accrued interest if you

purchase zero-coupon bonds as part of a tax-sheltered retirement account, such as a Keogh or IRA.

Zero-coupon securities come in a number of varieties: corporate zeros, municipal zeros, convertible zeros, mortgage-backed zeros, and Treasury zeros.

If you hold your zero coupon to maturity, fluctuations in interest rates won't affect you. However, if you have to sell your zero coupon bond before it matures, you should know that if interest rates rise, zero-coupon bonds fall in value—and usually more dramatically than bonds that pay current interest.

Conversely, when interest rates fall, zeros rise more rapidly in value, since the bonds are locked in at a specific, and favorable, reinvestment rate.

WHY: Zero-coupon bonds offer investors convenience. You invest a set amount today, and you can rest assured that it will grow to a specified sum when the bond comes due.

You aren't confronted with the problem of reinvesting the interest you earn. The only investment decision you make is to buy the bond in the first place. When you speak with a financial adviser, he or she can help you sort out exactly when zero coupons may be appropriate for your circumstances.

WHY NOT: You must pay annual taxes on your "income" from zero-coupon bonds, even though you don't pocket your earnings until maturity. For this reason, many financial advisers recommend that you buy them only for tax-favored accounts, such as IRAs or Keoghs, where taxes are deferred. Other advisers like these bonds for children's college accounts. Why? You know you'll have the amount you need by the year your child is ready for college. And $1,000 of an under-fourteen child's unearned interest is tax-exempt.

WHERE: Zero-coupon bonds are available from a variety of institutions—banks, brokerage houses, even the Federal Reserve.

You should expect to pay a small sales commission

when you buy zero-coupon bonds—2 percent is typical. The fee is often included in the price of the bond. Prices of zero-coupon bonds are quoted in *The Wall Street Journal* and most daily newspapers.

WHEN: Since the value of zero coupon bonds rises more rapidly than other corporate bonds when interest rates decline, they represent the best value during periods when interest rates are expected to fall.

Questions and Answers

I borrowed money to invest in some tax-exempt bonds. May I write off the interest?
Sorry, but the rules say that you may deduct interest only on money you borrow to purchase investments that produce *taxable* income.

What is Sallie Mae?
Sallie Mae is the nickname of the Student Loan Marketing Association, a publicly held corporation. The company pools government-guaranteed student loans and resells them to investors in two forms—bonds issued by Sallie Mae and Sallie Mae stock.

The bonds carry little risk—they are backed by the full faith and credit of the federal government—and they yield about a quarter of a percentage point more than Treasury securities with similar maturities. Sallie Mae stock is traded on the New York Stock Exchange.

CHAPTER 5

EQUITY INVESTMENTS

If we knew today what the stock market was going to do tomorrow, we would all be rich by the day after. But who knows? There's always someone who can tell you how you *should* have invested, what stock you *should* have bought, or what stock you *should* have sold.

That advice, alas, was valuable yesterday, not today. What you need now is information that will help you make investment decisions today and in the months ahead.

It's a fact. Historically, stocks have produced higher returns than almost any other investment vehicle over the long haul.

Since 1926, the annual return on small company stocks has averaged 12.6 percent, and on common stocks, 9.8 percent. These figures compare to an average return of 4.8 percent for long-term corporate bonds, 4.1 percent for long-term government bonds, and 3.4 percent for Treasury bills.

These historic results, of course, don't guarantee that the same will happen tomorrow. They do suggest, however, that at least a portion of most people's portfolio should be in stock or equity investments.

In this chapter, we tell you what you need to know before you put your money in the market. In the following section, we review the array of equity investments.

We begin, though, with a few key definitions. Just as you wouldn't take a job as a telephone operator in

Istanbul unless you spoke Turkish, you should also not invest in the stock market until you learn the language of Wall Street.

Return on equity is one way to measure how well a company is performing and to contrast its performance against others in its industry. You calculate this return—which is expressed as a percentage—by dividing a company's common stock equity (that is, its net worth) into net income.

Earnings per share is the amount of profit allocated to each outstanding share of stock. Say, for example, that a company reports after-tax earnings of $25 million for the year. The number of shares outstanding in the corporation is 12 million.

Its earnings per share would be $2.08—that is, its earnings of $25 million divided by the number of outstanding shares, or 12 million.

Price/earnings ratio, or P/E ratio, is a simple computation, but one that allows you to calculate how much you're paying for the current earnings of a company.

The ratio—which is also known as the P/E multiple—is determined by dividing the stock price by the earnings per share. Here's an example.

Say a stock is selling for $52 a share, and its earnings are $4 a share. Divide $52 by $4 and the result—13—is the P/E ratio.

P/E ratios are calculated using both earnings from the previous year and estimates of earnings for the current year. A *trailing P/E ratio* is based on earnings from the last year, while a *forward P/E ratio* is one that uses predictions of future earnings.

High P/E ratios—those with a multiple greater than 20—suggest a company that's on the fast track. Investors are willing to pay more for this stock's earnings, because they anticipate, rightly or wrongly, that the company will will experience rapid earnings growth.

Stocks with low P/E ratios are usually more solid, less risky, and less likely to provide high earnings growth.

These are the equities of blue-chip companies, mature industries, and stock groups that are currently out of fashion. Low P/E stocks usually provide high dividend yields, unlike most high P/E stocks.

Book value per share is a measure of value. If you divide a company's net assets by the number of shares outstanding, the result is book value per share.

You should know, though, that book value doesn't tell you the company's liquidating value—that is, what the company would be worth if it sold its assets for cash.

Debt-to-equity ratio measures the debt of a company compared to the company's net worth. You can calculate debt-to-equity ratio in two ways.

One is to divide total liabilities by total shareholder equity in order to see how well the shareholders' equity will fare against creditors' claims should the company liquidate.

The second way is to divide total long-term debt by total shareholders' equity to measure leverage, or the amount of money the company has borrowed to boost return on owners' equity.

Compare a company's debt-to-equity ratio to the ratios of other companies in the same industry. If there are significant differences, you might neeed to do some further research before you go ahead and invest in that company.

Dividends are payments to stockholders, usually paid on a quarterly basis. The amount is decided by the company's board of directors and usually reflects the company's earnings for that time period.

You may want to consider investing in an equity mutual fund, especially if you have limited money to invest. The fund can relieve you of the need to constantly monitor many companies.

Something else you should know: Customer accounts containing cash and securities at most brokerage firms are insured by the Securities Investor Protection Corporation (SIPC). The SIPC insures accounts at member firms up to $500,000 in cash and certain securities (not mutual funds), with a limit of $100,000 on the cash portion.

The SIPC covers your losses only if the brokerage firm fails. It doesn't help you out if your investments proved to be poor ones or your stock declined precipitously in price.

Stocks are traded on a variety of exchanges.

The New York Stock Exchange—or NYSE—traces its roots to 1792, when a group of securities salesmen met under a buttonwood tree at 68 Wall Street in Manhattan.

The men promised "not to buy or sell from this day for any person whatsoever, any kind of public stock at a less than one-quarter-percent commission on the specie value, and that we will give preference to each other in our negotiations."

It was this agreement—later dubbed the Buttonwood Agreement—that gave birth to the NYSE, now the largest in the United States with some 1,600 listed corporations.

The 1,300 or so seats on the NYSE are owned mainly by partners or officers of securities firms, although there are a few individual owners as well.

Stocks that trade on the NYSE—or "the Big Board," as it's often called—usually belong to older, more established companies. Examples of companies listed on the NYSE include such household names as Ford, IBM, and Kodak.

Stocks listed on the NYSE must meet strict requirements—a minimum amount of time in business, a record of earnings, a diversity of shareholders, and so on.

Stocks listed on the American Stock Exchange or AMEX must also meet stringent requirements. For example, the firm must have earnings of at least $400,000 and corporate net worth of at least $4 million. And the market price of the shares must be at least $5. Stocks traded on the American Exchange—which is also known as "the Curb"—are usually of established small- and medium-sized companies.

The *over-the-counter* market is a nationwide network

of brokers and dealers who buy and sell stocks that usually aren't sold on either the NYSE or the AMEX. In this market, transactions are made through a computerized telephone network rather than on the floor of an exchange.

In the past, over-the-counter stocks were mainly those that couldn't qualify for the NYSE or AMEX. That, however, is no longer the case. Over-the-counter stock trading is regulated by the National Association of Securities Dealers (NASD).

The initials NASDAQ stand for the National Association of Securities Dealers Automated Quotations System, a computerized network that's owned by the NASD and provides brokers and dealers with price quotations for over-the-counter securities.

In addition to these three major exchanges, there are a number of regional exchanges, such as the Pacific Stock Exchange (PSE).

Common Stock

WHO: If you count capital appreciation among your investment goals, you probably want to include common stocks in your portfolio.

WHAT: When you own shares of *common stock*, you own a part of a company. Your ownership stake depends on how many shares you hold. For example, if you own 1,000 shares of stock and the company has 1 million shares of stock outstanding, your ownership stake is 1 percent.

But even if you own only one share of stock, you're entitled to certain legal rights—among them, the right to receive declared dividends and the right to vote on certain issues that affect the company.

Common stockholders, for instance, elect the company's board of directors and vote on changes in company bylaws—including measures to ward off hostile takeovers.

Stocks of public companies are listed on a variety of

exchanges or may be traded over the counter. The stock of closely held companies is traded privately and isn't easily bought and sold.

Information about public companies is easy to obtain.

The law requires companies to file annual information reports—called 10-Ks—with the United States Securities and Exchange Commission (SEC).

You can look at these reports at local SEC offices. But most companies will, for the asking, send you their 10-K and most recent annual report free of charge.

And you should ask for both. The 10-K provides information that the annual report doesn't. For example, it presents more detailed financial statements and tells you how much corporate stock is owned by the company's top management.

You can also request 10-Qs—the report a public corporation must file quarterly with the SEC—and 8-Ks. A company must file an 8-K when an extraordinary event occurs, such as bankruptcy, mergers, or a change in auditor. (Over-the-counter companies file similar reports, known as 10-Cs, in these circumstances.)

All these reports are a matter of public record.

Common stocks normally fall into two categories—income stocks and growth stocks. There is also a combination of these two: growth and income stocks.

The least volatile of these are *income stocks*, which are usually issues of companies in mature industries. These stocks produce regular dividends.

But these stocks offer little chance of growth.

Unlike the demand for hot software programs or trendy running shoes, demand for the products or services of these companies is fairly stable. Electric utilities are good examples of income stocks. Income stocks are usually the mainstay of the conservative investor's portfolio.

Blue-chip stocks are common stocks of companies with a proven track record of stable growth, steady profits, and regular dividend payments. Because they usually have less volatile prices, they are on the lower-risk end of stock market investments.

There's no authoritative list of blue-chip stocks, but most people agree that in 1989 the stocks of companies such as American Telephone & Telegraph, Coca-Cola, Dow Chemical, Du Pont, General Electric, General Mills, ITT, and Merck qualify for the designation.

Growth-and-income stocks are more volatile than straight income stocks.

But, if you want dividends and also would like the possibility of increasing your investment over the long term, consider growth-and-income stocks. The drawback: as with any investment, the greater the chance of appreciation, the more risk involved. Growth-and-income stocks are slightly more risky than income stocks.

Growth stocks are stocks of corporations that have exhibited greater-than-average gains in sales or earnings over the last few years and are expected to continue their high levels of growth. Over the long haul, growth stocks tend to perform better than stocks in the previous two categories.

Of course, they are also riskier investments, since they usually have higher P/E ratios, lower yields, and are more volatile.

The primary benefit of investing in growth stocks is that they offer the potential for capital gains. But the prices of these stocks can also be extraordinarily volatile.

WHY: Investors may profit from stocks in two ways—by the payment of regular dividends and by a rise in the share price. But it's the possibility of capital appreciation that's the primary benefit of stock ownership. Stocks are also liquid investments. You can sell them at any time. (Of course, you can experience a considerable loss if you must sell when a stock's price is depressed.)

WHY NOT: If there's one lesson to be learned from the 1987 stock market crash, it's this: Common stocks may be extremely volatile in price.

Share prices often decline without warning and without

regard to the financial condition or prospects of a company. True, the stocks of older, more established corporations don't fluctuate as dramatically as the stocks of newer, emerging companies.

But even the shares of seasoned companies are subject to price fluctuations in cases of takeovers or disasters, such as the Alaska oil spill.

Dividends aren't guaranteed. If the earnings of a company plummet, so will its dividends. And many growth stocks pay no dividends at all, because the companies retain their earnings to plow back into operations.

WHERE: Common stock prices are listed each day in *The Wall Street Journal* and the business sections of most daily newspapers.

You may purchase shares of common stocks through full-service and discount brokers. Commissions vary by the firm and the number of shares you purchase. You'll usually pay less in commissions at a discount broker, but you'll forfeit the advice a full-service broker offers.

WHEN: Stocks provide some protection against inflation, because share prices usually rise with the rate of inflation. But rising interest rates usually drive stock prices lower, since an upturn in rates frequently signals a downturn in business activity. Moreover, when interest rates are high, people feel they can get a better return with less risk by buying cash equivalent investments.

Preferred Stock

WHO: If your goal is a steady stream of income and your time horizon for investing is long, preferred stocks may be right for you.

WHAT: Preferred stock comes in several varieties, but all pay dividends at a set rate. The most common type of preferred stock is *cumulative*—that is, if a company fails to make a dividend payment because of poor earnings, it can pay you later when earnings improve.

With *noncumulative preferred stock*, you receive no such guarantee. If the company misses a dividend payment, you're out of luck. You receive nothing later.

If you own *participating preferred stock*, you're entitled to share in the profits of the company above and beyond the stated dividend. With *nonparticipating preferred stock*, you're limited to the stipulated dividend, which is why you should opt for participating preferred.

Adjustable-rate preferred stock pays a dividend that's adjustable, usually quarterly, based on changes in the Treasury bill rate or other money-market rates.

You can exchange *convertible preferred stock* for common stock, so its price tends to fluctuate more than *nonconvertible preferred*, which behaves more like a bond.

Owners of preferred stock—like the owners of common stocks—have certain legal rights. But owners of preferred stocks usually give up some privileges to gain preferential treatment in other areas.

For example, preferred stockholders often forego voting rights in exchange for the privilege of receiving dividends before owners of common stock do. Being first in line can be a plus, especially if you own stock in a company that's strapped for cash and paying meager dividends.

Another advantage of owning preferred stock is in the case of a business that's liquidated. Preferred stockholders usually receive priority over common stockholders when assets are liquidated and the proceeds distributed. You should know, though, that preferred shareholders come after bondholders in the pecking order.

The order in which creditors and owners are paid usually goes like this: the Internal Revenue Service, creditors, bondholders, preferred stockholders, and, finally, common stockholders.

Preferred stocks are popular with institutional investors, thanks, in large measure, to the federal income tax laws.

Uncle Sam exempts from taxation 70 percent of the

dividends companies receive from preferred as well as common stocks. Individual investors get no such break. They pay taxes on dividend income at the same rates as ordinary income.

Although preferred stock is, by definition, an equity, it behaves more like a bond, rising in price when interest rates fall, and falling in price when interest rates rise. The only exception, as we saw, is convertible preferred.

In fact, preferred stocks are an attractive alternative to bonds. The yield is slightly higher than the return on bonds, because bonds are "safer"—that is, owners of bonds hold a higher claim on company assets in the case of a liquidation.

WHY: One plus of preferred stocks is their return on equity record. Only a handful of companies has ever failed to pay a promised dividend.

The yield on these stocks is higher than it is on most common stocks, and, unlike common stocks, the dividend remains fixed from year to year.

The price of preferred stocks is also much less volatile than is the price of common stocks. But share prices do respond to changes in interest rates.

WHY NOT: One drawback of preferred stocks is that they carry with them no legal obligation to pay the stipulated dividend. In addition, corporations enjoy a 70 percent exemption from taxes on dividends; this exemption is not available to individual investors.

As with any other stock, if the fortunes of the company decline, the price of the stock may fall. But if the fortunes of the company improve, the price of the stock may not rise.

And investors should keep in mind that these stocks are investments for the long term.

Here's another drawback: Usually preferred shareholders have no voting rights, and preferred dividends are paid at the discretion of the company's board of directors. These aren't legal debt obligations.

WHERE: You may purchase preferred stocks through a full-service brokerage firm. You pay a commission when you buy and sell your stock.

Not every brokerage firm tracks the records of preferred stocks. So you should deal with a firm whose research department follows these issues.

The prices of preferred stocks are listed in *The Wall Street Journal* as well as the business sections of the larger daily newspapers.

WHEN: As a rule of thumb, the return on preferred stocks is highest when interest rates are low and lowest when interest rates are high.

Questions and Answers

Should I invest in new issues?

If your goal is capital appreciation, new issues *may* be right for you. But these stocks aren't for safety-minded investors.

In fact, new issues are usually risky investments.

New issues come in two varieties.

One is *initial public offerings*, or IPOs, which are shares of stock that are sold on the market for the first time by a company that was formerly private. With IPOs, investors sometimes have the opportunity to "get in on the ground floor."

The other type of new issue comes in the form of additional shares of public companies that—for one reason or another—need to raise more capital.

New issues that are sold publicly are registered with the United States Securities and Exchange Commission. New issues that are sold privately avoid SEC registration, as long as a letter of intent establishes that the securities are purchased for investment and not for resale to the public.

New issues are most popular during bull markets.

You should realize, though, that it may be the market itself that's pushing up the prices of these stocks—not the underlying value of the company.

In bear markets, the reverse holds true. Demand is low and new issues are difficult to sell, even if the issuing company is financially solid.

Underwriters of new issues—that is, investment bankers—work to prop up the price of these stocks within the first few weeks of issue. Then the market takes over.

But here's a sobering fact to consider: Within one year, more than half of all new issues sell for less than their initial offering price.

Here's something else you should know if you maintain a stock margin account (that is, an account that allows you to borrow against your holdings): Most new issues don't qualify for margin. That means, you can't borrow against them.

Speculators in new issues may stand to pocket handsome short-term profits—25 percent to 50 percent or more—but usually only in bull markets.

Investors may stand to gain over the long haul, because new issues offer them the opportunity to get in early in emerging companies in exciting new industries.

The floor maintained by underwriters offers investors some protection, but this floor is maintained only for a short time—usually no more than four weeks.

You should know that the price of new issues can plummet once underwriting support is withdrawn and market forces assume control.

And the prices of these stocks are extremely volatile. In fact, they can lose as much as 50 percent of their value in a few weeks.

New issues rarely pay dividends. And you're betting on a company—and often management—without a long track record.

Where can I purchase new issues?

New issues are usually traded over the counter, and you may purchase them through your full-service or discount broker. You pay no commission on these trades, because the issuing company is compensating the brokerage firm for bringing its stock to the market.

However, since there sometimes is a great demand for these new issues, you frequently must be a favored customer of the brokerage to get in on the initial offering.

Most people end up buying these issues shortly *after* the offering, when the shares begin trading in the secondary market (that is, the broker is selling previously purchased shares). And at that point, of course, you do pay a commission.

I borrowed money to purchase stock. May I deduct the interest?

If you borrow money and use it for investment activities, you may deduct the interest from your income only up to the amount of your net investment income.

But you get a break in 1990.

In 1990, you may deduct 10 percent of interest expense in excess of investment income—up to $2,000. After 1990, however, you may deduct only the interest equal to your investment income. How does the IRS define *net investment income*?

It's your investment income—usually interest, dividends, and capital gains—minus the expenses you incur in generating that income.

These limits apply to investment interest only. They don't apply to interest you pay in borrowing money for personal uses, such as the mortgage on your home.

CHAPTER 6

REAL ESTATE INVESTMENTS

Groucho Marx, after much evasion, finally succumbed to the coaxing of a real estate agent who wanted to show him a palatial oceanfront estate.

The salesman drove the comedian up the mile-long, beautifully landscaped approach, then escorted him through the house, the stables, the gardens, and the kennels. Groucho patiently plodded after him, nodding gravely as the realtor extolled the virtues of the property.

Finally, he was ushered out onto the flagged terrace and the salesman waved proudly toward the broad expanse of the Pacific.

"Now, what do you think?" he challenged.

"I don't care for it," replied Groucho thoughtfully, and he gestured at the view. "Take away the ocean and what have you got?"

In his own way, Groucho was right, for in real estate—as any professional will tell you—location is practically everything. If you keep this traditional advice in mind, you may find that an investment in real estate may pay handsome dividends for you.

Before you get into the real estate game, though, you need to know your options—and to understand the risks and rewards of each type of real estate investment. After all, if it were that easy to profit from real estate, Donald Trump wouldn't be famous.

Which one of the many real estate investment vehicles makes sense for your portfolio? In the pages that follow, you'll find the information you need about a variety of real estate investment options. First, though, a few words about return.

Real estate—or so the conventional wisdom goes—is a resource in limited supply. And, as a result, its value will always rise.

But there are some problems with this analysis. For starters, who's to say the supply is all that limited? A hundred years ago, no one ever heard of a skyscraper. So there's no guarantee that ingenious new ways won't be found to stretch this limited resource.

Keep in mind also that real estate values rise and fall often for reasons that have little to do with the intrinsic worth of the property. Witness, for example, the oil glut and the subsequent free fall of real estate prices in Oklahoma and Texas.

That's not to say that you can't do extraordinarily well in real estate. But you should invest with realistic expectations. Now, let's take a look at the pluses and minuses of the real estate investment options available to you.

Real Estate Limited Partnerships

WHO: You say you want most of the benefits of owning real estate but few of the headaches of actually managing properties yourself?

Then these investments may make sense for you.

WHAT: A *real estate limited partnership*—or real estate syndication, as it is sometimes known—is organized by a general partner who buys and manages the properties.

Investors—known as *limited partners*—contribute money to the venture but don't get involved in day-to-day management. In most cases their liability is limited to their original investment, although they do share in any profits or losses.

Usually, partnerships exist for only a certain period of

time. Most aim to liquidate their assets in seven to twelve years and distribute the proceeds to their partners.

Real estate limited partnerships invest in a variety of properties—from hotels and nursing homes to apartment buildings, office buildings, shopping malls, even casinos.

Some partnerships concentrate their properties in specific geographic locations, while others look for promising real estate opportunities across the country.

Before the 1986 overhaul of the tax law, most people invested in real estate limited partnerships to cash in on big tax write-offs. They could then use depreciation deductions to offset some of their earnings or investment income.

The landmark 1986 Tax Reform Act mandated that investors could write off these passive losses only against passive income—that is, income defined by the law as generated by investments in which the individual didn't "materially participate."

As a result, some of the most popular real estate limited partnerships today are organized to produce passive income.

Popularly known as PIGs—for passive-income generators—these limited partnerships are sometimes used by investors to offset some of the passive losses they are still collecting from their old tax-shelter investments.

Essentially, these days you can buy into two types of real estate limited partnerships—those that are designed to produce current passive income plus capital gains when the property appreciates and is sold, and those intended to produce capital gains and tax deductions.

The minimum investment in a limited partnership is often as low as $1,000 for qualified retirement plans, $2,500 for individual investors. You should know, though, that you may be required to meet minimum net worth and income standards.

WHY: When you invest in a real estate limited partnership, you share in the advantages of a real estate investment without the headaches of direct ownership.

These partnerships also give you the chance to own part

of a large real estate project or undertaking that might otherwise be too expensive for you.

Moreover, you can collect current income and enjoy the possibility of price appreciation when the partnership sells its properties.

Since some of these partnerships buy real estate with all or mostly cash, there are no or few mortgages to pay off and thus no or little related debt service. That can mean a larger positive cash flow for you—plus the possibility of generating partially tax-deferred income.

How? Here's an example: Say your share in a limited partnership produces revenues of $12,000, expenses of $9,000, and depreciation of $3,000. For tax purposes, the partnership breaks even. But for cash purposes, you have a $3,000 positive cash flow.

When you consider these investments, remember too that their return is based on the underlying value of the property and isn't subject to stock market fluctuations.

In addition, these vehicles can still shelter some cash flow or pass along any tax losses, subject to the stringent passive loss limitations of the Tax Reform Act.

As with all investments, make sure to analyze the track record of the person who manages the partnership before you make your move.

WHY NOT: What happens if you want to get out of your limited partnership early? Traditionally, these partnerships have been extremely illiquid. But you do have a few options when it comes to selling a real estate limited partnership interest.

For one, you may be able sell your interest through a financial adviser. Or the general partner, or another partner, may want to buy back your interest.

Some firms have emerged that specialize in buying and selling partnership interests. But if you have to sell prematurely, you usually won't get back what you invested.

As a general rule, it's easier to sell your interest in a real estate limited partnership if it's structured to generate income rather than capital appreciation.

WHERE: Real estate limited partnerships are available through private or public offerings. Private offerings limit the number of investors who may participate. Moreover, investors must meet the strict income and net worth requirements of the partnership.

Public partnerships are registered with the SEC, and they must provide a prospectus that has been filed with that agency to all potential investors. You can buy public limited partnerships through your broker or financial adviser.

A word, however, about fees: As a rule, the partnership compensates the person who sells you the partnership interest for his or her services.

And that commission—which is detailed in the prospectus—is often quite high. In fact, fees can range from $600 to more than $1,000 on a $10,000 investment.

WHEN: Since real estate has historically served as a hedge against inflation, real estate limited partnerships make sense when inflation is on the rise. Many financial advisers say that every diversified portfolio should include at least some real estate.

Real Estate Investment Trusts

WHO: If you want to invest in real estate but preserve liquidity at the same time, *real estate investment trusts*, or REITs, may be right for you.

WHAT: REITs are similar to mutual funds. That is, you put money in a fund—a REIT—with other investors, and the REIT buys or finances such income-producing and growth-oriented properties as apartment buildings or shopping complexes.

The manager of the REIT uses some of the funds generated by the property to pay expenses, and you and the other shareholders pocket the rest in the form of dividends.

What happens if some of the properties in which the REIT invested are sold? Then the profits from these sales also are passed along to the investors.

Usually, when dividends increase, the price of the REIT shares goes up as well—but outside circumstances, such as interest rates, can also affect the share price.

The federal government doesn't tax REITs in the same way as it taxes corporations—as long as the REIT pays out at least 95 percent of its profits to its shareholders. The benefit for shareholders is obvious: more money goes into their pockets and less into Uncle Sam's.

When REITs perform well—which they do as long as dividends are generous and the properties continue to appreciate in value—investors can expect average total returns of 6 to 8 percent annually. REITs, however, are far from foolproof.

It's crucial to check out locations and market conditions before putting any money into real estate—even into a real estate fund such as a REIT.

Remember, real estate is only as good as its location and management. Poorly chosen and poorly managed properties can turn a reasonably sound investment into a nightmare, but one that can be avoided if you research the reputation of the management team before handing over your money.

An *equity REIT* is one of the two major types of REITs. (The other is a *mortgage REIT*, which we cover next.) Equity REITs invest directly in properties.

They tend to specialize in the properties they buy. For example, some choose to concentrate on nursing homes and other health-care facilities. Others invest exclusively in large shopping centers, while still others buy office and other commercial buildings.

But not all equity REITs are organized the same way.

Some pass along to their shareholders the rents they collect, while other equity REITs use these funds to buy more real estate.

Tip: Older equity REITs usually make better investments than newer ones. The reasons? For one, older REITs sell at the deepest discount from the property's appraised values, so that you as an investor are buying properties for much less than their resale value.

Older equity REITs are also appealing because their managers have had time to gain experience, and the properties are most likely to already be producing income.

In addition, investors in older REITs don't have to pay the heavy start-up costs associated with REITs that are just getting off the ground.

But they do have to pay brokers' commissions.

Here's something else you should know: Many REITs have a perpetual life. That is, when a property is liquidated, proceeds immediately go into another property.

However, some REITs have a finite life, usually seven to ten years. After that period, they liquidate all their properties and distribute the proceeds to shareholders.

Tip: If you're interested in even greater diversification, a handful of mutual funds invest in a portfolio of REITs.

WHY: A great advantage of REITs over other forms of real estate investment is their liquidity. So—even though real estate is usually illiquid—investors in REITs enjoy the same liquidity they would have if they put their money into a mutual fund investing in stocks or bonds.

You can buy your shares through a broker and sell at any time (although prices may vary considerably with the market value of the underlying assets).

And because you're buying shares in a fund, REITs allow you to enter the real estate market with only a small investment.

Still another advantage of REITs: You reduce your risk by buying into a diverse portfolio of properties—just as wary stock market investors spread their risk by buying shares in mutual funds that invest in a variety of securities.

WHY NOT: The value of your REIT shares—like stocks—can fluctuate considerably. So some risk-averse investors may want to steer clear of REITs.

Tip: You should take special care when it comes to investing in certain types of equity or mortgage REITs known as *blind pools*. These types of REITs usually don't specify the properties they intend to invest in before their shares are first offered for sale.

In fact, the managers of blind pools can take up to a year to make their real estate purchases. During that time, your cash is simply deposited in short-term securities.

Moreover, the share prices of these REITs usually drop once the initial offering is completed, reflecting the offering expenses associated with raising start-up capital.

Of course, if you have faith in the track record of the managers running a blind pool, you shouldn't rule it out as an investment possibility. The bottom line is, read the prospectus carefully so that you know exactly what you're investing in.

WHERE: About a third of all REITs are listed on the New York Stock Exchange and the American Stock Exchange. The rest are traded over the counter.

You can invest in REITs through a financial adviser or broker, and most full-service brokerage firms issue research reports on REITs.

WHEN: When inflation is high, REITs usually do better than the stock market as a whole. Like any real estate investment, they act as a hedge against inflation.

You should know, though, that the price of mortgage or equity REITs fluctuates with the financial markets—and that's true even if real estate prices are rising. The share price of a mortgage REIT generally goes up when interest rates fall and goes down when interest rates climb.

Direct Ownership of Rental Real Estate

WHO: If you're interested in a hedge against inflation and potential appreciation—and don't mind being a landlord—buying rental real estate directly may be a smart move for you.

WHAT: You can buy for rental purposes anything from a one- or two-family house to a multi-unit apartment building to an office building.

You know that investors who've been in the right place

at the right time have reaped huge profits with what seems like relatively little effort—and, in fact, you're right. Buying and selling property directly can be an extremely rewarding business.

Before you dive in, though, consider these words of caution: Never buy real estate without analyzing the area and the market in which you're interested. And remember, the dizzying appreciation of just a few years past is probably behind us now.

Also, consider these questions before you buy: Are condominiums selling well or is the demand behavior for apartments and single-family homes?

Is the property in question near shops, schools, entertainment, and public transportation? Are businesses moving into—or out of—the area? What types of rents can the local economy bear? Are there local zoning restrictions that may impede your plans?

And consider investing with a partner. You'd be surprised how much ready cash—and time—is needed for repairs and maintenance.

Then, too, go in with realistic expectations. Rental incomes aren't always adequate to cover mortgage payments. It may take the addition of tax breaks just to come out even. Worse yet, your property may remain unrented for a period of time.

Ideally, your property should generate enough income to cover your debt and operating expenses and provide a good return on investment when you consider appreciation.

Tip: As a rule of thumb, it's better to buy the worst house in the best neighborhood than the best house in the worst neighborhood.

Tip: You may not know it, but the more apartments a building contains, the lower the risk due to vacancies. In other words, you lose less on a percentage basis if one of eight apartments is vacant than if one of two is without tenants.

Tip: Make sure to have any property you're considering buying inspected by experts for termites, structural problems (including roof and fireplace damage), and potential weaknesses in the heating, cooling, and plumbing systems.

Remember, you can use the cost of these repairs as a bargaining chip to negotiate a lower purchase price from the seller.

WHY: No doubt about it. The biggest boons of real estate ownership are the possibility of appreciation and the opportunity for leverage. You may purchase rental real estate with a down payment as small as 10 to 15 percent of the purchase price.

Another benefit from rental property is the fact that real estate has tended to outperform most other investments during periods of moderate inflation—from around 7 to 9 percent. It has also done well during periods of high inflation.

WHY NOT: Real estate is one of the most illiquid of investments. Though you may find a buyer for your rental property in a week, it's possible for the property to remain on the block for months or even years before a suitable buyer appears on the scene.

Acting as a landlord can bring more than its share of aggravation and expense—from midnight calls about broken furnaces or leaky roofs to dripping faucets or frozen pipes.

Investors who want to buy and sell property directly should go into this venture with their eyes wide open. Not only can managing property be an unexpectedly time-consuming job, but the returns aren't always as high as one expects.

In fact, there may be no returns at all. Real estate is now relatively flat in some regions, as the boom moves on to other areas.

In addition, the tax breaks for rental property are less favorable than they were three years ago. For example, the 1986 Tax Reform Act capped the amount of losses from rental real estate that you can use to offset nonpassive income at $25,000 a year.

This full amount may be claimed only by taxpayers whose adjusted gross income is $100,000 or less, and only if they participate actively in the property's management.

WHERE: You can purchase residential rental property or commercial real estate directly from the owners, or you can go through a real estate agent.

WHEN: Rental real estate is no different from any other real estate investment. When inflation is high, it usually performs better than the stock market as a whole. So, like any real estate investment, rental real estate acts as a hedge against inflation.

Questions and Answers

We want to invest in rental real estate. Where should we start?

Start in the place you know best—your hometown.

While property may be appreciating faster elsewhere, you stand the best chance to profit in a place you know well. Also, it's difficult to be an out-of-town landlord.

Make a list of the up-and-coming neighborhoods. You should be able to make intelligent choices based on your knowledge of the area.

Which is the best investment, residential rental property or commercial rental property?

There's no hard-and-fast rule. We know people who make money investing in residential real estate and people who make money with commercial properties. Ask a real estate professional in your area which type of property is currently appreciating faster.

I borrowed money to help finance construction of a small office building. May I deduct the interest in the year I pay it?

It's a little known fact but, when you take out a loan to help finance the construction of a commercial building or residential rental property, you may not deduct the interest in the year you pay it. Instead, you must *amortize* it—that is, spread it out over time.

Here's an example.

Say you're a physician, and you're tired of paying rent. With the help of an architect friend, you begin construction of a two-story office building to house your booming medical practice. During construction, you rack up a hefty $20,000 in interest charges on building loans.

"Ouch," you say as you write the checks. But wait.

The pain isn't over yet.

Under the tax law, these interest charges are treated as part of your construction cost, so you may not deduct any of it as current interest.

The reason? The costs are for benefits that you receive over time—meaning the use of the building. So you write off these interest charges over the useful life of the building—a hefty 31.5 years for commercial real estate and 27.5 years for residential rental property.

CHAPTER 7

HARD ASSET INVESTMENTS

The tangible reality of hard assets—gold in a vault, for instance, or a diamond on your finger—doesn't assure a person who invests in them of absolute safety.

But when the economy becomes more uncertain than it normally is, these hard assets start to look awfully good. Are they, really? Should your portfolio include investments in natural resources? And what about that favorite long-term haven, gold?

There's a reason hard assets look attractive when the unpredictable winds of financial change start to blow. Read on to learn why.

Gems

WHO: A beautiful diamond, ruby, or emerald may make you feel like a million dollars, but for most of us, gemstones rarely make good investments.

WHAT: You may not know it, but most gemstones are actually colorless. Their color comes from impurities in the stone that act as pigmenting agents.

Rubies and emeralds aren't the names of actual minerals. A ruby is the red variety of corundum, and an emerald is the green variety of beryl.

In total, some one hundred different minerals qualify as

precious or semiprecious stones. And when it comes to investing in these gems, what you don't know can hurt you.

What criteria should you use to judge whether a gem is really a gem—that is, whether it's worth what you're paying? You take into account such factors as carat, cut, color, and clarity. *Carat* is a unit of weight equal to 200 milligrams.

"Carat" comes from the word *carob*—seeds of Mediterranean trees that were used to balance scales in ancient times because they were so uniform in weight. As a rule, the larger the number of carats, the more expensive a gem and the more rapidly it appreciates in value.

Cut is the way the gem is shaped. A gemstone increases in brilliance—and value—with the number of facets that are cut into it.

Color is just that—the color of the stone. Diamonds range in color from clear to yellow, with colorless stones the most valuable. With rubies, emeralds, and other colored stones, by contrast, the more intense the shade, the more valuable the stone.

Clarity refers to clearness. A universally accepted letter system is used to grade diamonds—the clearer the diamond, the lower the letter in the alphabet. A change of one letter grade in clarity can move the price of a diamond up or down by hundreds of dollars per carat.

There's no such grading system for colored stones, such as rubies and emeralds. So, while colored gems usually cost less than diamonds, they are also riskier investments.

Two rules of thumb to follow when investing in gems: Invest in gems as much for your pleasure as for profit. You're less likely to be disappointed that way.

And, if you do invest in gems or jewelry, get them appraised by an independent reputable gemologist. The American Gem Society at 5901 West Third Street in Los Angeles, California, 90036-2898, can refer you to reputable jewelers and appraisers in your area.

WHY: Gems—or jewelry that contains gems—are an investment that provide pleasure as well as potential profit.

WHY NOT: Dealers who sell gems—or jewelry containing gems—take a hefty markup, often as much as 100 percent. Yet, when you sell a gem or a piece of jewelry, dealers usually pay no more—and sometimes less—than the wholesale price.

What's most appealing about gems—their one-of-a-kind beauty—is precisely what makes them so difficult to invest in with any certainty. Since no two stones are absolutely identical, there's no standardized market for gems other than investment-grade diamonds.

Also, no agency of the federal government regulates or polices the sale of gems, so it's crucial that you buy only from reputable dealers.

Another drawback to gems is their illiquidity.

WHERE: You can purchase gemstones from jewelers and dealers. Make it a point never to buy gems over the phone from someone you don't know.

And never purchase stones that are sealed in plastic or in containers that make them difficult to examine. Disreputable dealers, for example, have been known to coat a diamond to disguise its yellowish color. It's difficult to spot this coating when the stone is sealed.

Deal only with reputable companies in the jewelry or gem industry. Ask dealers for references, then check those references.

Jewelers who belong to the American Gem Society are a good bet. This group requires its members to take refresher courses and pass examinations to maintain their expertise.

Buy gems only from dealers who guarantee to repurchase the stones if you're not completely satisfied. And purchase only gems that are certified by a bonded and insured gem laboratory—that is, one that guarantees the accuracy of its work.

If you would like more information about investing in

gems, ask the American Gem Society to send you a copy of its booklet, *The American Gem Society Consumer Kit*. The publication is free and includes a listing of its 3,000 member firms in the United States and Canada.

Also available free for the asking from the American Gem Society is *Diamonds—Facts and Fallacies*, a purchasing guide.

The American Society of Appraisers (P.O. Box 17265, Washington, DC 20041) will provide you—at no charge—a list of its members. (The organization requires members to substantiate their competence and adhere to a strict code of ethics.)

WHEN: The price of gems typically rises with the rate of inflation, so these stones can sometimes serve as a hedge against inflation.

Gold

WHO: Are you looking for a hedge against inflation? Then you may want to include gold in your investment portfolio.

WHAT: In 1848, when gold was discovered in the Sacramento Valley, thousands of Americans went west to stake out claims and become, they hoped, instant millionaires.

The stampede swelled the population of California to more than 100,000—thereby entitling it to statehood—but relatively few of these "forty-niners" ever struck it rich. In reality, gold proved to be as elusive as it was precious.

Investing in gold is easier than it used to be. In fact, you can speculate in gold in a host of ways. The two most common, though, are gold bullion and gold coins.

People who like their gold in solid chunks may want to buy *bullion*—that is, gold bars or ingots—and keep it in a depository.

Gold bars may remind you of Goldfinger's aborted attempt to take over Fort Knox, but buying gold bars is less practical for the average investor than buying gold coins.

These coins are sold for a small premium above the value of their gold content. (We aren't talking about rare gold coins here, but newly minted gold coins.)

Most coin dealers sell one-ounce coins for 5 to 7 percent above the daily spot market price of gold and repurchase the coins at 2.5 percent above spot. But you should be prepared to pay larger premiums for smaller denominations.

Popular coins available to investors include the Canadian Maple Leaf, the U.S. Gold Eagle, the Mexican Peso, the South African Kruggerand, and the Chinese Panda.

WHY: Historically, gold, like other hard assets, has served as a hedge against inflation. As the rate of inflation rose, so did the price of gold.

Another good reason for buying gold is that it's liquid. There's always an active market for gold, so you can sell it any time.

WHY NOT: You should know that the price of gold is volatile. In fact, it can fluctuate for reasons that are as much emotional as they are economic. Another drawback of gold—or any precious metal, for that matter—is that it yields no current income.

WHERE: You can buy gold bullion and gold-mining stocks through a financial adviser or stockbroker. Gold coins are sold by coin dealers.

WHEN: If you think inflation is about to take off, it might be a good time to invest a small portion of your portfolio in gold.

Oil and Gas

WHO: Oil and gas partnerships aren't for safety-minded investors. But if you're not averse to risk, and capital appreciation and a steady stream of income are your primary aims, these investments may be right for your portfolio.

WHAT: To begin—a few definitions of terms we use frequently in this and other chapters. Most oil and gas investments are organized as partnerships. A *partnership* is defined as two or more people who agree to do business together.

Unlike individual taxpayers, partnerships don't pay separate federal income taxes. Nonetheless, the IRS still requires them to file tax returns.

What's more, partnerships must provide each investor, or partner, with a Schedule K-1. This form lists partnership income and deductions. Each partner transfers the information contained on this schedule to his or her personal tax return.

Uncle Sam compares the information on each partnership return with the data reported on the personal tax returns of the partners. The reason for all these forms is that the IRS wants to make sure partners accurately report their share of partnership income—or deductions.

A partnership can include two types of partners: general and limited. *General partners* are personally liable for all partnership debts.

If a partnership goes bust, general partners may have to sell their houses, cars, and other personal assets to satisfy the partnership's creditors.

Limited partners, on the other hand, are usually not held personally responsible for any debts of the business beyond the amount they invested or promised to invest plus any profits or—in IRS jargon—distributions they received from the partnership.

Say you purchase an interest in an oil-drilling partnership, and you agree to contribute $35,000 over three years. In the first year, you put in $10,000, and, in the second year, $15,000. Then, with virtually no warning, the partnership goes belly up.

Your losses add up this way: You're out the $25,000 you invested to date. But you may also have to fork over the $10,000 you promised to invest in year three—for a total loss of $35,000. The money goes to satisfy the creditors of the partnership.

Uncle Sam classifies most limited partnership investments as *passive activities*—meaning businesses that you don't actively participate in managing.

Under the tax rules, you may use your losses from passive activities only to offset your gains from these activities. You may not deduct passive losses from other types of income—wages, salaries, interest, dividends, and so on.

Uncle Sam carves out an exception to this rule for *working interests* in oil and gas wells. He says that you may still use losses from these ventures to offset your ordinary income. The problem is, along with a working interest comes unlimited liability.

For most people, the drawback of unlimited liability far outweighs the advantage of deducting losses from their ordinary income. So, as a rule of thumb, many financial planners advise their clients not to invest in oil and gas partnerships for tax reasons alone.

Here's something else you should know: Oil and gas syndicates and pools are actually specialized forms of partnerships.

Syndicates are partnerships that own a single property—a gas well in Texas, for example—or a group of similar properties—dozens of gas wells in Texas and Oklahoma. *Pools* are similar to syndicates but invest in more than one type of property.

Now, on to the specifics of oil and gas partnerships.

These programs—each of which is a distinct business entity—are set up by independent oil companies or by oil investment managers. They typically range in size from $1 million to $30 million packages, and partnership units usually cost $5,000 to $10,000 each.

These partnerships use your money to lease land and equipment, then pay for the costs of drilling wells and, with luck, producing oil and gas.

The riskiest of all energy investments are *exploratory partnerships*. These are organized to search for undiscovered reservoirs of oil or gas. Some exploratory wells are *wildcat wells*, meaning they are drilled in an area of unproven oil or gas reserves.

Some are *controlled wildcat wells*—that is, they are drilled in an area outside the proven limits of an existing oil or gas field. And some are *deep test* wells, which means that they are drilled within a proven oil or gas field but to unproven depths.

Exploratory partnerships—unlike most other oil and gas programs—offer investors the potential of big profits down the road but little chance of near-term income.

Development partnerships are less risky than exploratory ventures, since they drill in areas of proven reserves to depths that were known to be productive in the past. These programs typically offer more of a chance of striking oil than exploratory programs do.

Balanced partnerships drill both exploratory and development wells. In so doing, they provide investors with the best of both worlds—that is, the higher potential returns offered by exploratory wells with the higher chance of striking oil.

Income partnerships—the least risky of these energy investments—differ from other oil and gas programs in one key respect: rather than drilling new wells, these partnerships purchase wells that are already producing oil or gas.

The key advantage of these programs is that investors receive a steady stream of income as long as the wells keep producing—perhaps between ten and fifteen years.

But as the oil or gas flows from the well and reserves are depleted, the income produced drops. Eventually, the well dries up and is abandoned by the partnership at some cost.

If you decide to invest in oil and gas, do it with the help of a financial adviser who is experienced in evaluating oil and gas programs. And make sure that he or she closely reviews the prospectus of whatever program you choose.

Tip: Look for ventures with low overhead and ones where the sponsors are also investors. (You'll find this information in the prospectus.)

WHY: Some oil and gas partnerships offer the potential for capital gains; others, current income; and still others, capital gains *and* current income.

WHY NOT: Investing in oil and gas partnerships is risky business. You can lose not only the amount you invested but—in the case of partnerships that require you to make payments over time—the amount you promised to invest. Safety-minded investors may want to look elsewhere.

WHERE: One of the best sources of information about oil and gas partnerships is the person who sells these units to you—that is, a financial adviser or stockbroker.

Most national and regional brokerage firms employ specialists to follow, evaluate, and make investment recommendations about oil and gas partnerships. And your broker or financial adviser should be more than happy to pass this information along to you.

WHEN: The price of oil and gas—like the price of most natural resources—typically rises with the rate of inflation. So oil and gas can serve as a hedge against inflation. (Obviously, this rule doesn't apply when the market is glutted with oil or gas.)

Questions and Answers

I believe the price of oil is at rock bottom, and I want to invest in the industry. But I'm not interested in limited partnerships. Any ideas for me?

You may want to consider purchasing stocks of companies in the oil industry. There are lots of stocks to choose from—energy stocks make up about 13 percent of the Standard & Poor's 500 Composite Stock Index. And stocks are more liquid than limited partnership investments.

You may also want to invest in an oil industry sector fund—that is, a mutual fund that invests only in oil industry stocks.

You should know, though, before you invest that energy stocks don't always directly reflect the ups and downs in oil prices. Like other stocks on the exchanges, oil company issues are subject to the fluctuations of the stock market as a whole.

Is there any way to invest in gold without buying the metal itself?

Buy shares in a gold-mining company.

Gold-mining companies in Canada and the United States offer certain advantages over their foreign counterparts: for example, these companies mine their gold in a relatively stable political climate, and the price of their shares is sensitive to changes in the price of gold.

But it's not unusual for shares of these companies to rise or fall more dramatically than the price of gold itself.

If you want to try your luck with foreign companies, you must buy *depositary receipts* rather than common stock. These receipts mean you receive dividends, but give up the right to participate in the management of the company—by voting for the board of directors, for instance.

One plus—or minus—of investing in depositary receipts lies in the value of the dollar. The value of the depositary receipts and dividends you receive varies with the exchange rate of the foreign currency. In other words, share prices and dividends decline with the dollar.

Another way to invest in gold stocks—or stocks of any other precious metals—is through mutual funds. Several mutual funds specialize in domestic and foreign mining stocks.

CHAPTER 8

MANAGED INVESTMENTS

Managed investments include mutual funds, real estate investment trusts (REITs), face-amount certificates, limited partnerships, and unit investment trusts (UITs), to name a few.

These vehicles are called "managed" because, in each instance, a manager is in charge of selecting and monitoring the underlying investments.

In this chapter, we'll concentrate on mutual funds, limited partnerships, and UITs.

Let's begin with some mutual-fund basics.

For many people, a mutual fund is the answer to the diversification that's so hard to attain on their own. Even institutions such as pension funds and college endowments invest in mutual funds.

A mutual fund is simply a company that makes investments on behalf of its shareholders. The fund pools the money of different people—each with a different amount to invest.

Money managers then take that pooled money and invest it in a variety of stocks, bonds, or other securities selected from a wide range of industries and companies.

Each shareholder owns a proportionate share of the fund. Investors who put $1,000 into the pool get the same rate of return as the ones who put in $10,000.

Mutual funds come in two varieties.

With an *open-end mutual fund*, investors may buy

shares from the fund or sell shares back to the fund at any time. So the amount of money under management constantly shifts.

You should know, too, that sometimes a manager may close a fund to new investors if the fund, in the manager's opinion, has taken in too much cash to invest optimally.

With a *closed-end fund*, there's a set number of shares outstanding. These shares are traded on the open market just like any stock.

Net asset value (NAV) *per share* is the price at which open-end funds sell or redeem their shares—minus any redemption or deferred sales charges.

It's arrived at by subtracting a fund's total liabilities from its total assets, then dividing the result by the number of outstanding shares.

Closed-end funds, however, sell for an amount that's higher than their net asset value—that is, a *premium*—or for an amount that's lower—that is, a *discount*.

The stock price of closed-end funds rises or falls with supply and demand. Typically, most closed-end funds sell at a discount.

You should know that all funds impose management fees, but some funds add other costs as well, such as initial sales charges and redemption fees.

So, what should you look for when it comes to the fee structure of a mutual fund? Start by asking for a copy of the fund's prospectus, its ''Statement of Additional Information,'' and the latest annual and interim reports to shareholders.

These documents will explain the fund's fee structure.

Most of the fees mutual funds charge fall into one of four categories: annual charges, front-end loads, back-end loads, and 12b-1 charges. Let's take a look at each.

Annual Charges

Mutual-fund managers charge annually—for operating expenses—about 0.5 to 1.5 percent of the value of your fund shares.

Front-End Loads

Should you decide to buy mutual-fund shares from a stockbroker or financial adviser, expect to pay a front-end load—that is, a commission on the shares you purchase, also known as an initial sales charge. That charge usually runs from 4 to 8 percent and is deducted from the amount you invest.

Say you invest $1,000 in a mutual fund and pay a 5 percent sales charge when you buy your shares. That leaves $950 invested in the fund.

Should you buy a large number of shares, the commission may be reduced. Many funds are structured so that your discount grows as the number of shares you purchase increases.

Many people avoid load funds in favor of low-load or no-load funds where the shares are bought directly from the mutual fund or its sponsor.

A low-load fund levies an initial sales charge of 0.5 percent to 4.0 percent, while a no-load fund charges no sales fees. (Some, however, charge a redemption fee of 1.0 percent.)

Whether a fund has a load or not has nothing to do with its performance. How well a fund does depends on the management of its portfolio.

Back-End Loads

As you might have guessed, back-end loads refer to charges you must pay when you take your money out of a fund. Not all mutual funds impose back-end loads—also known as contingent deferred sales charges—and those that do often vary in the amount of the fee.

Usually, you pay more if you take your money out within a year than if you take it out after six years (by then the fee might have been gradually reduced to zero).

12b-1 Fees

This fee takes its name from the section in the SEC regulations that allows mutual funds to charge an annual

12b-1 fee. The fee helps cover the costs of selling and advertising the fund. It's not unusual to find it used in conjunction with a back-end load.

A *mutual-fund family* is a group of two or more mutual funds that have the same investment advisor. An advantage to the investor is that usually no sales charges are levied on transfers—and you can generally switch your money from one fund in the family to another, usually by picking up the telephone.

Frequently the family will include one or more funds that offer a steady stream of current income, along with one or more that offer the potential for capital gains.

For example, if you think the economy is heading in a certain direction, you can move your money to a fund in the family that would perform well in the new economic climate.

Tip: Before you opt for a particular mutual fund, take time to examine its performance record. You should have no trouble getting up-to-date figures that evaluate how a certain fund is performing compared to funds with similar objectives.

It makes some sense to invest in funds that have posted solid returns over a number of years, rather than investing in a fund that has suddenly taken off but has no track record to demonstrate that it has staying power over the long haul.

Watch for any sudden changes in the structure of the fund, such as a dramatic increase or decrease in its size.

Now, you want to know, how do you decide when to sell your mutual-fund shares? And how do you go about redeeming them?

If you realize that your investment goals are changing in favor of higher-risk or lower-risk investments, you may want to opt for a new fund. Or if you decide that your fund isn't performing as well as you had expected, you may want to change to another.

Some other reasons to cash out of a fund: You see that the fund's current portfolio managers are jumping ship, and you're not comfortable with the new team. Or there's a change in the fee structure that results in higher costs, and you don't want to pay more.

When it comes time to sell your shares, consult your prospectus. It spells out the procedures for redeeming your shares—for example, whether you may telephone the fund and ask that your shares be sold, or whether you must put your instructions in writing.

If your fund requires you to write a letter, you usually must mail this document to the fund's transfer agent—in most cases, a bank.

In your letter, spell out your instructions: "Please redeem my 500 shares of Growth Stock Fund, Inc." Then specify whether you want a check mailed to you or whether the money should be wired directly to your bank or transferred to a money-market account.

Most funds—to prevent fraud—require that your letter include your signature, guaranteed by a trust company, FDIC bank, or recognized brokerage house.

Most transfer agents will send your money the day after your shares are redeemed, although the SEC allows funds up to seven days to pay.

Tip: Send your letter by registered mail, return receipt requested, so you'll know when the transfer agent received it.

Now, with the basics behind us, let's take a look at some broad categories of mutual funds that are available today.

Growth Stock Funds

WHO: If capital appreciation is your primary aim—and you can handle volatility—a *growth stock fund* may be right for you.

WHAT: When you invest in an aggressive growth or growth fund, you invest in a diversified portfolio of stocks, in this case, the stocks of fast-growing companies.

Aggressive growth funds are among the riskiest mutual funds, because they invest in stocks of companies with the potential for growth but often little or no track records.

Managers of aggressive growth funds seek to maximize long-term appreciation. What that means is that managers of these funds usually buy and sell stocks more often than do managers of more conservative funds. And, as a result, investors pay higher brokerage costs.

It also means higher costs for operating the fund. And any time operating costs rise, the return to the shareholder might be lower.

Finally, an investor should know that aggressive growth funds often don't reduce their exposure to the stock market even when the stock market dives or soars too high. (Other funds often put some of their assets into cash when stocks don't seem to be a good buy.)

So, be prepared for share prices to decline at times.

Growth funds are risky, too, but they are less risky than are aggressive growth funds. Growth funds invest in the stocks of companies that exhibit faster-than-average growth in earnings over the past few years.

The prices of the stocks purchased by both aggressive growth and growth funds are based, in part, on what investors expect the company's growth to be in the future—not on what it actually is today. Investors take the risk that the growth they are hoping for will materialize.

With aggressive growth and growth funds, you pay taxes on the income you receive at your ordinary rates. If you would like more information on how mutual funds are taxed, ask the IRS for a copy of its free booklet, *Mutual Fund Distributions* (publication 564).

WHY: Growth funds offer investors diversification and liquidity. The biggest boon of these funds, though, is the potential for capital appreciation.

WHY NOT: One drawback of growth stock funds—as well as stocks—is the potential for erosion of principal. A poorly managed fund may underperform the market.

Another negative is smaller dividends.

Aggressive growth and growth stock funds pay smaller

dividends, because the companies they invest in tend to reinvest earnings in their businesses.

WHERE: You may purchase shares of aggressive growth and growth stock funds from a financial adviser or stockbroker or directly from a fund family.

Mutual-fund prices are listed in *The Wall Street Journal* and most daily newspapers. A number of financial magazines also devote substantial space to mutual funds. Among these publications are *Business Week, Forbes, Money*, and *Changing Times*.

WHEN: Aggressive growth and growth funds—like all stock funds—perform best in bull markets. But that doesn't mean you should buy them when the market soars. You'll do best to use dollar-cost averaging to purchase shares. And plan to hold them for the long term, that is at least three to five years.

Growth-and-Income Funds

WHO: You say you're looking for a steady stream of income plus the potential for some capital appreciation? Consider a growth-and-income fund.

WHAT: Growth-and-income funds reduce your risk by investing in the stocks of companies that pay dividends. The fund's return is made up of two components: changes in the market value of the securities the fund owns, and the dividend income from these securities.

This income tends to soften the effect of price declines on your total return. The compromise is that growth-and-income funds usually don't produce the dramatic gains that are possible with funds that invest primarily for capital appreciation.

Companies that pay dividends are usually large and well established. There isn't as much room for capital appreciation as with smaller companies.

WHY: These funds offer investors steady dividends plus the chance for some long-term growth.

WHY NOT: You may not get the same gains from capital appreciation that you would in a growth or aggressive growth fund.

WHERE: You may purchase shares in a growth-and-income fund through a financial adviser or stockbroker or directly from a mutual-fund company.

WHEN: Growth-and-income funds provide dividends even when the stock market falls though their net asset value can still fall.

Equity Income Funds

WHO: If you depend on dividends for part of your living expenses—or if a high degree of uncertainty makes you nervous—an equity income fund may be right for you.

WHAT: Equity income funds are among the more conservative mutual funds. They invest in the stocks of stable companies in mature industries, such as utilities.

You pay taxes on your income from these funds at your ordinary rates.

WHY: Equity income funds offer investors regular dividends as well as lower risk. Equity income funds also offer the potential for capital gains.

WHY NOT: Equity income funds offer less potential for capital gains than growth or growth-and-income funds. They also offer less protection from inflation.

In fact, the value of these fund shares usually declines more dramatically than does the value of other stock mutual-fund shares when interest rates rise. The value of your mutual-fund shares will fluctuate as the stock and bond markets rise and fall.

WHERE: Equity income funds may be purchased through financial advisers and stockbrokers or directly from mutual-fund companies.

WHEN: As with all stock funds, you profit most from equity income funds during times of economic growth, rising corporate profits and falling interest rates.

Bond Funds

WHO: Bond mutual funds make sense for investors who do not have enough available cash—at least $50,000—to invest in a diversified portfolio of individual bonds. They also make sense for investors who want the automatic diversification a fund provides.

WHAT: There are as many bond mutual funds available as there are types of bonds. So you can invest in Treasury security funds, convertible bond funds, municipal bond funds, corporate bond funds, and high-yield (junk) bond funds, to name just a few. You can also invest in Ginnie Mae funds, Freddie Mac funds, and Fannie Mae funds. You can even buy shares in zero-coupon bond funds that mature at various dates. Or you can buy shares in international bond funds.

You should know that there are basically two types of bond funds. The first type—what most people think of when they hear the term *bond mutual fund*—invests in a wide variety of bonds (usually of one type, such as corporate bonds) that mature at many different times.

The other type is a unit investment trust, which we cover later in this chapter.

WHERE: You can purchase shares in a bond fund directly from a mutual-fund company. Or you may buy shares through a financial adviser or stockbroker.

WHY: Bond funds usually let you invest in bonds which you may not be able to purchase as individual issues. As only one example, Ginnie Maes cost $25,000 each. But you can buy shares in a Ginnie Mae fund for a minimum investment of $500 to $1,000.

Another advantage of bond funds, like all mutual funds, is the diversity they provide. For example, you may be justifiably leery about investing in an individual junk bond. But a junk bond fund invests in a variety of issues.

WHY NOT: If you buy shares in a bond fund, the value of your shares will rise or fall depending on interest rates.

WHEN: You should time your investing in bond funds exactly as you would when it comes to investing in individual types of bonds. In general, bond prices rise when interest rates fall. (See Chapter 4 for details.)

Sector Funds

WHO: You say you're willing to bet on the fortunes of a single industry or segment of the economy? And a lot of volatility doesn't trouble you? Then sector funds may be right for you.

WHAT: Sector funds invest in one industry or segment of the economy—chemicals, say, or high technology, or even waste management.

When you invest in a sector fund, you place a bet on the future of that industry—a bet that its fortunes are on the upswing. The problem is that, if you bet wrong, the return from your sector fund may not keep pace with the gains of the market as a whole.

But here's another way to look at sector funds.

They offer you the opportunity for selective diversification—that is, they allow you to choose how you'll diversify your portfolio.

Many people believe that you can boost return by investing in different sector funds at different times in the economic cycle. But few people can successfully time their investments.

You should know that your gains and losses from a sector fund are treated the same way for tax purposes as gains and losses from any mutual fund.

WHY: Sector funds offer investors the ability to invest in a particular industry or economic sector.

WHY NOT: With sector funds, you're not only betting that the stock market will do well in the years or months ahead and that your fund manager will choose stocks wisely, but that a particular segment of the economy will perform well. So, you're assuming additional risk.

Sector funds may pay smaller dividends. Sector funds

MUTUAL FUND COMPARISON

LOW RISK — HIGH RISK

MONEY MARKET FUNDS

These money market funds have three main goals: conservation of capital, constant liquidity and the highest possible current income consistent with these objectives. Capital growth is not an objective. **Very limited risk.**

FIXED INCOME FUNDS

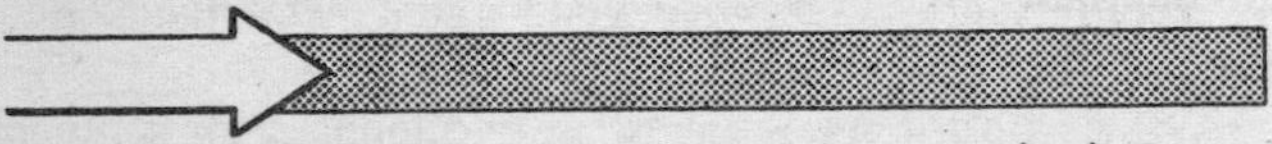

The funds in this group invest their assets primarily in corporate bonds or government securities to seek interest income. Secondary objective is capital growth. **Modest to moderate risk.**

TAX-EXEMPT INCOME FUNDS

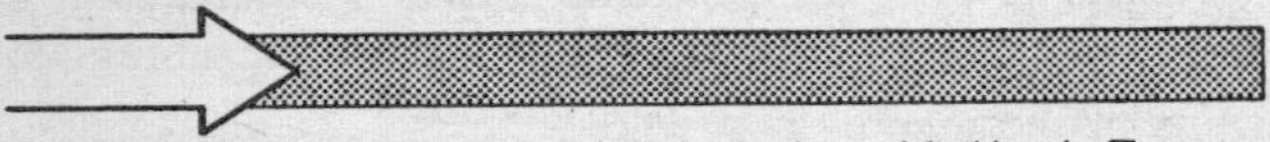

These funds provide tax-free income by investing in municipal bonds. The income is generally free from federal income tax and sometimes free from state income tax as well. **Risk varies by bond quality.**

GROWTH AND INCOME FUNDS

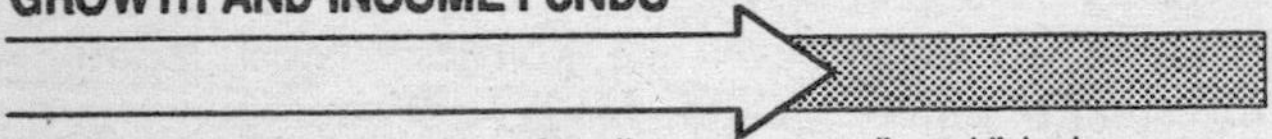

These funds focus on securities of medium to large, well-established companies that offer long-term capital appreciation and reasonable income from dividends and interest. **Moderate risk.**

GROWTH FUNDS

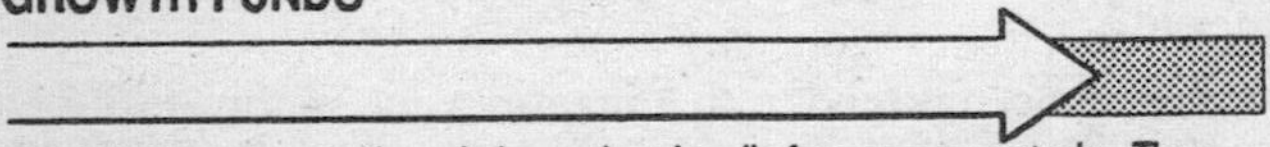

Funds in this group seek capital growth, primarily from common stocks. They are high risk mutual funds with a potential for high reward. **Income is not an investment objective.**

SPECIALTY GROWTH FUNDS

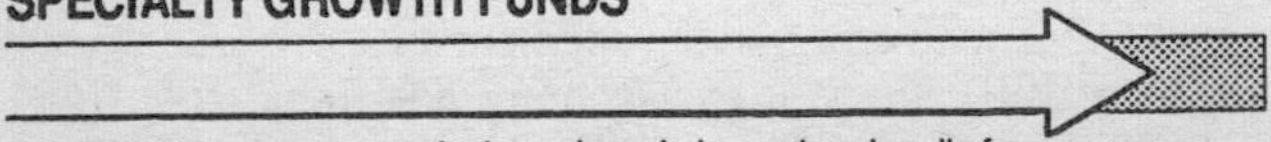

Funds in this group aggressively seek capital growth, primarily from common stocks in a specific industry or economic sector. They are high risk mutual funds with a potential for high reward.

that invest in utility companies are, as you might expect, the exceptions to this rule.

WHERE: You can purchase shares in a sector fund through a financial adviser or stockbroker or directly from a mutual-fund company.

WHEN: Sector funds make sense—many financial advisers agree—when an industry is in the early stages of recovery.

This chart at left matches preponderance for risk with appropriate investment vehicles.

Limited Partnerships

WHO: If you want to buy a stake in an investment you couldn't otherwise afford—a film, say, or a large real estate venture—limited partnerships may be for you.

WHAT: A limited partnership is like a mutual fund in that investors pool their capital to purchase a professionally managed portfolio of investments.

However, while most mutual funds invest primarily in stocks or bonds, limited partnerships may purchase various types of investments—from real estate to entertainment ventures to futures contracts.

Limited partnerships are organized to attain one or more of the following investment objectives:

- Capital accumulation: since a partnership's assets are expected to appreciate over time, investors have the potential to receive a sizable gain when the assets are sold.
- Tax benefits: while the partnership operates, investors receive tax benefits from expenses such as depreciation, operating costs, and interest payments. Investors may be able to defer taxes on capital gains, since they may not realize the gains (and therefore wouldn't be

◀ This chart at left matches preponderance for risk with appropriate investment vehicles.

of any cash generated by the partnership during operations.

As with many investments, there can be no assurance that a specific limited partnership will achieve its objectives.

Every limited partnership consists of one or more general partners and the limited partners.

As an investor in a limited partnership, you become one of the limited partners. A general partner, on the other hand, may be a person, corporation, or partnership that organizes and manages the partnership's affairs.

The general partner is ultimately liable for the partnership's obligations and directly responsible for its success. The general partner often contributes some capital and receives a share of the income, appreciation, and tax benefits.

Limited partners have no role in managing the partnership, but they provide most of the operating capital. Limited partners also receive a share of the income, appreciation, and tax benefits generated by the partnership.

Limited partnerships provide a number of benefits for investors, such as:

- Limited liability: you participate in the investment returns, yet your risk is limited to the amount invested.
- No double taxation: a corporation must first pay corporate taxes on its profits before distributing dividends. Stockholders must then pay tax on these dividends. Most limited partnerships, on the other hand, pass any earnings directly to you, without having to pay taxes at the corporate level.
- Diversification: most limited partnerships spread invested capital among a number of investments, often in different geographical locations; this strategy reduces the impact that any one investment's price movement will have on the overall portfolio.

- Professional management: most investors have neither the time nor the expertise to effectively manage a diversified portfolio of assets. Limited partnerships are managed by experienced professionals, which frees you from any decision-making responsibility regarding the operation of the assets owned by the partnership.

Limited partnerships are categorized by the type of industry they invest in. They are concentrated in several industries, such as real estate, oil and gas, communications, and equipment leasing.

WHY: Limited partnerships may make sense if you have passive income you need to offset with passive losses. Also, if they are run well, you could end up collecting current income *and* realizing a profit on your initial investment. And you don't have to worry about managing the investment. That's the general partner's job.

WHY NOT: Limited partnerships are illiquid, long-term, investments. When you invest in a limited partnership, you're tying up your money for the duration of the partnership. Because there's no established secondary market and none is expected to develop, it would be difficult to sell your partnership interests early. The success of the partnership largely depends upon the ability of the general partner to select and manage the partnership assets.

There are also specific risks involved in the type of investment made through limited partnerships. Some risks include: competition from other properties; government regulations, such as tax-law changes; and changes to the assets of the partnership due to specific market conditions and general economic trends.

WHERE: You can buy units of a limited partnership from a financial adviser or broker.

WHEN: Limited partnerships are risky business. You should buy them only after carefully evaluating individual partnerships with a financial adviser or broker.

Unit Investment Trusts

WHO: Unit investment trusts are best for people who want to invest for the long term, especially when the initial yield of the trust is high enough that you want to lock it in.

WHAT: A unit trust is a type of closed-end mutual fund that contains a fixed portfolio of bonds with the same maturity. The entire portfolio usually remains in the trust until the bonds mature.

These trusts try to lock in the highest yields possible on good-quality issues at the initial offering. Each trust has a limited number of shares for sale, but new trusts are being continually brought to the market.

Unit trusts are usually sold in $1,000 units. They have a one-time sales charge that typically ranges from 2 to 5 percent of the amount you invest. You also pay annual management fees of around 0.15 percent. You don't see either of these fees up front. That's because they're factored into the yield.

WHY: Investing in unit trusts makes sense if the initial yield is high enough that you want to lock it in for the long haul. Also, by investing in a unit trust, you usually get high-quality bonds and do not have to worry about individual issues.

WHY NOT: If you think you'll need your money in a hurry, you shouldn't lock it up in a unit trust. You can sell your units in the secondary market, if you need to, but you may incur a loss.

WHERE: You can buy units through a financial adviser or broker. Prices are based on the value of the securities in the portfolio.

WHEN: You should buy a unit trust when yields are attractive.

You now should have a good idea of the types of investments you can make in order to achieve your goals. In the rest of this book, we'll give you the information you need to shield yourself from financial disaster. We'll also tell you some ways you can—and must—protect the resources you're accumulating.

Questions and Answers

Should I invest in a balanced fund?

Investors worried about putting all their eggs in one mutual-fund basket may want to consider balanced funds. The managers of these funds invest in a variety of stocks, bonds, and money-market instruments on the theory that if one vehicle (such as stocks) takes a dive, then other vehicles (such as bonds) show improvement. The fund is thus protected from across-the-board losses.

These funds also try to achieve a balance between investments that provide current income and those that offer long-term capital appreciation.

What do I need to know about a tax-exempt municipal bond fund before I invest?

A tax-exempt mutual fund operates much as other funds. A portfolio manager oversees the pooled investments of thousands of shareholders. The manager is responsible for determining when to buy and sell the portfolio's holdings.

With a tax-exempt fund, at least 80 percent—usually up to 100 percent—of the investment portfolio consists of municipal bonds.

There are two kinds of tax-exempt mutual funds. One seeks, without too much risk, to maximize current income that's exempt from federal income taxes.

The other—a high-yield tax-exempt fund—tries to provide a high return that's exempt from federal income taxes. (Tax-exempt money-market funds also are available. For the most part, they invest in short-term municipal bonds and notes.)

Portfolio managers who oversee tax-exempt mutual-fund investments keep several criteria in mind when investing the portfolio's assets.

They keep a close watch on economic conditions in

various areas of the country, looking at such factors as unemployment, economic trends, industrial diversification, and fiscal management. Portfolio managers monitor tax-law changes that have an impact on tax-exempt securities.

The types of bonds purchased are often determined by interest-rate outlooks and the credit ratings of the individual bonds. For example, if it looks as if interest rates will fall, the manager may purchase bonds with longer maturities to lock in high rates for as long as possible.

I am an investor in a tax-exempt municipal bond fund. That means all income from the fund is tax-free to me. Right?

Wrong.

Even if your mutual fund purchases only public-purpose bonds whose interest is completely tax-free, the fund may still generate some taxable income to you. How?

Say, for example, that your fund sells some of its municipal bonds at a gain. This profit is distributed to you and other shareholders and is taxable as a capital gain. It's only the interest income from the municipal bonds that's exempt from federal taxes.

You can earn taxable income when you sell or exchange your tax-exempt fund shares at a profit. And—here's something else you should know—shifting money from one mutual fund to another is the same, in the eyes of the IRS, as selling those shares.

If you post a gain, that gain is taxable.

I am retired and considering investing in a municipal bond fund. Any advice for me?

The IRS taxes part of your Social Security benefits if your adjusted gross income (AGI)—plus any tax-exempt interest—tops a ceiling.

That ceiling is $32,000 for married couples filing joint

returns and $25,000 for single people and married couples who live apart and file separate returns.

You pay taxes on one half of your Social Security benefits or one half of the difference between your modified AGI and the base amount, whichever is less.

Confused? An example may help.

Say you're married, file a joint return, and your adjusted gross income—before your Social Security benefits—comes to $43,000. Your tax-exempt interest income adds up to $4,000. So, under the rules, you add this amount to your AGI.

The total—$47,000—tops the $32,000 ceiling. And that means that at least part of your Social Security benefits are taxable.

How much? Say, for example, your Social Security benefits for the year equal $9,762. Now, add to your $47,000 AGI one half of these benefits, or $4,881. The result—$51,881—is your income for the taxability test.

Next, subtract from $51,881 the ceiling of $32,000. The difference is $19,881, and one half of the difference equals $9,940.50. In your case, half of your benefits—$4,881—is less than half the difference between your AGI and the base amount, which is $9,940.50.

So you pay taxes on $4,881 of your Social Security benefits. For more information on this topic, ask the IRS to send you a copy of its free booklet, *Social Security Benefits and Equivalent Railroad Retirement Benefits* (publication 915).

PART 3

CHOOSING INSURANCE

- HOW MUCH RISK IS TOO MUCH
- DISABILITY INSURANCE
- HEALTH INSURANCE
- LIFE INSURANCE
- HOME AND PERSONAL PROPERTY INSURANCE
- AUTO INSURANCE
- UMBRELLA COVERAGE

CHAPTER 9

HOW MUCH RISK IS TOO MUCH?

Sit down with a financial planner, and one of the first questions he or she will ask is whether your insurance shields you from financial disaster.

Why? The answer is simple. Without adequate insurance, you put at risk everything you've worked so hard to achieve.

But how much insurance is adequate? That's what this chapter is all about. So roll up your sleeves and let's get started.

How much insurance do you need?

The types and amounts of coverage you need depend, in large measure, on your personal circumstances, including your obligations to others.

They also depend on how much financial risk you're willing to assume—that is, how much money you want to gamble on losing if disaster strikes.

Your willingness to take risks, in turn, is based on a variety of factors, such as your personality, your physical and financial health, and how much insurance you can afford.

You can examine your own attitudes toward risk by looking at areas where you know you're vulnerable to potential loss or accident.

Then determine how comfortable you are with these

risks and how much coverage you need to eliminate or reduce those risks that are unacceptable to you.

Start by looking at your risk in each of five general insurance categories: health, disability, life, automobile, and property/casualty.

You should know your potential losses in each category. Then transfer to an insurance company any potentially disastrous losses, such as a million-dollar lawsuit or a prolonged period of disability. These are losses that, if uninsured, could have devastating effects on your—and your family's—finances.

Here are a couple of rules of thumb to follow:

- For starters, always cover yourself against the threat of a major loss or a loss that could prove catastrophic—a serious and prolonged illness, say, or the loss of a house. After you make sure that you're covered against these major losses, decide which smaller risks you want to take on yourself.
- The bottom line: you want to make sure you're covered against huge losses. But you don't want to buy more insurance than you need.

It's not so important to be insured for small losses, such as bicycle theft—those that you can comfortably cover yourself. Nor does it always make economic sense.

Other examples of "small" losses not worth insuring might be the cost of having a dental cavity filled or the expense of a short period of disability. Don't pay for risks that you're willing to shoulder yourself; on the other hand, don't *exclude* risks for which you have decided you need coverage. Finally, once you decide that a risk is serious enough to transfer to an insurer, then examine with your insurance representative the types of insurance available.

And, above all, shop around. Insurance companies frequently offer different rates on similar policies. Moreover, you should examine the company's financial strength and its performance over the long term. Do business with companies that are rated A$^+$ or A by A. M. Best, a company that measures the financial stability of insurers. (You can find a copy of *A. M. Best's Insurance Reports* at your local library—or ask your financial adviser or insurance representative.) You can also check the financial health of these companies through Moody's Investor Service. Your library should have the latest Moody *Manuals*.

Getting Started

In the chapters that follow, we review five of the major types of insurance you need to know about.

We also tell you what to look for in insurance policies—and what to avoid. Read these chapters carefully. Then make a checklist of areas where you need better insurance coverage. Finally, discuss those needs with your insurance representative or financial planner.

CHAPTER 10

DISABILITY INSURANCE

How do you protect yourself should you become disabled? The answer is, with disability insurance, and that's what this chapter is all about.

What is disability insurance?

Disability insurance provides you income if you become sick or injured and are unable to work. It protects you and your family from financial disaster by giving you income even if you're off the job for one or two years or more.

Some disability policies cover accidents. Others cover illnesses. Still others cover both accidents and illnesses. Most people should have a policy that covers both.

Who needs disability insurance protection?

Anyone who depends on their earned income needs disability insurance protection. Why? Consider these statistics from the Health Insurance Association of America.

A forty-year-old executive, whether male or female, has a one in six chance of becoming disabled before his or her retirement. If you're between thirty-five and sixty-five, you're six times more likely to become disabled than to die.

Also, the average duration of a disability that lasts more than ninety days is five years. Insurance carriers shell out $18 every second in disability claims.

How much disability income insurance do you need?
When it's time to assess how much disability insurance coverage you need, most insurance representatives and financial planners will add up your monthly expenses, identify your sources of disability income, and then subtract the income—such as Social Security, distributions from employer-sponsored disability plans, or earnings from your investments—that you would receive while you're disabled.

You should have enough disability insurance to cover the difference between your monthly expenses and the income you will receive from other sources while you're disabled. Keep in mind that your expenses, if you're disabled, may be lower than they would be if you were still out in the workforce.

You should know, though, that most policies limit coverage to 60 to 70 percent of your gross earnings. (Companies don't pay more because they want to encourage people to return to work and because benefits are non-taxable if the premiums are paid by the individual.)

Something else you should know: Social Security is designed to pay benefits only for the most severe disabilities, meaning those that are permanent or expected to last at least twelve months.

One recent study shows that barely one quarter, or 26 percent, of disability claims filed with Social Security in 1986 were approved.

It's best *not* to count on Social Security to totally protect your income.

What else should you know about disability plans?
For starters, most people should avoid a policy that contains "*any occupation*" clauses. These are clauses that call for benefits to stop if you cannot work at your regular job but take a job in an occupation other than your own to help make ends meet.

Say you're an emergency-room physician and you

rupture a disk in your back while falling from a ladder at home.

You're unable to return to work for several months, but you do accept a part-time position as a consultant to the hospital.

Tip: If your disability policy is an any occupation plan, your benefits will stop or be significantly reduced. Not so with an "*own occupation*" policy. Own occupation plans cost more, but generally they are worth the extra expense.

Here's another scenario.

Say you're gradually recovering from your accident, and you want to return to work part time. Under most policies, your payments stop even though you're not working full time.

For about a 15 to 20 percent increase in your premiums, you can purchase a disability policy with a residual benefit rider attached. This rider allows you to continue to receive some benefits while you ease back to work on a full-time basis.

Here are a few additional points you should know about disability insurance before you decide which policy is best for you.

Your insurance carrier may cancel your policy at any time unless it's marked *guaranteed renewable*. Also, look for a policy that's *noncancellable* as well. A guaranteed renewable, noncancellable policy is one on which the premiums remain the same from year to year.

Riders covering spouses who become disabled are available from a few companies. That's the good news. The bad news? Only full-time homemakers are covered. Benefits are usually provided for fifteen months, and they generally equal 50 percent of the amount you would pay to a housekeeper for performing the duties normally performed by your spouse.

Always ask about restrictions on any policy you're considering. Know what is covered and what isn't.

Consider taking advantage of *step-rate premiums*. These allow you to pay lower premiums now, and higher ones later when presumably you can better afford them. Keep in mind that they'll cost more in the long run.

Some policies include *transition benefits*—meaning benefits that go to your spouse or dependents if you die while collecting a disability benefit. It's a good idea to find out how long these transition benefits last. You should also ask if your survivors are entitled to a refund of premiums in case of your death. These extra benefits, however, also increase your premiums.

How long does disability coverage last?

The length of coverage varies by the policy purchased, but is typically one year, three years, five years, to-age-65, or lifetime. Most insurance agents and financial planners advise their clients to purchase policies that cover them for their working lifetimes.

Unfortunately, not all carriers offer these policies, and those policies that are available are expensive. One alternative to consider is a plan that pays benefits until you're covered by your pension plan or Social Security retirement benefits.

How much does disability insurance cost?

The premiums you pay vary by age, sex, health, and occupation. A police officer for example, pays more for disability insurance than a loan officer in a bank, because the police officer is more likely to become disabled.

The premium you pay also varies by the *elimination*—or deductible—*period* you choose. The elimination period is the time you must be disabled before your policy starts to pay.

You may specify elimination periods of 30 days, 60 days, 90 days, 180 days, or longer depending on how long you want to wait for disability insurance to begin.

Tip: The longer you wait for your benefits to start, the less you pay in premiums. For example, if you chose a ninety-day elimination period, your premiums are 15 to

20 percent less than if you opted for your payments to begin after thirty days.

Here's something you may not know, but should. Your savings in premiums are less with waiting periods that are longer than ninety days.

Also, disability checks come at the end of the month, not the beginning. So, in effect, a thirty-day waiting period is really a sixty-day waiting period.

Which elimination period is best for you?

The answer depends on your circumstances. If you're single and have a large nest egg, or have a short term plan through your employer, a disability policy with a relatively long elimination period may make sense for you.

What if you think a waiting period of longer than a month would strain your resources? You may want to trade off higher premiums for a shorter waiting period—or build your emergency fund to cover an extra sixty days.

Who pays for your disability insurance coverage?

Many large companies provide disability insurance coverage for their employees. And if it's offered to you, you should not turn it down. However, this coverage isn't always adequate. Elect as much, or the maximum amount of coverage through your employer, so that you can take advantage of low group rates. Then buy additional individual disability insurance for full coverage.

Also, you should know the tax consequences of accepting coverage from your employer. If your employer pays your disability insurance premiums, and you later become disabled, all the income you receive from the plan will be taxed as ordinary income.

A different rule applies if you purchase a personal disability insurance policy and pay the premium. As a general rule, benefits you receive from this type of policy aren't taxable.

One idea: If your company offers disability insurance

within a so-called cafeteria plan—a plan that allows you to choose from among a menu of fringe benefits—it may make sense to bypass the disability package and elect to pay for disability insurance yourself with after-tax dollars. That way you may be able to elect another benefit on the menu, such as a child-care supplement or dental insurance.

Also, if your company provides a disability policy and includes the premiums in your income, the benefits will be tax-free. If you choose to purchase disability insurance under the cafeteria plan, arrange to pay for the policy on an after-tax basis, so the benefits won't be included in your taxable income.

Tip: Say you work for yourself. It may be a good idea to buy your disability insurance policy with your own money, instead of with funds from your business. If you pay the premiums out of your own pocket, any disability payments you receive aren't taxed as income.

How do you increase your disability coverage?

You should know that your carrier may ask you to take a physical examination any time you want to increase your personal coverage or supplement your company plan—unless your policy contains the clause "guaranteed future insurability," or a "future increase option."

These guaranteed policies allow you to increase your coverage at specific times in the future as your income increases, before a disability occurs. In this case, a physical examination isn't required.

If your disability policy includes a "cost of living [COLA] rider," it means your monthly payments, after you're disabled, will increase to coincide with increases in the cost of living.

Tip: You may want to consider supplementing any company plan with a policy of your own. Doing so could be especially important if your company gears its coverage to your base salary, not on what you earn in salary plus bonuses or commissions.

One final thought: It's better to purchase a disability policy when you're young. Contrary to conventional wisdom, young people are more likely to be disabled than older ones, because they have a more active lifestyle.

And since premiums are based on age, the younger you are when you buy the policy, the less money you'll pay out over the life of the policy.

CHAPTER 11

HEALTH INSURANCE

A sad truth is that the only time we appreciate good health insurance benefits is when we are ill. At those unhappy periods, we know how important a solid benefit package really is.

Health insurance, of course, is becoming one of the most hotly debated topics in the United States today. It's a subject that's bringing together some strange bedfellows—everyone from physicians to patients' rights advocates to company executives. Many individuals, it seems, are dissatisfied with the type of insurance system currently in place. In fact, many would like to see some sort of national health insurance plan.

While the debate rages on, however, we must choose—and choose wisely—from the types of health insurance plans currently available to us. In this chapter, we acquaint you with some of the factors you need to consider when selecting health coverage.

The past couple of years have seen carriers going out of business, a tightening of benefits, and rapidly rising costs of health care. It's a potent combination—one that makes it all the more critical that you select a health plan that meets anticipated, as well as unforeseeable, health needs.

Before we discuss the specifics, here are some general rules to follow when it comes to choosing a health insurance plan. With the increasing sophistication of medical technology these days, we can count on longer life expectancy and a continuing upward spiral in health costs.

- Investigate the array of plans in the marketplace, paying particular attention to items we will discuss such as deductibles, stop-loss provisions, and exclusions.
- Shop around for reputable, financially stable insurance companies, Preferred Provider Organizations (PPOs), or Health Maintenance Organizations (HMOs), and don't hesitate to ask your doctor which insurers are the best to deal with and why.
- Some company-provided health insurance does not kick in until thirty to ninety days after you begin employment. In that case, you should consider extending your old policy for a month or buying a stopgap policy (that is, a temporary medical policy that covers you for a short term, for example six months), to guarantee you have a safety net.
- Don't hesitate to ask your insurance agent or financial planner for advice. Other sources of information are the Group Health Association of America, 1129 20th St., NW, Suite 600, Washington, DC 20036, which represents all health maintenance organizations; and the American Association of Preferred Provider Organizations, 111 E. Wacher Dr., Suite 600, Chicago, IL 60601.
- Look for ways to cut costs without seriously cutting coverage. For example, boosting the size of the deductible and out-of-pocket expenses you're willing to pay will reduce your premium payments. Assuming the risk yourself for small losses (such as prescription medicines or dental X-rays) also makes sense, provided you're covered for catastrophic losses (such as a serious accident or prolonged illness).

Let's begin our review of health insurance coverage with a look at one of the newer kids on the block—Health Maintenance Organizations.

Health Maintenance Organizations

WHO: HMOs may make sense for you if you want comprehensive and coordinated coverage under one facility. These organizations are especially good for families with babies and small children who need preventive care, which isn't normally covered by private medical insurance.

WHAT: HMOs are prepaid health-care plans that provide most, or all, of your medical care. The broadest, and most expensive, plans cover everything from hospital and doctors' fees to outpatient visits, prescriptions, and emergency care out of state. More limited plans require members to pay a certain percentage of some services, such as office visits or visits to specialists who aren't part of the HMO.

WHY: Most HMOs are well run, have a variety of competent doctors from which to choose, and use highly respected health-care facilities, including hospitals and labs. You usually pay only one nominal fee (in addition to the premium) for each visit—$3.00 to $7.50 in 1989. You're not required to pay any deductibles or co-insurance costs, though with some plans there's a co-insurance cost for prescription drugs. (With a co-insurance plan, as we will see, you pay a certain percentage of your medical expenses, and the insurer picks up the rest.)

WHY NOT: The major difference between HMOs and private carriers, such as Blue Cross/Blue Shield, is that HMO members, except in emergencies, must use doctors and services provided by that HMO. Do you have a trusted dermatologist you want to continue seeing for a particularly persistent skin rash? If he or she isn't in the plan, you will have to pay for the visits yourself.

If you choose to forego your trusted physician for the sake of enrolling in the HMO, remember to check out whether or not the HMO you're interested in has a specialist who can treat your condition. (It most likely does.)

Also, not all HMOs are alike. Before you join one, do what you would before selecting a lawyer, an accountant, or any other type of professional: make a reference check.

Find out what the HMO's reputation is compared to other HMOs in your area; look at its financial statements and make sure you understand exactly what services it offers.

Ask about the reputations of the doctors employed by this particular HMO; and evaluate how well the HMO will meet the needs of you and your family. Do you have a specific illness that might be better treated by doctors who aren't in the HMO? Do you approve of the hospitals used by this HMO for obstetrics? Does the HMO cover the cost of organ transplants? Second opinions? Does it pay all or part of the fee for outside specialists or offer psychiatric counseling? How quickly can you get to see a doctor? (Some HMOs are booked months in advance.) What about dental and eye care?

Tip: You should make sure the HMO offers emergency out-of-state coverage. The last thing you want is to find yourself many miles from home with a broken leg and no health insurance coverage. In addition, you should find out if you can pick up coverage at this HMO yourself if you no longer work for the employer who sponsored the plan. (If you work for a company with more than twenty employees, the federal government mandates that you must be allowed to continue coverage for at least eighteen months after you leave your position.)

One last point: In the past few years, we have seen a weeding out of the suddenly crowded HMO field. So make sure the HMO you're considering isn't on shaky financial footing or planning to cut back essential services.

WHERE: Today, HMOs are available in just about every part of the country. For a list of HMOs in your area, write the Group Health Insurance Association of America, 1129 20th St., NW, Suite 600, Washington, DC 20036 (telephone [202] 778-3200).

Preferred Provider Organizations (PPOs)

WHO: In most cases, you must belong to a group, such as a group of employees, to participate in a PPO.

WHAT: PPOs are a relatively new variation on the HMO concept. In a PPO, doctors and hospitals agree to provide a company's employees with services at a discounted rate. What the doctors get in return is an increase in the number of patients.

Not all PPOs operate in the same way. Some charge employers a flat monthly fee. Others provide medical services to a company's employees and are paid by the company on a fee-for-service basis.

WHY: In general, PPOs offer a wider range of doctors than HMOs. Like HMOs, PPOs usually agree to cover the costs of emergency care, even though it's not provided by a PPO participant.

WHY NOT: Unlike HMOs, some PPOs provide treatment only on a fee-for-service basis at discounted rates. Also, they will take only groups of employees, not unaffiliated individuals.

Tip: One last note of caution. Although PPO doctors say they are offering discount rates, it's wise to check around and see if these rates are still higher than other doctors in the community are charging.

WHERE: These organizations are available in most areas of the country. For a list of PPOs in your area, write the American Association of Preferred Provider Organizations, 111 E. Wacher Dr., Suite 600, Chicago, IL 60601 (telephone [312] 644-6610).

Private Medical Insurance

WHO: You say you want the freedom to seek care from any physician you choose? Then health coverage through a commercial insurance carrier may make sense for you.

WHAT: Basic medical plans, such as Blue Cross and Blue Shield, provide varying degrees of coverage for hospital, surgical, and physicians' expenses. If you're not covered by a group plan at work, the amount you will pay for an individual plan depends on a number of factors. These include your age, sex, occupation, and health. Sometimes even where you live is taken into account, since some areas of the country, such as New York City and Houston, are known for their high hospital costs.

Most policies—whether group or individual—include an annual deductible amount, usually between $100 and $300. This means that you pay the first $100 or $300 of your medical costs for a given year and the insurer covers the rest within the policy's limits.

Many policies—particularly individual plans—operate with a co-insurance clause. That means you and the insurer agree to split expenses, with the insurer usually picking up around 80 percent of the tab. Most policies, however, impose a limit on how much you will pay in any one year. For example, with some plans, if you pay $2,000 in a year, the insurer will pick up 100 percent of any additional costs.

What kind of coverage do you get through these plans?

Most policies these days include major medical coverage, which we will discuss shortly. Most also include *hospital expense insurance*, which pays for any hospital stays. Based on what is considered a reasonable and customary fee for your geographic area, the insurer pays, wholly or in part, for room and board, nursing care, drugs, lab fees, X-rays, and medical supplies. It also pays for any necessary outpatient sevices, such as pre-admission tests.

However, the health insurance offered by many plans either limits the number of hospital days it will cover (anywhere from twenty days to four months) or puts a cap on the dollar amount it will pay. So be sure to check out any limits.

Surgical expense insurance covers the cost of operations,

but it doesn't always cover all related procedures. Nor will carriers give surgeons carte blanche to charge whatever they want for an operation. Most policies spell out the procedures they will cover, and they limit the amount of coverage to "usual, customary, and reasonable" fees.

Some physicians won't charge more than the insurer will reimburse them for, and, in some states they aren't allowed to charge more. In other states, physicians will ask you, the patient, to pay the difference between the insured amount and the actual fee. So it makes sense to check out the charges before you receive treatment. In this situation, it's a good idea not to sign any agreement to pay more than the "usual, customary, and reasonable" fees.

Instead, you should alert your insurer to the higher charge. The insurer can then choose to negotiate a fee acceptable to both parties. Or, an insurer may ask the physician to justify why the cost of a particular procedure is higher than the generally accepted fee. In rare instances, if the doctor makes a convincing case, the insurer may agree to pay the higher rate.

Physicians' expense insurance pays for a specified number of in-hospital visits; some plans also cover office visits.

Major medical insurance is the insurance that kicks in when your basic coverage, including hospital, surgical, and physicians' expenses, ends. If, for example, your regular insurance covers only twenty days in a hospital, and you're hospitalized for eighty-three days, major medical will cover you for the last sixty-three days of your stay. It will also pay for any related medical needs outside the hospital.

Most policies pay 80 to 100 percent of the expenses (minus a deductible that can range from $100 to $1,000). They usually cover intensive-care services, artificial limbs, reconstructive surgery, oral surgery (if it's provided in a hospital), and prescription drugs, among others. You shouldn't, however, expect routine dental work, cosmetic surgery, annual physicals, and other expenses to be covered.

WHY: These policies do give you complete freedom in selecting physicians and specialists. You're also assured of coverage no matter where in the country you may be. By contrast, you might have a problem getting your HMO or PPO to pay for emergency care outside the insurer's immediate area.

WHY NOT: Once you add in deductibles and possible co-insurance payments, these policies usually end up costing you more. You also have to put together your own "group" of physicians to meet special needs.

WHERE: Blue Cross and Blue Shield plans are available in every state. You can choose from a wide variety of commercial insurers throughout the country.

Dental Insurance

WHO: If you have the opportunity to sign up for a dental plan offered by your employer—and it costs you nothing extra—it makes sense to do so.

WHAT: These plans cover common dental expenses such as X-rays, teeth cleanings, fillings, root canals, crowns, and, in some cases, orthodontic work. For a single person, plans usually cost $15 to $20 a month; a family would pay about $25 to $35 a month.

WHY: If your employer is footing the bill for a dental plan, by all means enjoy its benefits.

WHY NOT: If your employer provides you with dental insurance at no cost to you, great. But you should think twice before buying a dental policy yourself. Why? Your dental insurance premiums may cost more than your dental bills, especially if your dental work over the course of a year includes nothing more than teeth cleanings and occasional X-rays or fillings.

WHERE: Dental insurance is available from a variety of insurance carriers. For more information on these plans, write the American Dental Association, 211 E. Chicago Ave., Chicago, IL 60611. Or you may telephone the group at (312) 440-2500.

Nursing Home or Long-Term Care Insurance

WHO: Americans are living longer than ever before. As they age, their chances of having to spend time in a nursing home increase, along with the cost of nursing home care. Considering that half of those in nursing homes stay an average two years, these plans could provide vital coverage.

WHAT: Long-term care or nursing home care policies can pay for nursing home expenses. Depending on the policy, they can pay for some home health-care expenses as well. Generally, the older you are when you apply and the greater the number of features a policy offers, the higher your premium.

Because long-term care policies vary widely in both features and premium levels, it's essential to compare policies carefully before you buy. Some important features to watch for include: coverage for all types of nursing home care (skilled, intermediate, and custodial); coverage for home health care; no previous hospitalization required before you enter a nursing home and qualify for benefits; coverage for organic nervous and mental disorders, such as Alzheimer's and Parkinson's disease; inflation protection; and guaranteed renewability (that is, the policy cannot be canceled by the company once it's issued).

WHY: With the cost of nursing care on the rise—already the average annual cost of nursing home care is $25,000—it's clear that many people cannot shoulder the expense themselves. That's where these types of policies come in.

WHY NOT: Many long-term care policies are very expensive and severely limited in their coverage. Compare policies carefully before you buy.

WHERE: This type of insurance is becoming available from most major insurance carriers. If you would like more information on these plans, ask the American

Association of Retired Persons to send you copies of these two booklets: *Before You Buy—A Guide to Long-Term Care Insurance* (stock number D12893), and *Making Wise Decisions on Long-Term Care* (stock number D12435).

The group's mailing address is 1909 K St., NW, Washington, DC 20049. The telephone number is (202) 728-4355.

Questions and Answers

I want to make sure my family and I are covered adequately when it comes to health insurance. But how much is enough?

One school of thought holds that you should purchase enough insurance to cover 75 percent of any medical expenses you may encounter. However, if you go by that rule of thumb, you ignore the possibility that major illnesses or accidents could rack up costs as high as, or higher than, hundreds of thousands of dollars. Could you afford to pay 25 percent of those expenses?

You should also find out if the policy you're offered at work—or the one you buy as an individual—includes deductibles, or has a co-insurance clause. If the answer is yes, figure out if you can afford to pay the deductibles or meet the co-insurance requirement for a catastrophic illness. Finally, check the list of ineligible expenses.

These questions aren't designed to cause you undue anxiety. The point is that you want to have enough medical insurance to be covered for huge losses, but you don't want to purchase more insurance than you need. You should ask your financial planner or insurance representative for advice.

What is a stop-loss provision? Do I need it?

It's a provision in an insurance plan that requires the carrier to pay your entire medical costs once your out-of-pocket medical expenses exceed a predetermined amount.

Yes, you do need it. Without this coverage, you could

be liable for certain portions of astronomical medical bills. But note that most major medical policies set a ceiling—usually $500,000 to $1,000,000—on what they will pay over your lifetime. And if you have an older policy or converted from a group medical plan, the ceiling may be lower—usually $250,000.

If you select your own policy, look for a stop-loss provision that has no such ceiling. It costs a minimal amount each month and could make a huge difference in your financial security.

Are there certain benefits I should look for in a health insurance policy that may not be obvious?

Yes, several. For example, look at your policy's coverage of psychiatric care. You may be willing to accept limits on the amount of coverage for outpatient services (such as group therapy), but you should try to get full coverage for inpatient psychiatric service. The cost can be staggering.

Check out whether your state is one that regulates how much an insurance carrier must pay for psychiatric outpatient treatment.

Other questions to ask: Does your policy cover kidney dialysis? Many policies specifically exclude this treatment. Does it pay for treatment of alcoholism? Finally, you should ascertain when your coverage under a specific plan begins.

If you're buying an individual policy, check to make sure it takes effect immediately. And see if the plan excludes so-called pre-existing conditions—that's a condition, such as diabetes, that you may have had before you purchased the policy. You will find that most plans have this exclusion.

What is the effect of the Comprehensive Omnibus Budget Reconciliation Act of 1986?

COBRA, as it's more familiarly known, requires companies that employ twenty or more people to continue to provide group health insurance for up to three years to widows, divorced or separated spouses, and dependents of active employees.

Companies of this size must also offer coverage for up to eighteen months to terminated employees and their dependents, or to employees who lose coverage because their hours are reduced.

However, the law allows employers to collect a monthly premium from individuals that equals the full amount the company actually pays for each employee, plus 2 percent extra. (That 2 percent surcharge goes to cover the company's administrative costs.)

When, and how, does Medicare kick in?

Medicare pays for health care for individuals who are sixty-five or older or disabled. It's financed by the contributions of employees and employers through Social Security taxes. But everyone is eligible for it—even if you never worked a day.

Medicare is divided into two parts. Part A covers hospital expenses, "limited" (that is, skilled) nursing home care, and some outpatient expenses. Part B is voluntary, financed both by the federal government and by monthly payments from participants. This part covers costs not included in Part A, such as doctors' services, medical supplies, and prescriptions.

Part B pays 80 percent of covered medical and surgical charges above an annual $60 deductible.

You must apply to receive Medicare benefits. If you decide to buy Part B, apply about three months before your sixty-fifth birthday. That way, you will have successfully cut through any red tape by the time you're eligible.

What is a conversion policy?

This is a plan that allows you to convert a group health insurance policy to an individual one. But you should know that the individual policy won't be as comprehensive as the group plan, and the cost may be higher.

CHAPTER 12

LIFE INSURANCE

We know—the mere mention of the words *life insurance* puts you to sleep. But consider these aspects of life insurance: a competitive rate of interest, generally tax-deferred earnings, and, in most cases, guaranteed principal. Moreover, when you die, your beneficiary gets the death benefit tax-free.

Now does the topic of life insurance interest you?

In this chapter, we discuss what you need to know about life insurance—how much to buy, what kind to buy, and where to buy it.

So roll up your sleeves and let's get started.

To many people, life insurance is like income taxes—an unavoidable but unpleasant fact of life. Yet, without the needed coverage, a single chance event can leave your loved ones with no money for even the basic necessities of life.

So, how much life insurance do you need? Think of life insurance as a way of maintaining—not improving—your family's standard of living. Now, take out a pencil and paper and calculate—as best you can—your family's financial needs should you die.

You should know before you begin that some protection is already in place—Social Security pays monthly benefits to a widowed mother with children under the age of sixteen.

Many financial planners say that the amount your family will need to live on each year is about 75 percent of its current annual after-tax income—and that amount doesn't cover capital goals, such as education. But, as a rule, you should buy enough life insurance so that your heirs can live off the interest or other income from the proceeds.

Times and situations change, though, and as your circumstances shift and you and your family grow older, your need for life insurance will change.

Now, on to our review of your life insurance options.

Universal Life

WHO: A *universal life policy* may be right for you if you want to own a flexible insurance policy that helps you defer current income taxes on policy earnings.

These policies combine pure life protection with a cash-value that earns a competitive interest rate. Earnings on your cash value accumulate tax-deferred.

Universal life policies are only about ten years old, but they are very popular. They make up more than a third of the life insurance policies sold today.

WHAT: Universal life insurance is flexible enough to match the protection needs of a lifetime. It allows you to choose—and change—the amount of coverage, the length of coverage, even the size and frequency of your premium payments.

How? Universal life separates the cash value of your policy from pure life protection, allowing you to adapt the plan to your circumstances.

Within limits, you can change the type and amount of insurance protection to fit your needs. For example, your death benefit can remain the same from year to year.

Or it can change over time as the cash value of the policy increases. (You may choose to have your death benefit equal the initial protection amount or face value plus the cash value.)

Or the death benefit can increase or decrease as your needs or circumstances change. (If you increase your coverage, you may have to provide evidence of insurability.)

Say, for example, that you're in your early thirties and have two children under the age of five. Chances are, you need life insurance—and lots of it. But as you grow older and your children reach maturity, your need for coverage may diminish.

With universal life, you can design a plan so that it pays a larger death benefit when you're young and a smaller death benefit when you're older.

And with universal life, you control how and when you make your premium payments.

You can increase or decrease your payments—or even skip payments—as long as your cash-surrender value is large enough to pay the cost of protection and any other expense change, and the premiums don't exceed tax-law limitations.

By paying extra premiums or depositing lump sums, you can add to your cash value and earn income on a tax-deferred basis. That is, you pay no income taxes on the interest earnings that accumulate unless they are withdrawn. However, if you exceed certain premium levels that are spelled out in the tax law, your contract may become what is known as a *modified endowment policy*.

What is a modified endowment policy?

A modified endowment policy is a life insurance policy with premiums paid faster than the tax law guidelines prescribe. The modified endowment policy status doesn't affect the major benefits of a life insurance contract—you still get tax-deferred earnings and an income tax-free death benefit. However, with a modified endowment policy, borrowings or partial surrenders are treated first as distributions of earnings, subject to income taxes and, if you're less than fifty-nine and a half years old, an IRS 10 percent penalty tax on the amount of earnings is charged.

On the other hand, if your policy is not a modified endowment contract under the tax law, Uncle Sam doesn't generally treat as taxable income the amounts you may borrow from your policy. Most policies allow you to borrow from your cash-surrender value after the first year of ownership and still keep the policy in force.

You may also make full or partial withdrawals, but keep in mind that most carriers levy surrender charges that are reduced over time for these withdrawals.

Death benefits are paid to your policy beneficiary free of income tax. However, the amount of the death benefit is included in the deceased's federal gross estate for estate tax purposes, unless you've made certain legal provisions ahead of time.

The majority of universal life plans are fixed-dollar policies—that is, they offer you a guaranteed rate of return. Your cash value earns competitive rates of interest and policies guarantee that the rate will never dip below a specified amount—typically, 4.5 percent during the life of the policy. But some are variable-dollar policies, called variable universal life. With variable universal life policies, you can direct your premiums into a variety of underlying nonpublic stock, bond, and other mutual funds sponsored by the insurance carrier. In addition, you may switch from one fund to another without paying tax.

Most universal life companies mail you an annual report updating you on your policy—the amount and cost of the insurance portion, the cash value of the policy, the current rate of return, and any fees the company charged to your account.

WHY: Universal life offers you security and flexibility; flexibility in the amount of your death benefit and the timing and amount of your premiums.

For example, in those years when you have more income than usual, you can pay higher premiums, thereby building up your cash value more quickly—and, remember, cash values grow without your paying income tax on the earnings.

In years that are lean, you may skip premium payments altogether if cash value is sufficient. In this case, the insurer will deduct the required premium from the cash that has accumulated in your account.

WHY NOT: Universal life offers long-term protection and isn't usually a place to park cash temporarily. Possible surrender charges and the fact that distributions from modified endowment policies may be subject to income taxes and a possible IRS 10 percent penalty make this product a vehicle for the long term.

WHERE: Universal life is available from most major carriers and is sold by financial planners, insurance representatives, and stockbrokers.

If you would like more information on universal life policies, write the American Council of Life Insurance (ACLI), 1001 Pennsylvania Ave., NW, Washington, DC 20004-2599. The group's telephone number is (202) 624-2000.

WHEN: The flexibility of the death benefit and premium with a universal life policy makes it appropriate to cover the life insurance protection needs of a lifetime. Whether you're young, middle-aged, or mature, a universal life plan can be tailored to meet your protection and capital accumulation or savings needs.

Whole Life

WHO: If you want lifetime protection, the assurance that your premiums won't rise from year to year, and the opportunity for your savings to grow tax-deferred, then a *whole life policy* may make sense for you. This type of insurance is also good if you're older and worried about the cost of insurance rising. With whole life, your costs are fixed.

WHAT: Whole life—the granddaddy of insurance policies—offers you premiums that stay the same from year to year. The amount of your insurance also won't change as long as your policy is in force.

One drawback of whole life is that you start out paying more in premiums than you would for a comparable amount of term insurance. These higher-premium payments in early years build up a reserve, so your payments in later years don't go up, even though the actual cost of insurance does increase as you age.

The difference between whole life and term is that with whole life policies, only a part of your premium goes to pay for the pure-risk portion of the policy in the early years.

The rest goes to cash value, which is like a savings account, where your earnings accumulate tax-deferred until they are withdrawn. (Generally, whole life policies don't allow partial surrenders.) Whole life policies typically pay lower-than-market rates of interest, because the interest rates are guaranteed for the life of the policy.

However, some policies—called *participating policies*—pay dividends. Dividends are refunds of premiums. These refunds are paid if the company has favorable mortality, investment, and expenses experience. Dividends aren't guaranteed. (Your policy spells out the specifics.)

You may borrow from your policy or cash it in.

WHY: Whole life offers you lifetime protection at a flat annual premium and guaranteed interest rates. The cash value also provides you an opportunity to save on a tax-deferred basis.

WHY NOT: Because whole life offers lifetime protection at a fixed rate, you should not buy it if you only need short term life insurance protection, or if your insurance needs are likely to change. In that case, term life insurance would be better.

WHERE: Whole life policies are offered by most insurance carriers and are sold through financial planners, insurance representatives, and stockbrokers. For more information on whole life policies, write the American Council of Life Insurance (See p. 147).

WHEN: These policies may make sense for you whenever you have a need for protection and capital accumulation and you want to pay a premium guaranteed to stay level.

Term Insurance

WHO: If you're in the market for insurance coverage only, and you want to spend the least amount possible over the short term, so-called *term insurance* may make sense for you. It also is a good way to purchase insurance if you have cash-flow problems.

WHAT: Term insurance is strictly no-frills. It offers you a set amount of coverage—$50,000, say, or $100,000—for a specified term or period of time.

If you die during the term, your insurance carrier pays your beneficiaries the *face value* of the policy. If you live, the insurance company keeps your premiums, and you start all over again.

The primary selling point of term insurance is that it's inexpensive when you're young. However, premiums increase with your age. Term insurance may cost—depending on your age—anywhere from $1 to $20 per year, or even more, for each $1,000 of coverage.

The exact amount you pay varies by your age, sex, health, and whether or not you smoke. A fifty-year-old man who smokes, for example, can expect to pay quite a bit more for a $200,000 policy than a twenty-year-old woman who doesn't smoke.

Term insurance comes in a host of varieties, but you only need to acquaint yourself with the most common—*nonrenewable term*, *yearly renewable term*, *five-year renewable term*, *ten-year renewable term*, and *annual reducing term.*

- Nonrenewable term is the least expensive policy you can buy. It requires you to reapply—and requalify—for coverage whenever the policy expires. With nonrenewable term, you run the risk that when you reapply, your carrier will turn you down if you become ill or disabled.

  You should know that many insurance carriers require you to fill out a health questionnaire or take a physical exam each time you reapply for coverage.

Renewable policies cost more, but you qualify for renewal automatically, no questions asked.

- Yearly renewable term is a policy that you may renew in yearly increments for a specified number of years or to a certain age. The carrier agrees at the outset that you may renew your coverage each year without providing evidence of insurability, such as a physical examination that shows you to be in good health.

  But renewability doesn't mean level premiums. Your premiums will go up from year to year, and for an obvious reason: as you grow older, you're more likely to die.
- Five-year renewable term is renewable in five-year increments, while ten-year renewable term is renewable in ten-year increments. With both policies, you may usually renew your coverage until you reach an older age, such as seventy, without providing evidence of insurability. Policy premiums increase with each renewal period.
- With annual reducing term, your premium doesn't change as long as the policy remains in force, but the death benefit decreases over a selected period of time.

  When does annual reducing term make sense? Say your dependents will soon become independent—that is, they will be able to support themselves. Annual reducing term takes into account that you need less and less coverage as your children grow older.

Most term insurance is *convertible*—that is, you may convert it to a whole life or universal life policy without providing evidence of insurability.

Many financial planners recommend that you opt for a policy that's convertible. That way, if you become ill, you can switch to a whole life or universal plan without taking a physical examination.

Tip: Here is something else you should know.

If you're buying a home or making a major installment purchase, you may purchase term insurance to complete the payments in the event of your death. But note: It's often cheaper *not* to buy this insurance from the seller of the loan.

WHY: The biggest boon of term insurance is that premiums are low, especially when you're young. It allows you to get protection at a time when you can least afford to be without it.

Many planners say it's a good idea to choose coverage that offers a level amount of protection for a specified period of time or that diminishes with your need for insurance.

WHY NOT: One problem with most term insurance policies is that your premiums increase as you grow older.

WHERE: Most major insurance carriers offer term insurance. You may purchase it through your financial planner, insurance representative, or stockbroker. For more information on term life policies, write the American Council of Life Insurance (see p. 147).

WHEN: You will pay a lot less for coverage if you take out renewable term insurance when you're young and less of a risk. At older ages, term insurance can become prohibitively expensive.

Single-Premium Life Insurance

WHO: You may not think of your life insurance policy as a savings vehicle, but it actually can be. When you purchase a single-premium life insurance policy, your earnings—interest, dividends, and so on—accumulate tax-deferred. Who should invest in these policies?

The answer is, first, people who need insurance protection; second, people who are looking for a tax-deferred savings vehicle, are buying for the long haul, and have a lump sum to invest. The most common reason for buying any kind of life insurance is to provide financial protection for loved ones when you die. However, the savings aspect of the policy may also provide a useful benefit. It depends on your objectives.

WHAT: If your insurance representative or financial planner comes calling to tell you about single-premium life insurance, it may pay to listen.

With these policies, you begin by paying a one-time premium—minimums are often $5,000 to $10,000, although many people put in as much as $25,000 to $50,000 or more.

In exchange for this sum, you receive a specified amount of life insurance protection—typically several times the amount of your premium, depending on your age.

The large premium becomes a nest egg that can be invested in a variety of ways. If you buy a *single-premium variable life policy*, you can direct your premium into a variety of underlying nonpublic stock, bond, and other mutual funds sponsored by the insurance carrier. You may switch from one fund to another without paying tax, and all your investment earnings compound tax-deferred.

On the other hand, if you want to eliminate the risk that any investment losses will erode your policy's principal—a valuable benefit in light of the 1987 stock market crash—you may want to consider a single-premium policy where the cash value is guaranteed by the company. In this case, your premium earns a fixed annual return—at a rate that's often comparable with long-term, tax-exempt bonds. Again, all your interest earnings are tax-deferred.

In the past you could borrow against these policies without incurring any adverse tax consequences. However, for contracts purchased after June 21, 1988, this is no longer true. They will be taxed like deferred annuities—that is, the IRS considers any distribution you get as earnings first and return of investment last. So there is no longer a tax advantage in borrowing against these types of contracts.

What else should you know about these plans?

If you buy more than one modified endowment policy (such as two single-premium life insurance policies) within a calendar year, you must treat them as one contract for tax purposes. This could result in additional amounts being treated as taxable income if you take a distribution from any one of the contracts.

The *death benefit* paid by the policy—minus the amount of any outstanding loans—passes to your beneficiaries free of income tax. (Your death benefit is the amount your insurance carrier will pay your beneficiaries if you die while the policy is in force.)

WHY: Single-premium policies offer you the opportunity to provide financial protection for your loved ones and to salt away money for retirement. Earnings on the dollars you invest grow tax-deferred as long as the dollars remain in the policy—that is, you don't withdraw or borrow the money. Death benefits pass to beneficiaries free of income tax.

WHY NOT: Single-premium life insurance policies are designed for people who want insurance protection and at the same time a tax-deferred savings vehicle. However, a person with little extra money for savings and a large need for insurance should consider term insurance or universal life rather than single-premium life insurance.

Most carriers levy so-called back-end loads during the early years of ownership in an effort to discourage policy holders from withdrawing money early and to reimburse the company for initial commissions and other expenses. This charge—along with a possible IRS 10 percent penalty for early withdrawal of earnings (that is, earnings withdrawn before age fifty-nine and a half)—make single-premium insurance policies inappropriate for people who are buying for the short term. However, if you're in for the long term, these back-end loads won't affect you.

WHERE: Single-premium policies are available from a variety of sources—financial planners, stockbrokers, insurance representatives, and so on.

Many people find insurance a complicated subject. Check with your financial planner or insurance representative to find out which choices are right for you.

For more information on single-premium life policies, write the American Council of Life Insurance (see p. 147).

WHEN: Single-premium policies make most sense for people who can afford to tie up their cash.

Questions and Answers

What is variable life?

One of the hottest insurance products of the 1980s, variable life combines old-fashioned whole life insurance with the freedom to direct the investment of your cash value as you choose.

This insurance product is structured just like variable universal life, except your annual premium is fixed. Your death benefit and cash value aren't fixed, however. They may soar or sink depending on how well your investments perform.

You may choose from among a variety of nonpublic stock, bond, and other mutual funds offered by your insurance carrier. You may not invest in any vehicle not offered by your insurer.

With variable life—as with other life insurance policies—you pay no ordinary income taxes on investment earnings until you withdraw the money.

What are my rights when it comes to life insurance?

You have the right to cancel a policy at any time. But you must pay the premium to keep the policy in force. You also have the right to request a report on the types and uses of personal information an insurance company may collect about you.

You have the right to know why a policy was canceled or your application for insurance was denied. (Medical information will be disclosed to your physician rather than directly to you.) If you're the owner of the contract, you have the right to change the beneficiary who will receive any death benefit that becomes payable.

You may correct any inaccurate information in the insurance company's files upon which a decision to issue or not issue a policy was based.

CHAPTER 13

HOME AND PERSONAL PROPERTY INSURANCE

Homeowners' insurance—the term applies to both homeowners and renters—is designed to protect you against catastrophic losses caused by anything from a fire or windstorm to vandalism, water damage, an accident on your premises, or an airplane crashing into your sun porch—a situation, incidentally, that happens more often than you may think.

Homeowners' policies come with varying degrees of protection. It's up to you to know what you're covered for and whether that coverage is adequate.

A general rule of thumb is that you should buy a policy paying benefits of 100 percent of the replacement value of your house or belongings. Don't forget that we are talking about relatively expensive items.

A policy that covers less than 100 percent of the replacement value of a house or even part of one means you have to cover the remaining percent yourself. These days, that could mean coming up with $100,000, or even more—just to replace the house you had.

Most carriers offer six types of homeowner's insurance. The first four are for free-standing single-family residences, the other two are for renters and owners of condominiums and co-ops. First, we take a look at the policies for homeowners. These are called Forms One, Two, Three, and Five.

Form One: Referred to also as Homeowner's 1 or HO-1, this type of policy costs the least and, as you may expect, offers the least protection. It covers damage to your home and personal possessions from ten named "perils" or causes: fire and lightning, windstorms and hail, explosions, riots and civil commotion, vehicles, aircraft, smoke, vandalism and malicious mischief, breakage of glass, and theft. If a cause of damage, called a "peril," isn't listed in your policy, it's not covered.

Form Two: Also called Homeowner's 2 or HO-2, this policy covers seventeen named perils and no more. Included are the ten perils from Form One plus damage from: falling objects; the weight of ice, snow, or sleet; the collapse of buildings; accidental discharge or overflow of water or steam; the explosion of steam or hot water systems; frozen plumbing, heating units, air-conditioning systems, and domestic appliances; and power surges. Form Two coverage costs slightly more than Form One—a price often well worth paying for the added protection.

Form Three: Homeowner's 3 or HO-3 provides "all-risk" coverage for your house and is the most popular type of plan available.

"All-risk" coverage means that your dwelling is protected against all losses, except those specifically excluded in the policy. What are these exclusions? They usually include earthquakes, floods, termites, landslides, wars, tidal waves, and nuclear accidents.

Personal belongings are also covered—but only for the seventeen perils listed in Form Two.

The cost of Form Three is roughly 10 percent to 15 percent more than Form Two—again, an amount well worth the increased protection.

Form Five: Under a Form Five policy, also known as Homeowner's 5 or HO-5 or Comprehensive Form, you receive the same "all-risk" protection on your dwelling as under Form Three and are subject to the same exclusions.

However, Form Five extends all-risk coverage to your

personal belongings. A policy offering this additional coverage costs about 30 percent more than a Form Three policy.

If your insurance company doesn't sell Form Five policies, ask if it offers Form Three with riders attached to include all-risk coverage of your personal possessions. The coverage won't be as comprehensive as a straight form Five policy, but it's better than the limited protection of a typical Form Three.

Now let's consider the two remaining types of homeowner's insurance: Forms Four and Six.

Form Four: Designed for renters, this policy protects only your personal possessions from the causes specified in an HO-3 policy. Other names for Form Four include Tenants Form, Renters' Policy, Contents Form, Homeowner's 4, and HO-4.

Form Six: Also known as Condominium Unit Owners Form, Homeowner's 6, and HO-6, Form Six is a policy specifically tailored to condominium and co-op owners. It protects your belongings from the same perils as those listed on Form Four. It also covers improvements and betterments inside your condo.

Most Form Six policies also include a rider that requires the insurer to pay if your condo association assesses you a fee for any uninsured losses. These are costs that can quickly add up to a hefty amount. For further protection, most condominium or co-op associations buy a so-called master property insurance policy to cover the building and property.

The terms of most homeowner's policies are fairly straightforward. Still, you should know the meaning of certain phrases and clauses when you're deciding which policy to buy.

Here are a few of the most common terms you may run across.

Actual cash-value policies

Sometimes these policies provide adequate protection for the cost of your house, and sometimes they don't. For example, if the floors of your home are old and worn out, an insurance adjuster will take depreciation into account when it comes time to calculate the value of your home.

These policies may not provide adequate coverage you need for the house's contents. Again, the reason is that insurance adjusters take into account depreciation when they figure out the value of your personal property. And depreciation can cost you dearly.

Here's an example. Say a fire destroys two floors of your house. A cash-value policy will probably pay for the cost of the floor minus depreciation. And when it comes time to estimate the value of your household items, the adjuster evaluates them on the basis of what the items are worth now, not what it will cost you to replace them.

So he or she figures, for example, that a four-year-old washing machine is much less valuable than a new one. And, instead of awarding you $500, the amount you will have to pay to replace it, the insurer gives you only $200, its estimated depreciated value.

Replacement cost endorsement

If your policy doesn't already have replacement costs built in and you want an insurance policy that will cover the *real* cost of replacing your household items, you need a "replacement cost endorsement" tacked onto your policy. This endorsement prevents the insurer from deducting for depreciation.

Adding this rider will boost the cost of your policy. However, it may be a wise investment on your part, given the difference between what items cost now and what the adjuster thinks they are worth after accounting for depreciation.

Exactly how much more will you pay for the endorsement?

If you're a homeowner, expect premiums to increase by 10 percent. Condominium owners can expect a 25 to 30 percent rate hike, and renters and co-op residents a 50 percent increase.

Why, you ask, should condo and co-op owners and renters pay a higher rate? Remember that their policies cover primarily the contents of their homes, not the structure itself. So, proportionately speaking, the replacement cost endorsement affects a much larger part of their policy.

One last point: Although most insurers will write you a check to pay for the damage to—or replacement of—your property, some insurers may want to do the actual repair work themselves. It's their way of monitoring costs that they think could get out of hand.

Limitations

These are high-value items, such as jewelry, furs, coins, and silverware, for which specific money limitations are built into all policies. For example, jewelry may be limited to $3,000 on a given policy, guns to $1,000, and so on.

A special rider may be purchased if you need additional coverage. These riders allow you to customize your policies to better protect valuable articles when the policy doesn't give you adequate protection.

Appraisals

These are professional estimates of what it would cost to replace your house or other items.

Appraisals are offered by such organizations as the American Institute of Real Estate Appraisers and the American Society of Appraisers, as well as by your insurance agent or insurance company.

If your house is valued at $200,000 or more, you may not need to worry about getting an appraisal. Your insurance company may do it for you. And the company may also offer suggestions on how to improve your new home's safety.

An insurance representative from whom you buy your homeowner's policy will probably do the appraisal free. A real estate agent or building contractor who performs an appraisal will charge either a flat fee or a fee based on a percentage of your house's appraisal value. (If you have a choice, opt for the former.)

In addition, some insurance companies often provide do-it-yourself appraisal kits. These help you itemize your possessions and may suggest you make a video inventory of them.

Just make sure when you get an appraisal that you get an estimate of your house's replacement value—the amount it would cost to build a house comparable to yours—and not the market value, the price you could sell your house for.

Inflation guard

This is a clause in a homeowner's policy that automatically boosts your coverage, as well as premiums, each time you renew your policy. It takes into account rising costs caused by inflation.

Questions and Answers

What property-related protection does my homeowner's policy provide besides my house and its contents?
In insurance lingo, the policy also covers *appurtenant structures*—that is, garages, storage sheds, and other buildings that stand on your property. In addition, you're covered for damage to family gravestones and markers located elsewhere.

Your policy also covers many extra expenses you and your family incur if your house is damaged and you have to stay in a hotel or motel.

Make sure to keep room and restaurant receipts, since

you will be reimbursed only for items and services for which you actually pay, less your normal living expenses.

Check to see whether your policy limits the total amount of reimbursement. It should offer you at least 20 percent of your house's value.

Can I get coverage for my mobile home?

The answer is yes. Not all carriers are willing to insure mobile homes. Those that do offer only Forms One and Two, and they will charge you higher premiums than usual. That's because mobile homes are more susceptible to damage, primarily from wind, than are regular homes.

I am concerned about liability. Does my homeowner's policy include any liability protection?

The answer is yes. You and members of your family—including your pets—get liability protection with your homeowner's policy. You're covered for medical payments for injuries to others, as well as for damages inflicted by you on other people's property.

The policy protects you if a limb from one of your trees, for example, falls on a person walking down your sidewalk—or your front steps collapse and break the leg of a visitor. Should that visitor sue, your defense costs would be covered and so would the costs of any judgments rendered against you (up to the limits included in your policy).

Are there any policies that offer earthquake protection?

Although most policies exclude earthquakes from their coverage, insurers do offer a separate earthquake policy, usually with a hefty deductible (as high as $10,000).

What about flood coverage?

Since private insurers consider flood coverage too risky, the U.S. Department of Housing and Urban Development has stepped in to fill the void. For about $35 per $15,000 of coverage, homeowners can get federal flood insurance in areas where flooding is considered a threat.

What kind of coverage do I get for jewelry from a standard homeowner's policy?

Standard policies limit the amount you will be reimbursed for jewelry—as well as for such items as furs or paintings—regardless of the value of the missing or stolen item. Dollar limits on personal property can range from $200 to $5,000, depending on the type of property and the insurance company.

I have heard the phrase "personal articles floater." What does it mean?

This floater is an addition to your homeowner's policy. As the name implies, the floater covers certain items of value, wherever they may be. The advantage of floaters is that the items you "schedule" are covered for "all risks," and the policy deductible isn't applied at the time of loss.

For example, should the jewelry be stolen from your luggage, or snatched off your neck on a dark street, you would be insured for the loss. You're also insured if the item is taken from your home or tumbles down the garbage disposal.

Your insurance company may require proof of the item's value before insuring you. Usually a sales slip or recent professional appraisal is adequate. Expect to pay premiums of 20 cents to $2 per $100 of value, depending on the type of home and the insurance company.

Personal articles floater limits are the maximum amount of reimbursement you can receive for the specific item described. However, the insurance company has the right to replace the lost or stolen item rather than pay you the amount listed. This is the normal way a claim gets settled, since the insurance company can buy a replacement ring, for example, at or near wholesale cost. Wholesale cost is considerably less than paying you the retail limit on your policy.

On replacement items such as a painting, ask for a "valued form" policy. This is a policy that reimburses you for the limit listed. You may find the additional cost per $100 of assessed value well worth the guaranteed reimbursement in case of loss.

Are there any riders that I should know about?

There are many you can ask about. For example, you can get a rider that protects you from liability claims from a cleaning person or other domestic worker who is injured while working in your house. Some states require "domestic worker's compensation" insurance as part of your homeowner's policy.

You can also get a rider that gives you additional coverage for everyday personal property, since most standard policies cover personal property only up to 50 percent of the value of your house.

There are also riders that can broaden your liability insurance to cover non-bodily injury suits, such as libel and slander, false arrest, malicious prosecution, and so on.

In any case, ask your insurance representative or financial planner what types of riders are available and which he or she suggests for your needs.

CHAPTER 14

AUTO INSURANCE

One of the biggest mistakes you can make is to skimp on your auto insurance coverage. A well-designed policy can shield you from financial disaster.

We know—as you do—that the cost of these policies is high. But so is the price of an accident. The cost of parts and labor to repair relatively minor damage to your car can add up to thousands of dollars.

Worse still is the liability you face from lawsuits brought against you by people injured in a car accident. The awards juries may make in personal injury trials can cripple you financially—not only by depleting your existing assets but by the garnishment of future earnings as well. Next to this potential loss, the cost of insuring the auto you own is, relatively speaking, negligible.

Many drivers make the mistake of not carrying enough protection. Often, they don't review their policies from year to year, which means that these policies never get updated. As a result, coverage that was once appropriate is now woefully inadequate.

In this chapter, we explain the various types of auto insurance and suggest the amounts of coverage you would be wise to carry. After you have read this chapter, you may want to go review your policy with your insurance representative or financial planner.

That way, you can be sure your coverage provides the protection you need. Remember, forewarned, as far as auto accidents are concerned, is indeed forearmed.

Bodily Injury Liability

WHO: Make no mistake about it. Bodily injury liability coverage is a necessity—not a luxury—and no driver should be without it.

WHAT: "What a day," you grumble to your secretary as you head out the door to the company parking lot. You don't know it, but your day is about to get far worse.

As you back your shiny new car out of its spot in the parking lot, you slam into the side of another car. The damage to the two cars is bad enough. But then you notice, the passenger in the other car is clutching his arm and grimacing in pain.

If you carry *bodily injury liability insurance*, relax. You're covered. Bodily injury liability insurance covers your liability as the owner of the car. It also covers the liability of anyone—family member or not—who is driving your car with your permission.

It pays the medical costs of—in this case—the injured passenger in the other car. Bodily injury liability also pays the cost of defending a suit and the amount of damages, if any, awarded by the court—but only up to the limit of your policy.

Some auto policies may carry a single limit for liability—$100,000, say. That amount is the maximum the insurer will pay for both bodily injury liability and property damage liability in any single accident.

Other policies called *split-limit* policies typically carry two bodily injury limits—$100,000 /$300,000, for instance. The first amount refers to the maximum the carrier will pay for injuries per person for a specific accident. The second number is the maximum the insurer will pay for all individuals injured or killed in that accident.

You should know that many states require you to carry at least a minimum amount of coverage—usually $10,000/ $20,000. But you shouldn't stop there.

That amount of coverage is simply inadequate. Our

advice is to purchase coverage for at least $100,000 per person and $300,000 per accident.

WHY: Without bodily injury liability coverage, you could lose your financial shirt.

WHY NOT: Unless your assets are large enough to cover any claim, there is no reason not to purchase bodily injury liability coverage.

WHERE: You purchase this coverage as part of your automobile policy from your representative or directly from the insurer.

WHEN: You should review your coverage every year to make sure it's adequate.

Property Damage Liability

WHO: Let's return to the car you backed into in your haste to leave the daily grind. You should be carrying *property damage liability insurance* to cover the cost of repairs—and of any potential lawsuit. Like bodily injury liability, property damage liability covers you as well as anyone driving your car with your premission.

WHAT: This insurance pays for repairing property damage for which you're responsible. The damage doesn't have to be to another car. It could be a fence, a house, or anything else you run into.

However, this coverage will *not* pay for damage to your own vehicle. For that, you need collision damage coverage, which we will discuss later.

And, like bodily injury liability, property damage liability covers you only up to the limits of the insurance you buy.

You, of course, want to make sure you have enough property damage liability. But how much is enough?

Today's roads are full of cars priced at more than $15,000. Some cars even cost $50,000 or more. Your property damage liability limit should be high enough to protect you from the total loss of two cars. We suggest a limit of $100,000.

WHY: You should have this type of coverage to protect yourself against potential lawsuits.

WHY NOT: There is no good reason not to have this insurance.

WHERE: Again, you buy this type of insurance as part of your overall policy from your representative or directly from the insurer.

WHEN: Review your coverage every year, and update it if necessary.

Uninsured Motorist Protection

WHO: It's unfortunate, but a good many drivers are uninsured. That's why everyone should carry *uninsured motorist protection*.

WHAT: This policy protects you if you're involved in an accident caused by an uninsured or hit-and-run driver. This insurance is mostly protection against bodily injury to you and your family members. Very few policies cover damage to your car by uninsured motorists. It also covers you and family members when you're riding in another car. Finally, it covers you if you're injured by a car while you're walking or bicycling.

A related type of insurance is *underinsured motorist protection*. In this case, the other driver may not have enough coverage to take care of your expenses. This additional insurance picks up where his or hers leaves off. Unfortunately, it's not available in all states.

WHY: Even though your state may require motorists to carry insurance, not everyone does. Or the driver who hits you may come from another state. That's why this type of coverage is so important.

WHY NOT: There is no good reason for not buying uninsured motorist's insurance—or underinsured motorist's insurance if the latter is available in your state.

WHERE: Don't use any state-imposed minimums as your guide. You can purchase $100,000/$300,000 coverage for less than $10 more than the minimum coverage.

WHEN: Again, review your policy annually with your insurance agent.

Collision

WHO: Here, you have an option. Not every driver needs *collision insurance*—or a lot of collision insurance.

WHAT: Say your car collides with another, and both cars suffer damage. In fact, the back end of your auto looks like a refugee from a scrap metal factory.

With collision insurance, your insurer picks up the tab for repairing your car—subject, of course, to your deductible.

What happens if the other driver causes the accident? Your insurance company pays for the damage to your car, then seeks reimbursement from the other driver's carrier.

WHY: If your car is new, and expensive, you want to protect yourself from the cost of repairs or replacement following an accident. In addition, if you have a loan on your car, the bank or other lending institution may insist you carry this coverage.

But that doesn't mean that you need maximum coverage. You can lower the cost of collision coverage by agreeing to pay for a larger part of the damage yourself.

The part you pay is called a deductible amount.

If you buy collision coverage with, say, a $300 deductible, you're responsible for the first $300 in repair costs any time your car is involved in an accident.

Buying collision coverage with a deductible makes sense for many drivers, because it cuts the cost of the premium substantially—by about 20 percent if you buy a

$500 deductible, or by nearly 50 percent if you agree to cover the first $1,000.

By buying insurance with a deductible amount, you're agreeing to take care of the affordable, small repair costs—and you're leaving the big bills, the kind that could really put a dent in your bank account, up to your insurance company.

WHY NOT: Unlike liability coverage, which you should never be without, it sometimes makes sense to carry no collision coverage at all. Why?

Perhaps you drive an older car with a market value of, say, $1,000. To you, this vehicle may serve as reliable transportation that would cost a lot to replace.

But to the insurance company, it's worth only $1,000.

And that's all you would collect from the company, even if the car were wrecked beyond repair. Still, you would be paying a high premium—several hundred dollars annually—to insure the car against collisions. Is the insurance worth that amount? The answer is, probably not.

Our advice is to weigh the cost of the coverage against the value of the car and your ability to pay for accidental damage. And consider taking a high deductible.

Tip: Here is another idea for you to consider. If you decide not to purchase collision coverage, put the money you save on that portion of your policy into a bank account and add to it each year. That way, you can painlessly save money to pay for any repairs that might become necessary.

WHERE: You purchase auto insurance from your car insurance carrier. Your premiums will vary with the type and age of your car, your age, sex, driving record, and location. Insuring a car in New York City where traffic bedlam reigns on city streets will cost a lot more than insuring the same car in, for example, Casper, Wyoming.

WHEN: It's particularly important to review this coverage annually or when you add new drivers—your sixteen-year-old with a new license, for example. Unlike many other types of coverage, you often want less coverage, not more, as the years go on.

The reason is simple. As a car gets older, it's worth a lot less, and you're frequently paying more in coverage than you're ever going to get back.

Comprehensive Physical Damage

WHO: Your need for *comprehensive physical damage* coverage depends on a variety of factors—not the least of which is the age and condition of your car.

WHAT: You don't have to be involved in an accident for your car to be damaged. A tree limb could fall on it while it sits in a parking lot. Hoodlums could break your windows or slash your tires.

Comprehensive physical damage insurance covers most noncollision damage—including damage sustained while the car is stolen.

It also covers the loss of personal possessions taken from the car. But you won't get the full amount for your cellular telephone or your custom stereo system, unless you have purchased a special rider covering those or other specific items.

WHY: You buy this insurance for the same reasons that you buy collision coverage—you want to protect yourself against the cost of repairs or a total replacement. Again, if you have a loan on a car, the bank or other lending institution may insist that you carry this coverage.

You may also want to purchase a rider if you own some expensive piece of equipment, such as a cellular telephone. But remember that you will pay a premium for this extra coverage. Weigh the cost of the extra insurance against the replacement value of the equipment. You may be better off without coverage.

Like collision insurance, comprehensive coverage can be purchased with money-saving deductibles. You should check out the rates before you buy.

WHY NOT: If you live in a low-crime area where the odds of nonaccident damage are minimal, you may be less likely to want this insurance.

You should know that you can buy comprehensive coverage without purchasing collision coverage—but not vice versa.

WHERE: Comprehensive insurance coverage varies in cost and depends heavily on where the car is located. In Boston—the reputed car theft capital of the country—it will, logically enough, cost you more than in a small, midwestern town.

WHEN: You should review this policy annually and reduce your coverage if necessary.

Medical Payments

WHO: Anyone who drives should carry at least a minimum amount of *medical payments insurance.*

WHAT: To return to your unlucky end-of-the-work-day accident: When you pulled too hastily out of your office parking lot, you—as well as the passenger in the other car—broke your arm in the resulting collision.

Your medical payments coverage will cover your medical expenses—and the medical expenses of any of your passengers who might have been injured in the accident.

The purpose of medical payments insurance is to cover the cost of immediate, necessary medical expenses for minor injuries sustained in an accident. If you're hurt in an accident, your insurer pays immediately and then may seek reimbursement if the other party is found to have been at fault.

With medical payments insurance, expensive litigation on small dollar claims is avoided. Serious injuries that require expensive treatment normally end up as the subject of litigation under bodily injury liability coverage or uninsured or underinsured motorists coverage.

WHY: You don't want to take a chance on not being covered for medical treatments. You will want your passengers covered as well. And prompt medical attention may well help avoid a lawsuit.

WHY NOT: There is no reason not to have this coverage, and in most states it's required.

WHERE: Typically, insurers sell this coverage in small amounts—as little as $500. But you should go for more—$5,000 is usually sufficient. The increased cost is only a few dollars and well worth the benefits.

In most cases, once your medical bills exceed the amount of your coverage, your health insurance kicks in. But remember, health insurance pays only your bills—not your passengers'. And the $15,000 of medical payments coverage isn't per person, but per accident. It doesn't go far. If the injuries to your passengers are serious, chances are you will be involved in a lawsuit under your bodily injury liability or uninsured or underinsured motorists coverage.

WHEN: Review your medical payments coverage annually to make sure it's adequate.

Questions and Answers

My state recently enacted no-fault auto insurance. What will this change mean to me?

Your state is among twenty that have enacted no-fault insurance laws. This new law may result in lower car insurance premiums for you.

With no-fault, your insurance carrier pays the bill for your own injuries if you're involved in an accident—no matter who is to blame for the accident. The idea of no-fault is that it saves the time and expense of going to court to ascertain who caused an accident.

But even in no-fault states, you may sue the other party to an accident. Your state law will specify when and on what grounds. Often, for instance, the law requires that death or permanent injury result from an accident before you may go to court.

Why is it that my twenty-two-year-old son pays more than $1,000 for his insurance, while my husband and I pay only $800? Our car is newer and more valuable than his, and he lives quite near us, though in a larger city.
Premiums for car insurance vary from state to state, city to city, and person to person. Most states allow insurers to offer lower rates to people with clean driving records or to classes of drivers with the lowest accident rates.

For example, statistics show that married women are involved in fewer accidents than other types of drivers. So their premiums are usually lower than other drivers'.

Likewise, unmarried men under age twenty-five are involved in more accidents than other types of drivers. So they usually pay higher insurance premiums.

No matter who you are, though, it pays to shop for car insurance. Except in a few states, such as Massachusetts, premiums vary from company to company.

My daughter is an excellent driver and has just completed a safe-driving course. Is she entitled to a break on her premiums?
Chances are, your daughter is eligible for a discount. Enrolling in a driver-training course often earns people a discount. So does making good grades in high school or college, reaching age sixty-five, installing antitheft devices, and insuring more than one car with the same carrier.

Some insurance carriers even give you a discount if you use public transportation regularly.

What if I forget to tell my insurance company that my eighteen-year-old son occasionally drives my car? Am I covered if he is involved in an accident?
The answer is probably yes.

However, at the very least, your insurer has the right to collect all the additional premiums it would have received if you hadn't forgotten to tell them your son is now driving. And the possibility of coverage being denied does exist. Although the courts have generally held in favor of consumers in these cases, the hassle you may be exposing yourself to just isn't worth it.

I own a small company, and I use my car 70 percent of the time for business. May I deduct my auto insurance premiums as a business expense?
Uncle Sam allows you to write off your insurance expenses, but only the portion that's attributable to business. If you use your car 70 percent of the time for business, you may write off 70 percent of your auto insurance premiums as a business expense.

CHAPTER 15

UMBRELLA COVERAGE

No matter how much you try to protect yourself from liability in the case of lawsuits, there's always the possibility that your automobile and homeowner's policies won't cover the judgment a jury or court might award a plaintiff.

That's where an *umbrella policy* comes in. In the case of liability claims, it picks up where your auto and homeowner's policies leave off.

Say your auto policy includes $300,000 in bodily injury liability coverage. If you're sued, and the jury awards the plaintiff $1 million, you're $700,000 short.

That money must come from somewhere—usually out of your pocket. And if your pocket isn't deep enough now, your future earnings could be garnished as well.

An umbrella policy—or *personal excess liability policy*, as it's sometimes called—makes good sense for anyone who owns a car or a home. The cost is minimal—typically, $125 for each $1 million in coverage if you own both a house and a car.

What if you don't own a car? Count yourself lucky. Since more liability suits stem from auto mishaps than accidents in the home, carriers charge less—often as little as $60 a year—for umbrella policies that cover people who are homeowners only.

You should know that you can purchase umbrella

policies with $5 million or more in coverage; but, in most cases, $1 million or $2 million is adequate.

Whatever the amount, though, it's a good idea to buy your umbrella policy from the same company that insures your car and home. That way, in the event of a claim, you avoid having different companies wrangling over who pays what and how much.

PART 4

YOUR HOME

- YOUR HOME AS AN INVESTMENT
- WHAT YOU NEED TO KNOW ABOUT MORTGAGES

CHAPTER 16

YOUR HOME AS AN INVESTMENT

Your home is more than an investment. It's also the proverbial roof over your head, and you want to exercise caution when you purchase it.

As a smart homebuyer, you should develop a game plan for each step of the process—from picking a neighborhood to selecting a house and choosing a mortgage.

In this part, we tell you some important facts about that most complicated of transactions, the purchase of a home. Let's start, in this chapter, with some answers to the most commonly asked questions about home ownership.

What are the tax benefits of home ownership?
Interest you pay on a mortgage is usually deductible for tax purposes. In fact, a mortgage remains one of the best tax shelters available to the average person. The only limit on the interest deduction is that the loan must be for the purchase of your primary home or a second home that you don't rent out more than fourteen days a year. (The IRS has special rules on deducting interest on second homes that you rent out.)

The only people whose mortgage deduction is restricted are those with mortgage interest on aggregate loan amounts in excess of $1 million or on aggregate home equity loan amounts in excess of $100,000, provided the home equity loan amounts don't exceed the fair-market value of the residence reduced by any acquisition indebtedness.

If you would like more information on the tax aspects of home ownership, telephone or write your local office of the IRS and ask for a copy of *Tax Information for Owners of Homes, Condominiums, and Cooperative Apartments* (publication 530).

The booklet, which is free for the asking, provides detailed information about home ownership and federal income taxes. It discusses itemized deductions for mortgage interest, real estate taxes, and casualty and theft losses.

And it explains how to treat closing costs and how to calculate the value of repairs and improvements that you make to your home.

You may also find *Tax Information on Selling Your Home* (publication 523) of interest. It explains how you may postpone the tax on part or all of the gain on the sale of your home and how you may exclude part or all of your gain from your gross income if you're fifty-five or older.

What price home can you afford?

Here's a rule of thumb to follow—and one that many bankers recommend to mortgage applicants: Spend no more than 25 to 35 percent of your gross income on housing.

Keep in mind that you should include as housing costs not only your monthly mortgage and interest payment but also the monthly cost of home insurance, real estate taxes, any private mortgage insurance you may be required to buy, and any condominium or co-operative fees.

How large a down payment *must* you make?

Don't make the common mistake of assuming that you must raise 10 to 20 percent of the purchase price of a home before you can buy one.

If you're a veteran of the United States armed forces,

you may qualify for a Veterans Administration (VA) loan for 100 percent of the purchase price of a home.

But you don't need to be a veteran to qualify for a Federal Housing Administration (FHA) loan that covers up to 95 percent of the purchase price.

Many banks and thrifts offer mortgage loans for up to 95 percent of the purchase price—as long as you can afford the mortgage payments and your credit is impeccable.

How large a down payment *should* you make?

If you're cash-poor, you'll have to scrape together as much as you can for a down payment. But if you're flush with cash, you should think about boosting your down payment.

Why? You may not know it, but increasing your down payment to 20 percent often may earn you a slightly lower interest rate on your mortgage loan. You may not be able to earn as much on your cash as the bank is charging for your loan.

In addition, if you do *not* put at least 20 percent down, many lenders require that you purchase *private mortgage insurance*—an additional expense.

Private mortgage insurance—PMI for short—protects the lender or mortgage holder in cases of default. As a homebuyer, you pay a single premium at *closing*—meaning the day you sign your mortgage loan and take title to your new home.

If your down payment is 15 percent, expect to pay a premium of 0.3 to 0.4 percent of your purchase price at closing. Put 10 percent down, and you pay about 0.5 percent on closing. With 5 percent down, you should expect to pay a full percentage point at closing. You also pay a small amount each month as long as the mortgage is outstanding.

So a larger down payment is an option worth considering. Our advice is to think of your down payment in the same way you would think about any other investment: where can you get the highest return with the lowest risk?

The *after-tax* cost of a mortgage is easy to figure. Simply multiply the interest rate by one minus your tax rate. (Your effective tax rate would include your state income tax rate if your state allows you to deduct mortgage interest.)

Say, for example, your tax rate is 28 percent and the mortgage interest rate you're offered is 10 percent. Your actual cost of borrowing is 10 percent times 0.72 (1 minus 0.28), or 7.2 percent.

If you can earn a higher after-tax return by investing your money elsewhere, you should probably do so and reduce the size of your down payment.

What if 7.2 percent is *more* than you think you'll earn after tax by investing your money elsewhere? Then, it pays you to make as large a down payment as possible—consistent, of course, with your financial situation and other demands on your money.

How do you raise money for the down payment?

One of the best ways, of course, is to systematically save or invest for a period of time. But if you have trouble meeting your goal, you have some other options.

It may come as a surprise to you that a lot of first-time homebuyers tap into their Individual Retirement Accounts (IRAs) for a down payment.

It's true that Uncle Sam will slap you with a 10 percent penalty for early withdrawal. And you must pay ordinary income taxes on the money you withdraw. But the tax benefits of home ownership—such as the ability to write off mortgage interest—may go a long way toward offsetting the extra taxes.

If you would like more information on the tax consequences of withdrawing money from your IRA, telephone or write your local IRS office and ask for a free copy of *Individual Retirement Arrangements* (publication 590).

Another idea for raising down payment money is to

take a loan from your employer-sponsored 401(k) plan. Uncle Sam is generous when it comes to 401(k)s. He allows you to borrow $50,000, or one half of your 401(k) account balance, whichever is less. However, interest on loans from 401(k) plans isn't deductible, even if you use the loan to purchase a home.

For more information on borrowing from 401(k)s, telephone or write the IRS and ask for a copy of *Pension and Annuity Income* (publication 575). It, too, is free.

Your parents—or grandparents—may want to help you out with your down payment. The rules allow each of them to give you $10,000 a year—generally with no gift or income tax consequences on either side. And this rule applies not only to parents and grandparents, but to any individual—related or not.

Still another source of money for a down payment, and one that's often overlooked, is the seller of the property you're buying. You may want to rent the home for a year or so, with a portion of the rent going toward the purchase price.

CHAPTER 17

WHAT YOU NEED TO KNOW ABOUT MORTGAGES

For homebuyers, obtaining a mortgage need not be cause for raising the roof—but waiting until the last minute to shop for a loan can be.

Lenders and loans vary enormously, and it takes time to sift through the options that are available to you. Chances are, you're going to have to live with your decision for at least several years—maybe even for decades.

What kind of home mortgage loan is right for you? And where do you get it? In this chapter, we describe various types of mortgage loans and mortgage lenders. We also tell you what you need to know *before* you refinance an existing home loan.

We start with two key definitions.

A *mortgage* is an agreement to repay a debt. With a mortgage, a borrower gives a lender a lien on the property as security for the loan. In return, the borrower gets the use of the property. The lender removes the lien when the debt is fully repaid.

A *lien* is a claim by a lender against a piece of property. It gives the lender the right to seize your home if you don't repay your loan.

Types of Mortgages

One question our clients often ask is, Should I shop first for the mortgage or the mortgage lender? We suggest that you decide first on the type of loan you want, then shop for that particular loan among the institutions that offer it.

Mortgages come in a number of varieties—from *balloon* and *fixed-rate* mortgages to *graduated payment* and *variable-rate* mortgages. Let's take a look at each.

Fixed-Rate Mortgages

WHO: The people best suited to fixed-rate mortgages take comfort in knowing what their obligations are and don't want to worry about them changing.

Fixed-rate loans make sense if you expect your income to level out in the years ahead or you think that interest rates are going to head up over the next few years.

If you're approaching or are beyond your peak earning years, you're living on a relatively fixed income. If you're older and buying a retirement home, you might also want to consider a fixed-rate mortgage.

WHAT: The initial interest rate on a fixed-rate mortgage will usually be higher than on a variable-rate loan, but you're getting something in return—security.

With a fixed-rate mortgage, you know what your payments are. You also know that they won't change—no matter how high interest rates soar or what happens in the financial markets after you take out your loan.

A variation on the fixed-rate mortgage looks deceptively like the next type of mortgage we are going to discuss, the variable-rate mortgage. But it's not.

It's called a *graduated payment mortgage* (GPM).

A GPM—also called a JEEP—carries a fixed rate of interest, but the monthly payments vary according to a schedule that you and the lender agree to at the outset.

Your first payments are low, possibly even lower than the interest charge on the loan.

Then, year by year, they increase.

The idea is to match the size of the monthly payment to the growth in your income and, consequently, your ability to pay the higher amount.

Three cautionary notes about GPMs: First, you may have negative amortization during the early years of the loan. In other words, by keeping your payment artificially low, you're actually going a little more into debt every month.

This is a potentially serious situation. Here's why. If you have to sell the house and cannot find a buyer who will pay enough to allow you to fully pay off the now-larger loan, you may not be able to sell the house or you may end up paying money to sell it.

Second, even if you're not building negative amortization, you may have to pay some stiff penalties if you pay off the loan early. So, basically, this amounts to the same thing.

The third note of caution? You should be fairly confident that your income will indeed rise to keep pace with your increasing monthly payments.

Another variation on the fixed-rate mortgage is a balloon mortgage—or a partially amortized loan, as it's sometimes called.

Say you believe that interest rates are coming down, and you want to make sure that you can refinance your mortgage loan when they do. Or say that you soon expect to come into a large sum of money—an inheritance, perhaps, or a big gain on the sale of a business. Or you know your job will cause you to transfer locations in a certain period of time.

Then a balloon mortgage may make sense for you.

With a balloon loan, your interest rate is fixed from year to year and your monthly payment is the same as it might be on a mortgage that runs for, say, twenty or thirty years.

But your payments don't run for that long.

Instead, a balloon loan actually runs for a shorter period—five years, for instance. And then you have to pay it off in one big, final "balloon" payment. It equals the amount of principal that's outstanding at the time the loan matures.

Of course, your mortgage agreement might include a provision allowing you to refinance your loan at that time. But even if it does, you'll have to refinance at what are then current rates, which, obviously, could be higher or lower than the interest rate you were paying.

WHY: The appeal of balloon mortgages is that they offer homebuyers a reduced rate of interest compared to fixed-rate and other, more conventional mortgages. Some require payment of interest only.

WHY NOT: When you take out a balloon mortgage, you're gambling that you'll have the cash to pay off the remaining debt at the end of term. What if you lack the money?

You must refinance your home at current—and possibly higher—interest rates or you'll lose it. It's as simple as that. And what if your home falls in value—a valid concern these days, especially in light of the soft markets in some parts of the country?

In this case, you may be able to refinance only a portion of your existing mortgage. You still must come up with a large chunk of cash—or lose your home.

WHERE: Nowadays, there are almost as many different types of lenders as there are different kinds of loans. One good source of information about home loans is your real estate agent. But take the initiative to do some shopping on your own, too.

A real estate agent may have a reason for preferring one lender over another, and that reason may have little or nothing to do with your best interest.

Thrift institutions are the traditional sources of fixed-rate mortgages. But these loans are also available from a variety of other financial institutions.

For example, credit unions, commercial banks, mortgage companies, mutual savings banks, real estate groups, and savings banks all offer fixed-rate loans.

You may be able to secure a fixed-rate loan from the seller of the house you want to buy or even from your employer.

WHEN: Fixed-rate mortgages make the most sense when interest rates are low. That way, you lock in a favorable rate.

Variable- or Adjustable-Rate Mortgages

WHO: If you believe that interest rates will fall, you may find *adjustable-rate mortgages* (ARMs) attractive. You must be careful, though, if you lack a financial cushion. As many people have discovered to their sorrow, ARMs can be devastating if you have guessed wrong on rates. That is, if rates go up, you could be stuck with a much higher monthly payment than you're comfortable with.

ARMs are also a popular choice if you're starting out in your career, not wealthy, fairly mobile, and expect to move up as well as move on within the next few years. Of course, ARMs can be appealing to people in any income category. In fact, those with more wealth may be more likely to take the risks associated with ARMs.

WHAT: With adjustable-rate mortgages, or ARMs, the interest rate you pay varies over the life of the loan.

ARMs usually offer a fixed interest rate in the early years of home ownership—sometimes just for the first year and sometimes for as long as five or seven years. Frequently, this rate is lower by a percentage point or more than the interest on fixed-rate loans.

But at the end of the specified period, the rate will rise or fall. It all depends on what has happened to the level of interest rates in the market since you took out the loan and on the specific provisions of your ARM.

Why are ARMs often a good deal for people with

relatively short residency and the potential for rising income? Here's the reason.

By the time the loan rate—and your monthly payments—go up, you have the income to handle the increase. Or, you may have already sold the house. And, of course, rates may *not* go up.

People who think interest rates are going to fall may also choose an ARM to get the lower initial rate. Then they can refinance when the rates on fixed-rate mortgages fall several years down the road. These people tend to be comfortable with some level of risk.

And make no mistake. There's risk associated with almost any ARM. You have much more to understand about the terms of this kind of mortgage than with the fixed-rate variety. Of course you'll want to know what the initial rate is, but you'll also want to make sure you understand:

- when the rate can first change;
- what index the rate is tied to;
- how much the rate can change and how often;
- whether there's a cap on the total amount the rate can change;
- your monthly payment under the initial rate;
- your monthly payment under the highest rate your loan can reach.

If you would like additional information about adjustable-rate mortgages, the Mortgage Bankers Association of America publishes two booklets on the topic: *What You Should Know About ARMS* (45 cents) and *Consumer Handbook on Adjustable Rate Mortgages* (20 cents).

WHY: Adjustable-rate mortgages sometimes make home ownership affordable when it otherwise might not be. That's because you can start out with a lower rate—sometimes a *much* lower rate—than you would with a fixed-rate mortgage. And that makes your monthly payments lower, which makes it easier for you to qualify for a mortgage.

WHY NOT: Just as with GMPs, some ARMs involve *negative amortization*, a dangerous trap under some circumstances. Here's what happens with negative amortization.

If the interest rate on your mortgage goes up, your monthly payments remain the same. But the amount of the loan increases each month.

In other words, depending on how much the interest rate on your ARM increases, you could end up owing more after your mortgage payment than before you made it. If this situation were to keep up for long, you could end up owing the lender more than your house is worth.

Maybe you don't care—unless you want to sell your house. Then the price you could get might fall short of paying off your loan.

Negative amortization loans were designed to make housing affordable to people who otherwise couldn't afford them during times of high interest rates.

And they were fine—provided you knew what you were getting into—when real estate prices were rising fast enough to keep pace with your mortgage balance.

However, today, when prices in many parts of the country are at best flat, these loans may no longer make sense.

WHERE: Most of the institutions that offer fixed-rate mortgages—commercial banks, credit unions, thrifts, and so on—also offer adjustable-rate mortgages.

WHEN: Variable- or adjustable-rate mortgages make the most sense when interest rates are on the way down.

VA and FHA Mortgages

WHO: If you're a veteran of the United States armed forces, you may qualify for a Veterans Administration (VA) loan for up to 100 percent of the purchase price of a home.

But you don't need to be a veteran to qualify for a Federal Housing Administration (FHA) loan that covers up to 95 percent of the purchase price.

WHAT: A VA mortgage—which is always a fixed-rate mortgage—is a loan that's backed by the full faith and credit of the Veterans Administration. An FHA mortgage is backed by the Federal Housing Administration.

WHY: If you can get a lower fixed rate, by all means do so.

WHY NOT: There's really no reason not to consider either of these types of mortgage loans as long as you can put up with some red tape.

WHERE: VA and FHA loans are made through banks, thrifts, and other commercial lending institutions.

If you would like more information on VA mortgages, telephone or write your local VA office or write the Veterans Administration, Washington, DC 20420.

For more information on FHA loans, write the Federal Housing Administration, U.S. Department of Housing and Urban Development, 451 7th Street SW, Washington, DC 20410.

WHEN: These loans make sense at most times. The exception: If rates are very high, but you think they are going to fall. In this case, an ARM might be a more suitable choice.

Monthly or Biweekly?

Biweekly mortgages are another mortgage innovation.

These mortgages start with a conventional fixed- or adjustable-rate mortgage. However, instead of paying monthly, you pay half the monthly amount every two weeks.

Say, for example, you have a biweekly, thirty-year $100,000 mortgage at 10 percent. With a regular thirty-year mortgage, you would pay $878 in principal and interest each month. However, with your biweekly mortgage, you divide the payment in two and pay $439 every two weeks.

What is the point? You pay off your loan sooner and you save on interest expense over the life of the loan. That's because you're actually making twenty-six payments during the year—or a whole extra month's worth of payments.

Tip: Another way to save a bundle on interest charges is to take out a shorter-term mortgage. Fifteen-year mortgages, for instance, are becoming increasingly common. The monthly payments are a bit higher than with longer-term mortgages—but not by as much as you may think.

For example, if you have a thirty-year, $100,000 mortgage at 10 percent, you would pay $878 in mortgage and interest costs each month. But if you have a fifteen-year mortgage at 10 percent, you pay $1,075 a month—$197 a month more. Also, most lenders offer lower rates on fifteen-year mortgages than they do on thirty-year mortgages.

Today's lower tax rates make these shorter-term mortgages more attractive than ever. Why? When marginal rates went as high as 70 percent, $1 of interest paid used to be worth as much as 70 cents in lower taxes. Now that the top tax rate is just 28 percent (33 percent in some circumstances), a dollar spent on mortgage interest saves you only 28 cents, or at most 33 cents.

One other nice point about shorter-term mortgages: The interest rates are frequently lower by a quarter or a half a point.

If you need a large loan—larger than $187,600 on a single-family home—you're looking at what the lenders call a *jumbo mortgage*. Those loans are more expensive because most, but not all, lenders sell their regular loans on the so-called secondary market, either to government agencies, such as the Government National Mortgage Association (GNMA), or to private buyers who may bundle lots of mortgages together and sell the bundle, in shares, to private investors.

But loans greater than a certain size—$187,600, as we mentioned, on a single-family home—cannot be sold as easily in the secondary market.

So the lender either must sell the loan to private investors or, less typically, keep it in its own portfolio. Therefore, it will charge you a premium rate—perhaps a half to a full percentage point more. However, you can frequently cut this rate slightly by increasing your down payment to 20 percent or more.

So, now you know about fixed- and variable-rate mortgages, and we have told you about most of the variations you're likely to run across. Still, lenders are always coming up with new loan or payment variations. So don't be bashful about asking your lender or checking with your real estate agent about current offerings. Don't assume that you have to stick to the tried and true. However, make sure you understand all the wrinkles that go along with new loans.

Shopping for the Lowest Rates and the Best Service

Now that you have a good idea what you're looking for, it's time to comparison-shop for rates. No matter which type of mortgage you decide on, you don't want to pay more for it than you have to.

So shopping around for the lowest interest rate among lenders makes sense. And, we are going to give you some ideas about how to shop efficiently. Bear in mind, though, that interest rates alone aren't the sole criterion of loan cost.

You also have to consider the cost of your application, the number of points you'll pay (we explain "points" shortly), and when you can lock in an interest rate. Still, it makes sense to begin by examining the interest rates various lenders are charging.

Don't assume that because they are competing in the same market, all lenders have pretty much the same rates. Not true. You'll find differences of at least one point, and sometimes more, on otherwise similar loans. It does pay to shop.

The easiest way, of course, is by using the telephone and the Yellow Pages. You should make sure the information you're obtaining is current, and ask questions as you go. Just make a chart that compares the offerings of various institutions.

In addition, local newspapers usually run—either weekly or monthly—a list of local lending institutions and mortgage companies and their rates.

Make sure to check this information with the lenders themselves, however. That's because the newspapers often don't include exceptions or qualifications that might apply to your situation. Lenders have been known to use bait-and-switch techniques, too.

When you're shopping around for loans, make sure to ask about *points*, or loan origination fees. Most lenders require you to pay these fees. One point equals 1 percent of the loan principal. So, if your loan is for $50,000, one point comes to $500.

Points are often negotiable. Or, if they aren't, you at least may have options from which to choose.

Some lenders, for example, will charge you two points at one lending rate but one point at a higher rate. Others vary the point charge depending upon the amount of your down payment.

Finally, once you find an attractive rate and add in the points you'll pay, you'll also want to know at what point in the loan application process your interest rate is set. Some institutions let you lock in a rate the moment you apply for the loan. Others make you take the rate that applies on the day of your closing—which could be higher than the rate the institution originally quoted.

Certainly, there's no easy formula to follow when you're mortgage-shopping. But if you take the steps we suggest, you'll find the lender who is right for you with no more than minimum pain.

Choosing a Lender

Should you care *where* the money for your home comes from so long as you get the loan on the terms that you like? The answer is no—with some qualifications. Once you get the loan, it hardly matters to what address you send your monthly, or biweekly, check.

But there are two matters you want to pay careful attention to when you choose a mortgage lender. The first is the ability of your lender to handle the loan application and the real estate closing in a smooth, professional, and pleasant manner.

Applying for a mortgage means exposing your financial backside. And it's a process that doesn't involve just you, the applicant. It requires you to ask other people and institutions—banks, employers, creditors—to supply information that the mortgage lender needs.

A good lending officer will remove most of the administrative burden of collecting this information from your shoulders. He or she will try to help you make sure that all the responses get in before the various deadlines pass.

Then there's the closing to consider. Real estate closings—as anyone who has ever sat through one knows—can be composure-rattling experiences.

You're relying on lots of other people—your attorney, the seller, the seller's attorney, the lender, appraisers, real estate agents, and others—to cover a plethora of fine points and accurately transfer a substantial amount of money, both in cash and on paper.

So, what you're looking for in these respects is a lender with administrative competence—the ability to handle details well—and a willingness to be helpful.

One of the best ways to locate a lender with these

characteristics is to ask for recommendations from friends who recently purchased homes.

Another point to consider when choosing your lending institution—aside, of course, from the terms of the loan and the cost of obtaining it—is whether you're ever going to need or want to do additional business with the lender in the future. In fact, you can hold out the possibility of future business as a bargaining chip.

Questions and Answers

Is seller financing worth considering?
Sometimes a seller, eager to dispose of his or her property, can give you better terms than an institution. And with no extra costs, such as points.

Obviously, this type of loan can make sense for you. You should consider a seller-financed loan (commonly called a *contract for deed*) if you can get better terms than you can elsewhere.

The downside: You don't actually own the property until the contract is fulfilled. And foreclosure under these circumstances isn't a pretty picture.

What is a wraparound mortgage?
The *wraparound mortgage* is—as the name suggests—a mortgage that wraps around your first mortgage. That is, it's really a second, or junior, mortgage. In case you default, the first, or senior, mortgage holder has first claim on the property.

You make your monthly payment to the wraparound lender, who in turn pays the senior lender. A wraparound mortgage is just a way of getting more credit without having to pay off your first loan and refinance your house.

I understand that some states and counties provide help for low- and moderate-income homebuyers. True? And, if so, where can I get information on these loans?
If you're a low- or moderate-income homebuyer, you may be able to borrow mortgage money at a bargain rate. To

date, more than $49 billion of such loans have been made.

As only one example, the state of Kentucky has made below-market-rate loans to low- and moderate-income families through a network of some seventy commercial lenders. Families at the lowest end of the income scale may qualify for loans with interest rates as low as 1 to 7 percent.

Other states help low- and moderate-income home-buyers by lending money—at low rates—for down payments and closing costs and offering extra tax breaks.

The qualifications for participating in these programs vary considerably from state to state. However, the average household income of participants in all state programs is about $27,200, the average down payment is $5,400, and the average purchase price is $60,000.

Would you like more information on state-sponsored loan programs? Real estate agents, lenders, local housing agencies, and state housing agencies are all good sources of information. For more information on state housing agencies, write to the National Council of State Housing Agencies, 444 N. Capitol St., NW, Suite 118, Washington, DC 20001.

PART 5

MANAGING YOUR DEBTS

- SHOULD YOU BORROW?
- WHAT YOU NEED TO KNOW ABOUT CREDIT
- THE RIGHT WAY TO BORROW

CHAPTER 18

SHOULD YOU BORROW?

You may not know it, but *debts*—the amount of money you owe to other people and institutions—are as important to your overall financial health as your assets.

That's why—as a smart money manager—you want to watch not only how much you owe but also the type and cost of each of your debts.

In this section, we tell you what you need to know when it comes to borrowing for consumption. And we start, in this chapter, with that most basic question: Should you borrow?

Can you afford to borrow?

Whether you make a purchase with a credit card or take out a car loan, it all amounts to the same thing: you're agreeing—in writing—to pay a fee for the use of someone else's money over a period of time.

The first question you should ask yourself—or your financial adviser—before exercising this privilege is the same question you should ask before making any purchase: Can I afford it?

We know, it sounds obvious. But you would be amazed at the number of people who, when they take out an auto loan, for instance, see only a shiny new car. They don't add the amount of *principal* and *interest* they must pay on that loan to their existing monthly obligations to see if they can make the additional payments.

Another issue to consider is whether a loan is the best

way for you to finance the car. Maybe you should sell an asset instead. Or consider other alternatives.

However, after all options are considered, you may determine that taking out a loan is your best alternative—particularly if the after-tax interest rate you pay on a loan comes to less than the interest you could earn by investing your money.

The question is one of making the best use of all the resources available to you. And that's how you should think about it.

What is your real cost of borrowing?

Let's stay with the example of buying a new car. It's a familiar situation to most of us, and it lets us ask ourselves all the right questions about debt.

If you have no cash and no liquid assets, you have no choice. Taking on debt is the only way you're going to acquire a car. Of course, this approach raises other issues, such as how expensive does the car have to be and what are the terms of the loan?

Stretching car payments over, say, five years lowers the monthly payment, but it increases the total cost of the car. What's more, cars lose their value rapidly.

With an extended loan, you may easily wind up in year four, for instance, owing more than the car is worth. That isn't a problem unless you have to sell. Then the cash you get for the used buggy won't pay off the principal and interest due.

The more likely case is that you do have a choice—or at least a partial choice. You can borrow to buy the car. You can pay for it with cash. Or you can convert an asset to cash and use that money. The question is, How do you sort out those options?

Take a look at your investment assets. It might be less expensive overall to convert one of them to cash to pay for the car than to take out the loan.

To make the point, let's use an unlikely situation.

Let's say that the car costs $15,000 and you happen to

have exactly that amount sitting in a bank passbook savings account earning 5 percent interest.

If you took that money out of the bank and used it to buy the car, the cost to you would equal the interest you're giving up. You're giving up 3.6 percent (the after-tax yield on your savings account) to avoid paying 14.16 (after-tax) percent in 1989—clearly a wise choice in anyone's mind.

Of course, the issue isn't always so clear-cut. First, you probably wouldn't have $15,000 invested in a 5 percent savings account.

Your dollars should at least be in a money-market account. But even here, the interest you're earning is almost certainly less than the interest you would have to pay a lender. Also bear in mind that the interest income is fully taxable, while the interest expense on the car loan is only partially deductible. You're better off using the money to buy the car than taking out an auto loan.

On the other hand, if the money you're thinking of using is, for instance, in a bank certificate of deposit that hasn't matured, you'll incur a penalty for early withdrawal. And you have to consider that penalty as part of the cost.

Perhaps you own stock or bonds or shares in a mutual fund. To sell them now in order to finance a car means that you're giving up the income, if any, they generate as well as their future capital appreciation, if any. How do you estimate that cost?

Doing so is tricky and partly subjective. You can probably estimate pretty accurately the income you'll earn from these investments as dividends or interest. Their appreciation over the period of the loan, which is your alternative, is harder to know.

But make a reasonable estimate because that, too, is part of the cost you'll want to compare. Say that you own $15,000 worth of stock in Growth Co., Inc., which pays no dividends. But in each of the past two years the value of the stock has risen by 20 percent.

You don't know for certain that this growth rate will continue, but you believe it's likely to. So, do you sell the stock and give up an estimated 20 percent annual return to buy the car, or do you take out a $15,000, 15 percent loan? Which is cheaper?

It's a close call.

The after-tax cost of the loan is, as we figured earlier, 14.16 percent in 1989 and will be 15 percent after 1990. On the other hand, the after-tax return on your stock is 14.4 percent (20 percent times your 28 percent tax rate). Of course, you won't pay the taxes on your growth in the stock until you sell it. How sure are you that the stock will continue to appreciate?

Now, let's look at this debt issue from a different perspective. We have been talking about incurring debt. What about paying it off? How do you know when you should?

Some people have a strong aversion to debt of any kind. But even here it's possible to be shortsighted in your enthusiasm to clear the debt side of your ledger.

In general, the interest rates you, as an individual, will pay on borrowed money will be higher than the rates of return you're likely to earn on investments. So it usually does make sense to reduce your debt level when you can. But that's a general rule.

You also must consider, for instance, what your future borrowing needs will be. Say, for example, that you're going to buy a new car next year, and you want to clear up your current debts. So you liquidate some investments and pay off your credit card bills and your home equity loan.

That's nice, but now you have no money for the car. And, to take out a new home equity loan next year, you'll incur the cost of points, lawyers' fees, and so forth all over again. And the home equity loan interest may be completely deductible.

The smarter move might have been to pay off the expensive credit card debt, but keep the home equity loan as it was. And, next year, you would have just that much more cash to put toward the car without incurring the added cost.

CHAPTER 19

WHAT YOU NEED TO KNOW ABOUT CREDIT

If you do decide that borrowing is the right choice for your circumstances, you now face other issues: when to borrow, where to borrow, how to borrow, and so on. In this chapter, we provide answers to frequently asked questions about credit and borrowing.

Who qualifies for credit?

When you apply for credit, a lender decides whether you're creditworthy by examining two primary sources—your loan application (which lists your place of employment and, in some cases, any references you have) and your *credit bureau* report.

What your potential lender is trying to determine, of course, is whether you *can* repay the debt. He or she also wants to know if you *will* repay the debt. And—in most cases—the lender wants to be protected in the event that you fail to repay.

Specifically, a lender will ask whether you have ever borrowed money. Did you pay these loans off promptly? Will your income allow you to cover basic expenses and still make your loan payments? Does your employment record suggest that you'll continue to receive this income?

Do you possess savings or other assets that you can use to repay the loan should you lose your job? Do you have other debts, and would they have first claim on your assets?

Many creditors use a scoring system that assigns points for a number of factors—income, length of time on the job, whether you own your home, freedom from other debts, and so on. Usually, the higher the number of points, the more likely you are to obtain credit.

The second item the lender looks at, your credit bureau report, contains a variety of information, including many of your outstanding debts and your repayment record.

It may also list the name of your employer, the amount you make, plus information from public court records, such as bankruptcy filings and tax liens.

The information in the report must be as current as possible. In fact, the law requires credit bureaus to delete most information that's older than seven years. However, a personal bankruptcy remains on your credit report for ten years.

You may want to call your local credit bureau (check the Yellow Pages) for a copy of your report *before* you apply for a loan. That way, you can check the report for accuracy.

The fee for the report varies from bureau to bureau but ranges from about $10 to $30—unless you were denied credit within the last thirty days. In this situation, the report is free for the asking.

What if you find something wrong in the report? Notify the credit bureau of the error. Even if it refuses to erase the disputed item, it must include with your report your written protest or explanation of fewer than one hundred words.

When is the best time to apply for credit?

The best time to apply for a loan—or so the conventional wisdom goes—is when you least need the money. In this case, the conventional wisdom is right.

If you plan to apply for a loan in the next few years, it pays to get your financial house in order. For example, pay off overdue balances and slash your existing debt.

If you want to reduce the amount you owe, start by adding up all your debts—installment loans, dealer loans, credit and charge cards, retail store charge accounts, student loans, and so on. (But don't include in this total the mortgage on your home.)

Say that the total comes to $4,000, and the interest rate you pay averages some 15 percent. Say, too, that your goal is to become debt-free in three years. Then, to reach your goal, you must make payments of about $140 a month.

What if you have never borrowed and don't have a credit record? You're at a disadvantage in obtaining credit—even if your finances are in impeccable order.

It could improve your chances if you maintain savings and checking accounts. Opening a charge account with a local store and paying off the balance within the terms of the credit agreement will establish a history of responsible credit management.

Where should you borrow?

One answer is, from the place that offers you the best terms. Typically, the least expensive loans are offered by *credit unions*, the most expensive by *finance companies.* You also want to take into account such factors as the company's reputation and integrity, the amount of service it provides, its financial stability, and its expertise.

You should do your loan shopping before you apply for credit. That way, you avoid filling out complicated applications for loans or credit that you wouldn't accept or aren't competitive.

When you shop, compare terms. You may want to call several lenders to ask about rates. Make sure you tell the lender, if you can, the size of the loan you need, the amount of the down payment, the term of the loan, and the reason you're borrowing—to buy a new car, for example.

A good indicator of the cost of borrowing isn't, surprisingly enough, your potential monthly payment. Rather, it's the *annual percentage rate* (APR), which takes into account several loan charges—including finance charges and processing fees.

You may want to consider consolidating your debts by borrowing from a single source—a bank, thrift, or credit union, for example. The interest rate you pay one of these institutions may be less than the amount charged by some credit card issuers.

How much debt is too much debt?

A friend of Richard Brinsley Sheridan (1751–1816), the Irish dramatist and politician, once observed, "Given that you come from such an illustrious Irish family, it's strange that your name has no 'O' in front of it."

"True," the amiable Sheridan replied, "and no family has a better right to it. We owe everybody."

Was Sheridan too much in debt? Probably, if he thought so. How much debt is too much debt? That's a question that you, too, must answer for yourself.

Many financial planners—and lenders too—argue that no more than 15 percent to 20 percent of your disposable income should go toward paying installment debts (excluding your rent or mortgage).

But don't make the mistake some people do and consider this percentage a perfectly acceptable upper limit. You have to take your own personality and spending habits into account.

And, for many people, 10 percent going toward servicing installment loans is too much. Why? They value their disposable income more, or they are just uncomfortable with debt.

Many financial planners also advise their clients to avoid borrowing heavily for luxuries, such as vacations, because it may mean that the person—now laden with debts—may be unable to later borrow for necessities, such as a car or a house.

How do you keep from getting in over your head?

The best way is to buy only what you can afford and borrow only what you can afford to repay. It's a hard rule to follow but one that's vital to your financial health.

What are your credit rights?

The Equal Credit Opportunity Act makes it illegal for lenders to discriminate against you on the basis of race, color, religion, nationality, age, sex, or marital status. You may not be discriminated against also if a portion of your income comes from public assistance programs or because you exercise any right under the Consumer Credit Protection Act.

If a lender denies you credit, it must notify you within thirty days after receipt of your completed application and explain the reasons you were refused.

The Truth in Lending Act requires lenders to disclose in writing the cost of borrowing, including the annual percentage rate and other charges. It also requires lenders to use an approved method for computing the annual percentage rate.

It's not important for you to understand the formula that lenders use to compute the APR. What is important is that the law requires that a uniform system be used throughout the financial services industry so that the consumer can compare the cost of credit.

For loans that are open-ended, such as credit card balances, lenders must explain in writing how they calculate finance charges. They must also specify when finance charges are first assessed—from the date of sale, posting, billing, or thirty days after billing.

The Fair Credit Billing Act allows you to challenge charges to your credit or charge card accounts that you think are incorrect.

If you have a problem with merchandise or services you charge, you may withhold payment on the item as long as the amount is more than $50 and the charge was made in your home state or within 100 miles of your home.

How do you exercise your rights under the act? Write the issuer of your charge card or credit card within sixty days after the bill is mailed and pay the portion of the bill that isn't in dispute. The issuer must correct the charges within ninety days or explain in writing why it didn't.

Always state your case in writing—a telephone call won't preserve your legal rights. With your letter, include copies of any disputed bills—for example, a receipt that lists the purchase price of an item as $10.93, not the $100.93 that appears on your bill.

The card issuer must look into the matter and, while doing so, may not charge you a finance fee or a late charge. Nor may the issuer close your account for nonpayment of the disputed bill or report it to a credit bureau.

The Fair Credit Billing Act also covers defective products for which you paid with a charge or credit card. The law allows you to withhold payment until the dispute is resolved. But you must make an honest effort to resolve the problem with the merchant.

The Fair Debt Collection Practices Act prohibits collection agencies from threatening you, calling you at all hours of the day or night, or embarrassing you by contacting people you know—such as your employer—and informing them of your unpaid obligation.

The Fair Credit Reporting Act protects you in cases where you're denied credit or even employment because of false information that appears in your credit report.

As we noted earlier, it gives you the right to review your credit report, contest information it contains, and attach a short statement about any disputed item.

If you would like more information about your rights in the area of credit, write the Federal Reserve Board (Washington, DC 20551) for a copy of its booklet, *Consumer Handbook to Credit Protection Laws*. The publication is free for the asking.

If you want to make a complaint about a financial institution, write the Division of Consumer and Community Affairs, Federal Reserve Board, Washington, DC 20551. This organization only handles complaints against banks that are members of the Federal Reserve system. But it will refer complaints against federally regulated savings and loan associations or credit unions to the appropriate federal agency. You may want to contact your state banking regulators for help, too.

Do you need credit insurance?

Not too long ago, a young man applied for a loan at a local bank. "Do you want credit insurance?" the banker inquired.

"Sure," the young man replied. "That way, I am guaranteed to get credit, right?"

"Wrong," the banker replied, then explained that *credit insurance* isn't, as its name implies, insurance that you'll get credit.

Rather, it's a life, unemployment, or disability policy that you purchase, naming your creditor as beneficiary.

If you die and the debt is outstanding, the policy pays up to the insured amount. If you lose your job or become disabled, the policy makes your payments—again up to the insured amount—until you find another position or your good health returns.

Credit insurance may make sense if you or your co-borrower will have difficulty keeping up with loan payments should you become disabled or unemployed or die.

Credit insurance also may make sense if you're on the line between getting accepted for credit and getting turned down. With credit insurance, a lender is more likely to get repaid, a loan becomes less risky, and you become a better prospect.

And, if you're older or in ill health, credit insurance premiums are sometimes less expensive than term insurance policies you buy on your own to cover your debts.

Credit insurance makes less sense for people with adequate insurance. Why pay twice for life and disability insurance protection?

You should know that some lenders receive commissions for selling credit insurance, while others write credit insurance policies themselves.

So, lenders profit from you in two ways—from the net

interest they earn from the payments you make on your loan and the premium payments you make on your credit insurance policy. You should know that federal law prohibits a lender from requiring you to obtain credit insurance as a condition of receiving a loan.

If you think credit insurance is right for you, examine the terms of the policy your lender offers. Then compare these terms to policies you can buy on your own.

Are you liable in cases of credit-related crime?

If a person uses your credit card without *authorization*—be it a thief or someone you know—your maximum liability after you notify the creditor is $50. And it makes no difference how much the person charges.

Your exposure—before you notify the issuer that the card is missing—can include any charges made before notification, so call as soon as you suspect your card is missing.

What about after you give notice? Then the card issuer—not you—is 100 percent liable for any unauthorized charges to your account.

The law requires card issuers to provide you an easy way to give notice that a card is missing or stolen, such as a toll-free telephone number.

It makes sense to keep in a safe place a list of your credit card numbers—plus the telephone numbers to call in case of loss or theft.

It's also a good idea to keep your credit cards separate from your wallet. That way, a pickpocket is unlikely to get his or her hands on them.

Tip: Always tear up the carbons when you receive a receipt for a credit card purchase. And never give your credit card number to someone who calls you and is unknown to you. Thieves can—and often do—use your card number to purchase merchandise by telephone.

CHAPTER 20

THE RIGHT WAY TO BORROW

If your credit history is solid, you could be eligible for a great deal of credit. So what are some potential sources of money? In this chapter, we take a look.

Let's start with a few basics.

Credit cards and charge cards—small, plastic emblems of financial responsibility—are an increasingly common feature of our cashless society.

Not all credit and charge cards are alike, but all are convenient, more secure than cash and, assuming your account is in good order, you won't get caught short. These cards also provide identification and they give you records that help you itemize your spending and prepare your income tax returns and other reports.

And you're not limited to charging in the United States. Merchants in many foreign countries also honor these cards. In some cases, you may also borrow money by presenting the card at a member bank or using an automated teller machine.

This *cash advance*—as the bank card systems like to call it—is actually an unsecured loan with the maximum amount prearranged by the bank. This maximum amount the bank or card issuer allows you to borrow is called your *cash limit*. (Your *credit limit*, by contrast, refers to the total amount—cash and purchases—you can borrow on your card.)

Caution: There's usually no grace period on cash advances, and they may cause you to incur extra fees.

What is the difference between a *charge card* and a *credit card*? With a charge card, you're usually required to pay the entire amount due each month. With a credit card, you generally get a choice—you may pay the entire amount or you may spread out your payments over time.

Charge Cards

WHO: Have you heard the story of the young woman who tried to rent a car without a charge card or credit card? She had the cash on hand to pay for the rental. Nonetheless, the rental car company turned her down flat.

Charge and credit cards, it seems, are almost an indispensable fact of life in our fast-paced society. Almost everyone needs at least one such card.

What if you're temperamentally opposed to debt? Keep your card on hand for emergencies, but don't use it otherwise.

WHAT: Listed in *The Guinness Book of World Records* is the name of a man who applied for—and received—a total of 1,173 credit cards. No one, naturally, needs 1,173 cards. Chances are, you can get by just fine with one or two cards.

What exactly do you need to know about charge cards?

Charge cards are ideal for business travelers, among others. Buy an airplane ticket, stay a few nights in a hotel, and watch the credit line on your bank credit card disappear. But with a charge card, there's no limit set in advance for the amount you can charge; charges are approved based on your ability to pay as demonstrated by your past spending and payment patterns as well as your personal resources.

Charge card companies bill you every thirty days, and you're required to pay this amount in full. The statement usually includes your new balance and any late charges that are due.

Annual membership fees for charge cards run upwards of $25. You pay more for prestige, Gold, or American Express Platinum Cards. But with the extra fees come extra services.

For example, some card issuers offer free flight insurance and free rental car insurance—when you charge these items to your prestige card.

Charge card issuers may also provide you a preapproved line of credit of $2,000 to $10,000 or more. Most credit cards don't charge interest unless you've paid late. If you use them correctly, you'll never pay interest on a charge card. However, the interest on your line of credit is usually the same as on your charge card. You may use your charge card credit line to purchase goods or services—or even pay your charge card bill.

WHY: With charge cards, you pay no finance charges—as long as you pay the entire amount due each month. (You do, however, pay a "delinquency" or "late" charge, if you don't pay until after the deadline for that month.) Many charge cards also offer travel accident insurance automatically when you charge airline, ship, train, or bus tickets to your card.

Card companies usually also make provisions for check cashing up to a specified limit, so travelers won't find themselves stranded without cash. And they have detailed statements of charges, which are useful for budgeting or business purposes.

WHY NOT: Do you prefer to pay cash or extend payment on all your credit purchases? Then charge cards may not be for you.

WHERE: Charge cards are issued by a variety of financial institutions. The largest are American Express, Diner's Club, and Carte Blanche.

Credit Cards

WHO: Most people—and virtually every business traveler—need at least one charge card or credit card.

WHAT: Like all forms of credit, credit cards permit you to budget your spending, allowing you to buy goods and services when the price is right for you.

Credit cards come in a number of varieties, but the most common are retail store credit cards and bank credit cards such as Visa and MasterCard.

Retail credit cards are issued by department stores, specialty shops, oil companies, and other retail merchants. These cards permit the holder to charge purchases to an account with the individual store or shop. You usually have a choice of a number of payment methods.

Either the purchaser pays in full once a month, in which case there's no finance charge, or the unpaid bill rolls over or revolves until the next month. With these deferred-payment or *revolving accounts*, the company imposes a finance charge each month.

Bank credit cards are issued by thousands of banks across the country, usually through MasterCard or Visa, the two largest bank credit card issuers.

As a cardholder, you may charge at retail stores, restaurants, service stations, airline ticket counters, and other facilities affiliated with the bank card plan.

In contrast to charge cards, bank cards also carry a maximum limit on how much you may charge. This limit, too, is prearranged by the bank or issuing institution.

You can pay your card balances in full after billing (usually within twenty-five days). Or you can make the minimum payment the card issuer requires, let the balance roll over to the next month, and pay a finance charge. With many bank cards, you'll pay a finance charge regardless of whether you made payment in full. These cards begin charging interest from the date you make a purchase.

These finance charges naturally increase the total purchase price of the items you may have bought during the month. The interest rate on unpaid balances is typically 14 to 22 percent, depending on the issuer and the state where it's located.

When you sign up for a bank credit card, you usually agree to pay an annual fee of at least $15 a year, and sometimes more. However, there are bank cards still offered with no annual fee.

A list of institutions offering these is available for $1.95 from BankCard Holders of America (460 Spring Park Place, Suite 1000, Herndon, VA 22070).

WHY: Again, you need at least one credit card or charge card these days—if only for identification and in case of emergencies.

WHY NOT: Choose a charge card over a credit card if you prefer to pay what you owe each month—and don't like to be tempted to spend more than you should.

WHERE: Most banks, thrifts, and other financial institutions offer credit cards. You apply for department store and other specialized cards through that specific company.

Credit Lines

WHO: Everyone encounters a financial storm or two during a lifetime. A credit line offers you the protection of extra cash when these storms hit.

WHAT: Many banks and thrifts—even charge card companies—offer credit lines of $5,000 or more. Usually, all you need do—in addition to having a solid credit history—is satisfy the institution's income, net worth, and length-of-employment requirements. You should know that these requirements are often stricter than those for other types of loans, since credit lines are generally unsecured.

Once you qualify for a credit line, it's available for your use year in and year out unless canceled by the issuer.

WHY: A credit line is an easy way to raise cash in an emergency. It also can help ease any temporary cash-flow problems you might experience.

Say you're self-employed, and you experience sharp but

temporary dips in your income. A credit line may provide you with the cash—and peace of mind—you need.

WHY NOT: A credit line can tempt you to spend more than you should. If you have a line of credit, you should exercise caution in utilizing it. Remember, you'll have to pay back the money with interest—no one's giving away cash for free.

WHERE: A variety of financial institutions offer credit lines—banks, credit unions, issuers of charge cards and credit cards, thrifts, brokerage firms, and so on.

Dealer Financing

WHO: It's a rare person who possesses the resources to pay cash for big-ticket items such as cars. So you need credit. Sometimes, a dealer offers the best terms.

WHAT: When it comes to financing a new car, you may do better on the showroom floor than at your local bank or savings and loan, but compare rates to be sure.

Chrysler, Ford, General Motors, and other auto makers are in the business of selling cars, and their finance divisions often slash rates as a sales incentive.

So, decide on the car you want. Then compare financing terms offered by dealers before you apply for a loan at a bank or thrift institution.

WHY: The biggest boon of dealer financing is low interest rates. Another advantage is convenience. You buy a car and apply for a loan in the same location.

WHY NOT: Interest on consumer loans won't be tax-deductible at all after 1990. So, in most cases, it makes sense to pay cash whenever possible. And you may be entitled to a hefty reduction in the price if you pay cash.

WHERE: Dealer financing is available where you purchase big-ticket items—automobile showrooms, appliance stores, boat dealers, and so on.

Home Equity Loans

WHO: You say you're a homeowner, and you're in need of cash? You may be able to tap the equity in your house for the money you need.

WHAT: Based on your eligibility and the terms the lender offers, you may be able to borrow up to 80 percent of the equity in your home—that is, the difference between the amount you owe on your home and its current market value.

And the interest rate you're charged is usually about two percentage points above prime—much less than you would pay on installment loans and credit cards.

There's usually no penalty if you pay off your loan early. You also gain access to these funds at any time, because with your home equity loan comes a checkbook. And in most cases you may write off interest on loan amounts up to $100,000.

WHY: Home equity loans are among the least expensive ways to borrow. Rates on these loans are often as much as five percentage points below the amount charged on installment loans and eight to ten percentage points below the rate charged on credit cards.

In most cases, the interest you pay on a home equity loan is tax-deductible—unlike most of the interest you pay on installment loans and credit cards.

WHY NOT: When you sign up for a home equity loan, you assume that you'll be able to repay the money you borrow. What if the unthinkable happens and you default?

You stand to lose your home. So, you should use this source of funds only for important major purchases, such as home improvements or college tuition. You should also keep in mind that you may have to pay hefty closing costs.

WHERE: Home equity loans are available from a variety of sources. Primary among them are banks and thrift institutions.

Installment Loans

WHO: Say you want to finance the purchase of a big-ticket item such as a car. Or you're looking for seed money to start a small business.

An installment loan may be the answer for you.

WHAT: *Installment loans* are, as the name implies, money lent to you that you must repay over a period of time in regular monthly payments—installments. The usual term of a personal installment loan is one to three years.

The amount of interest you pay will vary with the lending institution. Some will charge you as little as 6 percent, while others levy as much as 36 percent.

Loans are either *secured* or *unsecured*. Unsecured personal loans are backed up solely by your ability and willingness to repay. These loans are sometimes called *signature loans* and require a good credit rating—and a friendly banker.

Secured or *collateralized loans* are loans in which you offer security, such as a tangible pledge of goods or real estate lien to guarantee payment.

For example, your *collateral* or security may be the automobile or furniture you're buying, or it can be stocks and bonds that you deposit with the lender.

Whatever form the collateral takes, it's your guarantee to the creditor that his or her institution won't suffer a loss should you fail to honor your debt.

When you take out an installment loan, your lender will ask you to sign a *note*, which creates a legal obligation to repay the amount you borrowed.

The note is a listing of the terms of the loan—the APR, the amount you financed, any finance charges, your total payments and, if applicable, the circumstances under which the lender may seize your collateral. Make sure you fully understand the terms of any loan before you sign.

For example, the note may allow the lender to declare

you in default if you lose your job—even if you don't fall behind in your payments.

Tip: Try not to spread out payments for purchases over a time period that's longer than the useful life of the item. Say you plan to trade your car in after three years. You should finance its purchase price for three years or less.

WHY: One advantage of installment loans is convenience. You fill out an application, have a brief conversation with a loan officer, and that's it. Lenders notify you quickly if your application is approved or denied.

And the interest rates charged on installment loans usually compare favorably with rates offered on other types of loans, such as credit lines from credit card issuers.

WHY NOT: An extended repayment schedule can sometimes lull people into a false sense of having a larger positive cash flow.

You should know that some installment loans are precomputed—that is, you pay most of the interest in the early years of the loan. So, if there's a chance you'll repay a loan before it comes due, stick to "simple interest" plans.

WHERE: Installment loans are available from a variety of sources. Most common are banks, credit unions, thrift institutions, finance companies, and insurance companies.

The activities of all these institutions are covered by state and federal laws. These laws can govern the amount of interest the institutions may charge and the method of repayment. (But you should read the fine print, anyway.)

Margin Accounts

WHO: Do you own stocks, bonds, or other publicly traded securities? If so, you may qualify for a *margin loan* from your brokerage firm to finance additional purchases of investments.

WHAT: The amount you may borrow on margin depends on (among other things) the securities you pledge as collateral.

Say, for example, that the current market value of your portfolio is $20,000, and you want to borrow $10,000 to buy stock in a fast-growing company.

Most margin accounts allow you to borrow up to half the value of the securities in your portfolio.

The interest rate you pay is usually one to two points above prime and, in most cases, is compounded once a month and charged to your brokerage accounts.

WHY: The interest rate you pay on margin loans may compare favorably with loans available from other sources such as banks.

WHY NOT: If you borrow half the value of your securities and those securities decline in price, you may be subject to a *margin call*—that is, your broker will ask you to come up with the difference between the amount you borrowed and one half the current value of your portfolio.

WHERE: Brokerage firms offer margin accounts.

Policy Loans

WHO: Did you know that one of the least expensive sources of money is to borrow against the cash value of your whole life insurance policy?

WHAT: The amount you may borrow and the interest rate you pay varies by the amount of the death benefit, your age when the policy was written, and the year it was issued.

Policies written before 1980 let you borrow at a rate as low as 6 percent, while policies written after that date offer rates as low as 8 to 10 percent.

WHY: One of the biggest boons of policy loans is that they allow you to repay the money you borrowed at your own pace—or, in some cases, not at all. However, you should realize that, if you die, any outstanding loan will be repaid out of the insurance death benefit, which means your heirs will receive less.

Policy loans offer borrowers privacy. You're not required to disclose the reason you're borrowing. Nor are you required to bare your financial soul.

WHY NOT: Whole life insurance policies are a form of savings. Borrowing against those policies depletes your savings.

The interest charged on your policy loan may not be deductible, depending on your individual policy. What is worse, depending on the issue date and type of policy, your policy loan may be treated as taxable income to you when you borrow.

WHERE: Policy loans are available from your insurance carrier.

Questions and Answers

You say policy loans offer an inexpensive way to borrow money. But is that the least expensive way?

The answer is no. Parents or family members are often the source of the least expensive loans. They may charge you nothing or they may charge only the interest they would have earned on the money.

Such loans can complicate family relationships. So you may want to think twice before you ask a family member if you can borrow.

If you do decide to take out a loan from a relative, handle the transaction in a businesslike way. Draw up a promissory note that details the interest charged and the repayment schedule. Then stick to your agreement—no matter what.

My son is authorized to use my credit card. I gave him permission to buy a new sport coat, but he didn't stop there. He bought shoes, trousers, a tie, jogging shoes, a tennis racket, and so on. Am I legally liable for these charges?

Although the law limits your liability for charges by *unauthorized* users to $50, you're 100 percent responsible for charges made by *authorized* users.

Your best hope is to collect from your son.

I am in the process of a divorce. Am I liable for charges made by my former spouse to my credit cards?
Unless you notify the card issuer or merchant that you're no longer responsible for debts of your spouse, you may be held jointly liable for any charges made to any cards held jointly. One idea is to do away with all your joint accounts. Then open new accounts in your name only.

I applied for a loan and the banker asked me for a copy of my tax return. Is that request standard?
Lenders often ask borrowers to substantiate that they receive the amount of income they claim. People who are employed by someone else are often asked to provide copies of payroll check stubs or W-2 forms. Self-employed people are often asked to provide copies of their tax returns.

I am the owner of a small business. My employees and I would like to establish a credit union. How do we go about it?
Your situation isn't unusual. A growing number of small companies are offering credit union services to employees.

In southern California, for example, more than 650 small businesses offer these services. In central Florida, the figure exceeds 300, according to the Credit Union National Association, Inc. (CUNA), an industry group based in Madison, Wisconsin.

Credit unions are attractive to companies because they enable business owners to offer a fringe benefit to employees at a relatively low cost. Credit unions are cooperatives and, as such, they are nonprofit. They return the money they make to credit union members in the form of dividends.

The two big selling points of credit unions are that they typically pay higher-than-average interest on savings and charge lower-than-average rates on loans.

The law allows credit unions to be formed by almost any sort of group that has a common bond—for example, employees who work for the same company, stores in a shopping mall, or businesses in an industrial park.

However, the easiest way for small companies to offer credit union services to workers is to affiliate with an existing credit union.

Local credit unions will provide the forms and other necessary literature, and they will send a representative to explain credit union services to your employees.

If you're interested in affiliating with an existing institution, write CUNA's public relations department (P. O. Box 431, Madison, WI 53701).

It will put you in touch with credit unions in your area and will send you a brochure, *Credit Unions: What They Are, How to Join and How to Organize One*.

Another source of information is the federal National Credit Union Administration (NCUA), which operates six regional offices. Ask for the NCUA booklet, *Chartering and Organizing Manual for Federal Credit Unions*.

What's a bad debt?

Uncle Sam defines bad debts as accounts or notes that are entirely or—in the case of business bad debts—partially uncollectable, despite your good-faith efforts to collect them.

He allows you to claim a deduction for a bad debt when it becomes worthless, and the only way for you to determine that it's worthless is to make a full-faith effort to collect it. Until you attempt to collect what you're owed, the IRS maintains, the debt isn't deductible.

IRS agents know from experience that people seldom do all they can when it comes to collecting bad debts, so they scrutinize these deductions on audit. If you claim a bad-debt deduction on your tax return, be prepared to prove that you attempted and failed to collect what was due you.

I lent money to a friend, and he failed to repay me. May I write off that amount as a bad debt?

If the loan is entirely worthless, you may deduct it as a *nonbusiness bad debt*.

What is the difference between a nonbusiness bad debt and a business bad debt? Business bad debts are deductible from your ordinary income, and you may also write off the portion of a debt that's partially worthless.

Nonbusiness bad debts are treated as short-term capital losses, and Uncle Sam caps short-term capital loss deductions at an amount equal to your capital gains plus $3,000 per year. You may, however, carry unused capital losses forward into future years.

I own a small retail clothing store. May I write off as bad debts bills that my customers fail to pay?

You may not think of your accounts receivable or extended payment plans as loans but, in fact, they are. When you allow customers to pay you over time for items they buy, you are, in essence, lending them money to cover the cost of their purchases.

If they don't repay you, you may deduct the unpaid balance as a *business bad debt*. Here's something else you should know.

Uncle Sam allows you to deduct as business bad debts only those amounts that you previously reported as income. He also lets you write off a business bad debt if you have sustained an actual cash loss. As a result, this write-off is usually available only to people who keep their books on the *accrual method*. It may not be taken by anyone who uses the *cash method*.

With cash accounting, you record income when you receive it and expenses when you pay them. With accrual accounting, you record income as you earn it, regardless of when you collect the money. And you record expenses as you incur them, without regard to when you shell out the cash.

Say, for example, that you're a freelance writer, and you use the cash method of accounting. You submit a bill for $700 to a magazine for an article you have written.

The bill is never paid. Under the rules, you're not entitled to a bad-debt deduction. The reason is that you never reported the $700 as income on your tax return.

Uncle Sam does provide one exception to this rule governing cash-basis taxpayers. He says that you may deduct as bad debts cash advances and expenses you incur in providing services to people or companies that don't pay up.

Our writer, for example, could deduct as a bad debt any costs associated with writing the article—telephone calls, paper, typewriter ribbons, travel expenses, and so on. He or she could also write off these costs as ordinary business expenses.

Where can I write for additional information about writing off bad debts?

Ask the IRS to send you a copy of its Publication 548, *Deductions for Bad Debts*. The booklet is free.

PART 6

YOUR INCOME TAXES

- HOW INCOME IS TAXED
- TAX DEDUCTIONS FOR INDIVIDUALS
- TAX DEDUCTIONS FOR BUSINESSES
- WINNING TAX STRATEGIES

CHAPTER 21

HOW INCOME IS TAXED

"There is nothing sinister," the noted jurist Learned Hand once pointed out, "in so arranging one's affairs as to keep taxes as low as possible. Everyone does so, rich or poor. And all do right, for nobody owes any public duty to pay more than the law demands."

How, then, do you guarantee that you'll pay no more in taxes than you should? The answer is to engage in some solid nuts-and-bolts tax planning.

And the first step in tax planning is to master the basics of the tax code. This task, we know, is a difficult one—no less a person than Albert Einstein once complained that "the hardest thing in the world to understand is the income tax."

But with your knowledge of the tax rules and appropriate consultation with your tax advisor will come power—the power to slash hundreds, perhaps even thousands of dollars from your annual tax liability.

So, roll up your sleeves and let's get started.

What do you need to know about tax basics?

Most people know that a *tax deduction* is an amount that they subtract from their income before they calculate their annual tax bill. But a *tax credit* allows you to reduce dollar for dollar your total tax liability.

A tax credit—by definition—is an amount you subtract directly from your tax bill. Suppose your tax liability for the year adds up to $4,000. If you're able to claim a $900 tax credit—for child-care expenses, say—you would owe Uncle Sam only $3,100.

Your *taxable income* is your income after you subtract all your deductions and make any allowable adjustments, such as claiming contributions to a retirement account.

Once you know your taxable income, you calculate your total tax liability by checking the Internal Revenue Service (IRS) tax tables or rate schedules. These tables and schedules are included in the package of forms that the IRS mails to you each year.

Don't make the mistake some taxpayers do and confuse taxable income with *gross income* or *adjusted gross income*. They are something else entirely.

Your gross income is the sum of all your earnings—wages, salaries, dividends, interest, profits from your business, profits from your investments and so on.

As for your adjusted gross income, or AGI, you calculate it by subtracting from your gross income your contributions to an Individual Retirement Account and Keogh plans, alimony payments, and certain other items.

Your AGI—in other words—is your income before you claim *itemized deductions*, meaning expenses you subtract on Schedule A of your tax return. Examples of itemized deductions are medical expenses, charitable contributions, interest payments, and state and local taxes.

The *standard deduction* is an amount claimed by taxpayers who don't itemize. The amount of the standard deduction depends on your filing status, whether you're sixty-five years or older, or blind, and whether you're claimed as a dependent on someone else's return.

A *tax bracket* is a tax rate. The law includes only three—one at 15 percent, one at 28 percent, and one at 33 percent (more on this topic in the next chapter).

Your *average*, or *effective*, *tax rate* is calculated by dividing the total amount of tax you owe by your AGI. Confused? Consider this example.

Say your AGI adds up to $40,000 and you're single. First, you subtract your standard deduction—which for

1990 Individual Income Tax Information

Personal Exemption: **$2,050**

Filing Status	Standard Deduction
Single	$3,250
Married Filing Jointly	5,450
Married Filing Separately	2,725
Heads of Households	4,750
Children	500
Blind or Over 65	
Single	800
Married	650

single taxpayers comes to $3,250 in 1990—from the $40,000. (Our example assumes that you're not itemizing your deductions.) Then you subtract your 1990 personal exemption of $2,050 from the 36,750 to get your taxable income—that is, $34,700. In 1990, singles pay 15 percent on the first $19,450 of taxable income, for a tax of $2,917.50.

You pay 28 percent on the balance of $15,250, for a tax of $4,277. Your total tax bill, then, comes to $7,187.50—that is, $4,270 plus $2,917.50. So your effective tax rate is 17.97 percent—your tax liability of $7,187.50 divided by your AGI of $40,000.

Your *marginal tax rate* is the rate that you pay on your last dollar of income. Your actual marginal rate depends on your income, your filing status—single, married filing jointly, and so on—and the number of personal deductions you claim.

A single person reporting $28,000 in taxable income in 1990 would be in the 28 percent bracket—that is, he or she pays 28 cents on the last dollar earned to Uncle Sam.

1990 Tax Schedule

Marginal Rate	Taxable Income	
	Joint Return	Single Return
15%	$0–32,450	$0–19,450
28	32,450–78,400	19,450–47,050
33	78,400–208,690*	47,050–109,100**
28	Greater than $208,690	Greater than $109,100

*Assumes four personal exemptions
**Assumes one personal exemption

All figures for 1990 have been derived based on an inflation factor prescribed by the Internal Revenue Code.

Two more terms you should know: *above the line* and *below the line*. Above-the-line deductions reduce your taxable income whether you itemize deductions or not. Below-the-line deductions aren't worth anything if you don't itemize.

The *line* that these two phrases refers to is your adjusted gross income. Perhaps the best way to illustrate what we mean is with an example.

As we saw, some items, such as unreimbursed employee business expenses, used to be deductible above the line—that is, before you figured your AGI.

But no more. Say, for instance, your income is $80,000 and you incurred $1,000 in unreimbursed employee business expenses during the year.

Before recent tax law changes, you subtracted that $1,000 from your gross income to give you an AGI of $79,000. Then, you either took your other itemized deductions or the standard deduction, whichever was larger.

Under current law, however, your AGI is the same as your gross income, $80,000, because you cannot deduct your unreimbursed employee business expense unless you itemize. So, unless your deductible expenses, including the deductible portion of your $1,000 employee business expense, total more than your standard deduction, the old above-the-line deduction isn't a tax savings to you.

How is ordinary income taxed?

The amount of your income taxed at the 15 percent and 28 percent rates varies with your tax status. And it also varies with inflation.

For example, as inflation rises, so will the amount of income taxed at the lower 15 percent rate. For 1990, the 15 percent rate applies to the following amount of your AGI:

- $32,450 for married individuals filing joint returns and for surviving spouses;
- $26,050 for heads of households;
- $19,450 for single individuals; and
- $16,225 for married individuals filing separate returns.

Income greater than those amounts is subject to the 28 percent tax. How big a bite, then, does Uncle Sam take from your income?

Let's say you and your spouse together have taxable income of $50,000. You'll pay taxes on that amount of $9.781.50. Here's how you do the calculation.

The first $32,450 is taxed at 15 percent. That comes to $4,867.50. Your taxable income between $32,450 and $50,000 is taxed at 28 percent. That (the difference between $50,000 and $32,450 times 28 percent) comes to $4,914. These sums add up to $9,781.50—your total tax.

So, with $50,000 in taxable income—and as a married couple filing a joint return—your marginal tax rate is 28 percent. But your average, or effective, tax rate is 19.56 percent—that is, $9,789.50 divided by $50,000.

As your income rises, however, Congress has decided that it wants your marginal and your average tax rates to be the same. In other words, beyond some income level (see the list below), the tax code begins to remove the benefit of the lower 15 percent bracket. It does this by imposing a 5 percent surtax on your taxable income between certain levels. At the high point of this range and beyond, all your taxable income is taxed at a flat rate of 28 percent.

How does the surtax work?
First, here's a list showing the taxable income ranges over which the surtax applies to individuals in different tax categories:

- $78,400 to $162,770 for married individuals filing joint returns and surviving spouses;
- $67,200 to $134,930 for heads of household;
- $47,050 to $97,620 for single individuals; and
- $39,200 to $123,570 for married individuals filing separate returns.

Now, here's an example to show you how the surtax works—or, in other words, how the tax code converts a graduated tax into a flat tax.

Let's take the same married couple as before, only their taxable income has climbed to $162,770. The first $32,450, just as before, is taxed at 15 percent, yielding a tax of $4,867.50. Between $32,450 and $78,400, their income is taxed at 28 percent, yielding a tax of $12,866. Their taxable income between $78,400 and $162,770 is also taxed at 28 percent plus the 5 percent surtax. In other words, it's taxed at 33 percent, yielding a tax of $27,842.

So, altogether, their tax on $155,320 of taxable income comes to $45,575.50 ($4,867.50 plus $12,866 plus $27,842). Divide this tax by their taxable income ($45,575.50 divided by $162,770), and you see that the result is a 28 percent flat tax.

What has happened to the personal exemption?
Where the surtax we just explained leaves off, another begins. It's the same 5 percent, but it's levied for a different reason.

Congress figures that people in these upper-income reaches don't need the benefit of personal exemptions. So, the tax law takes them away by continuing to apply the 5 percent surtax to income in excess of the upper limits in the table above. In other words, our joint filing married couple will continue to pay tax at a 33 percent rate until Uncle Sam has recaptured the full tax savings resulting from any personal exemptions they may have claimed.

Suppose, for example, they claimed two personal exemptions, one for each of them. In 1990, personal exemptions reduce taxable income by $2,050.

Since our couple is taxed at the 28 percent rate, each exemption saves them $574 in taxes ($2,050 times 28 percent). To recapture $574 with a 5 percent tax, the IRS must apply the 5 percent surtax to $11,480 of income ($11,480 times 5 percent equals $574).

But our couple claimed two personal exemptions.

So, the 5 percent surtax will continue to apply to the next $22,960—two times $11,480—of their taxable income in excess of $162,770. When their taxable income reaches $185,730—$162,770 plus $22,960—the surtaxes cease and their marginal tax rate falls back to 28 percent.

How is capital gains income taxed?

Capital gains taxes—someone once quipped—are a cruel and unusual form of capital punishment, an observation with which most people would agree.

These days, you pay taxes on capital gains—whether they are short term or long term—at the same rates as ordinary income. So it makes no difference—tax-wise, at least—how long you hold onto an asset before you sell it.

But don't make the mistake some taxpayers do and assume that you no longer have to keep track of your long-term and short-term gains. Uncle Sam still requires you to categorize your gains as long term and short term and report them separately on your tax return.

What about capital losses?

Here's what happens if you rack up capital losses.

First, you may deduct all capital losses against any capital gains you may have. If you have reduced your capital gains to zero and still have losses left, you may deduct up to $3,000 of those remaining capital losses from your ordinary income in any one year.

If you don't use up all your losses in one year, don't despair. The rules say you may carry forward to future years any losses you cannot write off in the current year.

If you would like more information about how capital gains are taxed, ask the IRS to send you copies of these publications: *Investment Income and Expenses* (publication number 550), *Basis of Assets* (publication number 551), and *Mutual Fund Distributions* (publication number 564).

How are children taxed?

You should know that the law requries you to obtain a Social Security number for your chidren by the time they reach the age of two.

And you're required to write those Social Security numbers on your return. That way, the IRS can prevent double dipping—two taxpayers taking, for instance, an exemption for the same child.

In addition, every child with at least $500 in *unearned* income must file a return. Here are some other tax rules you should keep in mind.

Any money a child earns at a job is taxed at his or her marginal tax rate. But it's a different story if the child collects unearned income, such as interest.

If your child is under fourteen, unearned income that totals more than $1,000 is taxed at the parents' marginal rate—which is usually higher than the child's. When your child reaches fourteen, he or she is again taxed at his or her own rate on unearned income as well as earned income.

And if you're divorced?

Children under fourteen pay the same rate on unearned income as the parent with the higher tax rate. This rule also applies if you're married but file separate returns.

What exactly is the alternative minimum tax?

You may be one of those smart, successful individuals who has managed to reduce his or her tax bill to an amount you consider reasonable.

Well, don't pat yourself on the back just yet. What might seem reasonable from the taxpayer's point of view may appear quite the opposite to the IRS.

Moreover, the government—not too surprisingly—has found a way to make taxpayers in this situation pay their fair share.

It's called the alternative minimum tax (AMT)—and it applies to individuals who have reduced their tax bite significantly by means of a generous helping of credits and deductions. Here—in a somewhat simplified way—is how the AMT operates.

You figure your tax in the usual manner. Then you calculate your tax again, adding back to your income many of the deductions and other "preference" items you wrote off the first time around. Finally, you subtract a special exemption, which totals $40,000 for married couples filing jointly or $30,000 for single filers (this exemption amount is phased out for certain high-income taxpayers), then multiply the result by a flat 21 percent. If this AMT amount adds up to more than your regular tax, you pay the higher AMT sum.

Are you one of those taxpayers who has to worry about the AMT? You might be if you took an unusually large amount of the targeted deductions—you wrote off appreciated property donated to charity or received interest from some tax-exempt bonds that aren't exempt at all under the AMT.

Other write-offs that *may* trigger the AMT: large amounts of miscellaneous deductions, oil and gas partnerships, investment interest that is greater than investment income, and accelerated depreciation write-offs that top straight-line write-offs for the identical property.

Usually, those subject to the AMT have a combination of these deductions, not just one. So make sure to ask your tax adviser if you think you may fall under the AMT.

Where can you write for more information?

Just telephone or write your local office of the Internal Revenue Service. The IRS publishes a host of free tax guides. When ordering, remember to specify both the titles and publication numbers.

Here are two booklets that you may find useful: *Your Federal Income Tax* (publication 17) and *Tax Guide for Small Business* (publication 334).

Consulting your tax advisor is also a good idea in some situations.

CHAPTER 22

TAX DEDUCTIONS FOR INDIVIDUALS

It may come as a surprise to some people, but the goal of tax planning is *not* to get a sizable refund from Uncle Sam. After all, why should you let the government keep a big chunk of your money—on which it pays no interest—for the better part of a year?

Instead, the object is to pay no more in federal and state income taxes than you should and to pay no sooner than you're required.

The first step in achieving these ends is to claim all the deductions to which you're entitled. However, you cannot benefit from these write-offs unless you know what they are. Here, then, is a checklist of expenses that the IRS allows you to deduct on your personal income tax return.

Standard Deduction

WHO: Uncle Sam gives you a choice. He allows you to itemize your deductions on Schedule A of your Form 1040 or claim the *standard deduction.*

You take whichever amount is larger.

WHAT: The amount of the standard deduction depends on your filing status and is adjusted each year for inflation. In other words, as inflation rises, so does the deduction.

In 1990, a married couple filing jointly may claim a

standard deduction of $5,450; a married couple filing separately, a standard deduction of $2,725 each. A head of a household may take a $4,750 standard deduction in 1990; and a single person, a $3,250 standard deduction.

Here's something else you should know.

The rules allow you to claim an additional amount if you're sixty-five years of age or older. In 1990 single individuals in this age category may add $800 to their standard deduction. If you're married, add $650 for each spouse who is age sixty-five or older.

Moreover, if you're blind, sixty-five or older, and single, you may add $1,600 to your standard deduction for 1990. If you're in this situation, married, and file jointly, you may add $1,300. The amount climbs to $2,600 if both you and your spouse are blind and sixty-five years of age or older.

WHERE: Subtract the standard deduction on Form 1040.

WHEN: The rule is simple. You claim the standard deduction in years when it exceeds the amount of your itemized deductions.

Charitable Contributions

WHO: The IRS allows you to write off charitable contributions only if you itemize deductions on your personal tax return.

WHAT: You may deduct donations but only to *qualified* charities—that is, those that meet the government's requirements. If you write off contributions to an organization that isn't qualified, Uncle Sam may—if you're audited—disallow the deduction.

Qualified organizations are—by definition—nonprofit groups that are operated solely for charitable, religious, scientific, literary, or educational purposes. They don't include groups that try to influence legislation or get involved in political campaigns.

Here's something else you may not know, but should:

the government allows you to deduct contributions of both money and property. The rules?

If you contribute money, write off the amount of your gift. If you donate property, deduct an amount equal to the *fair-market value* of the property—that is, the amount the property would bring if it were sold by a willing seller to a willing buyer, on the open market.

Gifts of property may make sense if the property has increased in value since you bought it. It usually doesn't make tax sense to give *depreciated* property to charity.

Also, special rules apply to donations of property that's valued at $500 or more. If you do donate property worth more than this amount, you must file Form 8283, "Noncash Charitable Contributions," with your personal tax return.

You must also attach to your return an appraisal of property you donate that's valued at $5,000 or more—unless the property consists of publicly traded securities.

As for the appraisal itself, it must be made by someone who is a qualified appraiser and who is *not* a member of your family or the organization to which you're making the contribution—in other words, by someone who has no stake in overvaluing the property. The appraiser must be in the business of regularly appraising the type of property you're giving.

The good news is, you may be able to deduct the cost of the appraisal on your tax return as a miscellaneous itemized deduction (more on these deductions later).

Usually, the IRS limits charitable contributions to 50 percent of your adjusted gross income. (A lower percentage applies to gifts to some charitable organizations and to gifts of appreciated property.) If you make a charitable deduction that's greater than the 50-percent-of-AGI ceiling, you may carry forward the excess for five years.

Most people don't need to concern themselves with this ceiling. However, you might run afoul of the rule if your adjusted gross income is limited, for example, if you're retired and make large gifts to charities out of your assets.

If you would like more information on how to value donated property, ask the IRS to send you a copy of its Publication 561, *Determining the Value of Donated Property.*

WHERE: The place you write off charitable contributions is on Schedule A of your Form 1040.

WHEN: You deduct charitable contributions in the year you pay them or charge them to a credit or charge card.

Medical and Dental Expenses

WHO: Uncle Sam makes it difficult for you to write off medical and dental expenses on your personal return. How? He says that you may deduct only those medical and dental expenses that exceed 7.5 percent of your adjusted gross income.

That means if your AGI comes to $60,000, say, your medical and dental expenses must exceed $4,500 before you can deduct a dime.

You may write off only the amount that's greater than $4,500. That is, if your medical and dental costs add up to $4,520, you may deduct only $20.

The law does allow you to claim a write-off for medical and dental costs that you pay for qualified dependents.

WHAT: Any valid medical or dental expense not covered by insurance—including transportation to and from needed medical and dental care and the cost of medical insurance—is deductible. (You may write off a flat amount of 9 cents a mile plus parking and tolls for automobile travel or your actual transportation costs.)

What is the official IRS definition of *medical costs*?

Sums you pay for the "diagnosis, cure, mitigation, treatment, or prevention of disease or for the purpose of affecting any structure or function of the body." And these expenses also include any amounts for medical and dental insurance.

Among the expenses that are deductible: treatment for drug or alcohol abuse (including the expense of inpatient treatment), and the cost of sending a handicapped person to a special school (as long as that school is primarily oriented to treating the person's handicap).

Also: fees for medical and hospital services (such as private nursing care, costs for labs, surgical, diagnostic, and obstetrical services) and ambulance services.

Fees paid to physicians, dentists, acupuncturists, chiropractors, optometrists, podiatrists, and psychologists are deductible. So are medical insurance premiums, including those for Medicare B and insurance against breaking or losing glasses or contact lenses.

What other expenses may you write off?

The costs of prescription drugs, mental-health counseling or therapy; nursing services or a stay in a nursing home; special equipment you require for medical reasons, such as a wheelchair; artificial limbs; eyeglasses or contact lenses; guide dogs; and oxygen equipment.

Finally, Uncle Sam allows you to write off money you spend to modify your home to make it suitable for a handicap or some other medical condition. For example, you could deduct the cost of building a ramp or installing an elevator.

However, your deduction is limited in this situation.

Uncle Sam says you may write off only the difference between the cost of a modification and the value it adds to your property.

Say your doctor recommends—in writing—that you install a whirlpool bath to treat your severe arthritis. The price tag is $1,000.

An appraiser tells you the bath adds $900 to the value of your home. The law allows you to deduct only $100—that's the difference between $1,000 and $900. You may, however, write off the entire amount of an improvement if it doesn't increase the value of your home at all.

You should know, too, that if you're self-employed and pay for you own health insurance, you may, before

September 30, 1990, write off 25 percent of the cost of this insurance.

What about the other 75 percent? You may deduct it only if it—plus your other medical and dental expenses—exceeds 7.5 percent of your AGI. Another rule: You're not allowed to deduct more in health insurance premiums than you earn from your self-employed business.

Tip: When it comes to writing off medical and dental expenses, follow this strategy: Bunch as many of your medical payments as possible in one year.

WHERE: You write off medical and dental expenses—like all itemized deductions—on Schedule A of Form 1040.

WHEN: You deduct medical and dental expenses in the year you pay them. But what if you pay for medical or dental expenses in the year *before* you actually receive treatment? These advance payments may not be deductible in the year they are paid.

And what if you mail a check or charge services on a credit card at the end of the year? You claim the expense in the year you write and mail the check or make the charge.

Miscellaneous Itemized Deductions

WHO: You may claim *miscellaneous deductions* only if you itemize and only to the extent that these deductions top 2 percent of your adjusted gross income.

Say your AGI totals $60,000 and your miscellaneous deductions for the year come to $1,500; 2 percent of $60,000 is $1,200. You may write off only $300—that is, the difference between your miscellaneous deductions of $1,500 and 2 percent of your AGI, or $1,200.

WHAT: Miscellaneous itemized deductions are as the phrase implies—a grab bag of expenses. They include costs that relate to your investments, your job, and your taxes. They include, for example, fees for tax planning advice and subscriptions to professional journals.

Specifically, you may write off those expenses that relate to your job—as long as you pay those expenses yourself.

If your employer does reimburse your business expenses *and* includes the reimbursement in your income, the amount qualifies as an itemized miscellaneous deduction.

What qualifies as job-related expenses?

Fees for job counseling (as long as you're looking for a job in the same field, and it's not your first position); and dues for professional associations or unions. Job-hunting expenses, including the cost of preparing a résumé and fees to a headhunter or employment agency (as long as you're looking for a new job in your same field).

Also, employment-related education expenses for courses that help you maintain or improve your current work skills and education that's required by your employer or by law to keep your job, status, or present salary are deductible. However, the cost of classes to prepare you for a new trade or business or to meet the current minimum requirements for your present job isn't deductible.

You may also deduct 80 percent of business entertainment costs and up to $25 per person per year of business gifts. (The law says, however, that gifts you give your boss are personal and, therefore, nondeductible.)

Other job-related expenses that fall under the miscellaneous category: uniforms (if you're in the military reserves); work clothes, uniforms, or protective clothing that you cannot wear outside your job; and subscriptions to professional or trade journals.

Also: unreimbursed business-related telephone expenses (including the cost of an answering service or beeper); supplies and tools you need for work; and unreimbursed work-related travel expenses (though not for commuting).

And you may write off business meals that aren't reimbursed by your employer, but the cost is only 80 percent deductible.

The IRS also allows you to write off many expenses that are associated with investments that produce taxable income. This rule means you may write off costs associated with stocks, for example, but not those that relate to tax-exempt municipal bonds.

You may *not* deduct fees you pay—such as sales commissions—to buy investments. These, the IRS says, are capital costs and you must add them to the cost, or basis, of your investment. (*Basis* is the term used to describe your total cost or investment in an asset for tax purposes.) When you sell an investment—a stock, say—you may subtract the basis, including the commissions, from your sales proceeds to determine your profit.

So, what expenses are deductible when it comes to your investments?

They include: fees you pay an accountant or financial planner for help with your investments; 80 percent of entertainment expenses directly related to the management of your investments—the cost of a business dinner with your broker, for instance. (Of course, you must substantiate these expenses according to strict IRS rules.)

Also: bank custodial fees for dividend reinvestment plans; fees you pay separately to a money manager or investment adviser; legal fees for investment counseling; IRA maintenance fees (as long as you pay by separate check); the cost of renting a safe-deposit box; investment-related supplies and postage; and investment-related subscriptions.

Deductible, too, are telephone expenses that relate to your investments; travel and transportation cost (but—and here's where some taxpayers get tripped up—not the costs associated with traveling to an investment seminar or convention and not the cost of the seminar itself).

What about expenses related to your taxes?

You may write off the cost of tax advice your lawyer, accountant, or financial planner gives you; tax preparation and planning costs; tax preparation and planning books;

and appraisal fees you pay to calculate the value of property you donate to charity.

Uncle Sam also lets you write off expenses you pay for determining, collecting, or securing a refund of any tax. You may even deduct the cost of mounting a defense for yourself if you're audited. Who says Uncle Sam doesn't play fair?

Here's something else you should know. If you take a job in a new city, Uncle Sam allows you to deduct the cost of your move—under certain conditions.

Moving expenses fall into the category of miscellaneous itemized deductions. However, you get a break as far as they are concerned: they aren't subject to the 2 percent floor that applies to other miscellaneous deductions.

You may deduct all expenses that relate to the move: the cost of the mover, hiring someone to pack for you, and the expense of making trips to the new city to find a home. You may even deduct the cost of moving your car and pets.

You should know that you may lose the deduction if you don't stay in your new job for at least thirty-nine weeks during the twelve months after your move.

You may also lose your deduction if you don't relocate within a year of the date you sign on with your new employer. One other caveat: Your new job must be at least 35 miles further away from your old home than your old home was from your previous job.

If you own your home, you may also write off the cost of selling your old house and buying the new one. If you rent, you may deduct any costs associated with canceling your old lease or getting a new one, though you may not write off rent payments or security deposits at your new home.

You also may write off the cost of any temporary living expenses at the new job—up to thirty days—and the cost of travel, meals, and lodging to get to the new location.

Although you're not subject to the 2 percent floor, the

law does impose a cap on some of these costs: you may not deduct more than $3,000 for buying and/or leasing expenses, house-hunting costs, and temporary living expenses. Moreover, the temporary living and house-hunting expenses may not together top $1,500.

When it comes to writing off miscellaneous deductions, you should follow the same strategy as with medical and dental expense.

Bunch as many of these deductions as possible in a single year. That way, you improve your chance of exceeding the 2 percent ceiling and claiming a write-off.

WHERE: You write off miscelleanous itemized deductions on Schedule A of your Form 1040.

WHEN: You write off these expenses in the year you pay them or charge them to a charge or credit card.

State and Local Taxes

WHO: If you itemize on your tax return, you may deduct amounts you pay for state and local taxes, including property taxes.

WHAT: You may write off all sorts of state and local taxes. For example, you may deduct state and local income taxes. It makes no difference whether these taxes are withheld from your paycheck or forwarded in the form of estimated taxes. (Don't forget to deduct any refund of taxes to which you were entitled, but applied to next year's estimated tax rather than collected in cash.)

You may also write off any state and local real estate taxes. However, the rules don't allow you to deduct real estate taxes that you place in escrow—that is, in the hands of a third party—until those taxes are actually paid. What does this rule mean in practice?

Say you include an amount for property taxes when you pay your monthly mortgage. You may deduct only the amount that the bank or other financial institution actually pays to the taxing authority during the year. You may not deduct the entire sum you pay into the escrow account—

unless, of course, the entire amount goes to pay that year's taxes.

Also, you may deduct taxes on rental properties you own. However, the IRS imposes some qualifications on all these deductions. For starters, you must be responsible for the tax, not some other taxpayer. For example, if you pay your daughter's auto excise tax, you may not deduct it.

This means, too, that if you and your spouse file separate returns, each of you may deduct only the taxes that each of you pays.

However, the IRS treats income taxes paid on community income on a fifty-fifty basis.

Finally, the IRS says that you may write off taxes on your personal property—but with some restrictions. The tax must be based on the value of the property. It must be imposed annually. It must be imposed on the personal property itself—not for the "exercise of a privilege."

For example, say you pay a tax on your automobile. Your city says that you're paying this tax for the privilege of registering your car and driving it. Moreover, the tax isn't based on your automobile's value, but on its weight. Under these conditions, you couldn't write off this tax. (Remember, too, that you may no longer write off sales taxes of any kind.)

WHERE: You deduct most of these taxes on Schedule A of Form 1040. Taxes on rental property are deducted on Schedule E.

WHEN: You deduct these taxes in the year you file your return. You must also actually pay the tax in the year you file. You may not write off this year, for example, a tax you paid last year. The IRS considers the date you mail or deliver your check the date of payment.

Interest Expenses

WHO: Uncle Sam allows you to deduct interest on your personal return, but only if you itemize on Schedule A of your Form 1040.

WHAT: Let's face it. Interest deductions aren't what they used to be. In the not-so-distant past, you could write off 100 percent of the interest you paid on car loans, credit cards, and charge accounts, but not any more—thanks to the 1986 Tax Reform Act.

Now, so-called *personal interest* deductions are being phased out. In fact, after 1990, personal interest isn't deductible at all. That's the bad news. The good news? You face a less bleak prospect when it comes to other interest expenses, such as mortgage interest.

The 1986 Tax Reform Act opened a Pandora's box of tax complications by forcing taxpayers to classify interest they pay into several categories. Today, some interest payments you make are fully deductible, some are partially deductible, and some aren't deductible at all.

Let's take them in order. First, *consumer interest.*

In 1990, you may write off 10 percent of the interest you pay on credit cards or on other personal loans—a loan you take out to buy an automobile, for example. After 1990, you may not deduct any consumer interest.

One way around these rules is take out a home equity loan and use the money for personal purchases. That way, the interest is still deductible.

Tip: You should know that there's some real danger in borrowing in this way. If you're unable to pay back the money, you might have to forfeit your home.

Mortgage interest is the interest you pay on mortgages for your primary residence. The law says you may also deduct in full mortgage interest on a second home (subject to the limitations we discuss below). First, the IRS divides your mortgage debt into two categories: *acquisition indebtedness* and *home equity indebtedness.*

Acquisition indebtedness is defined as any loan, secured by your primary or second home, which you take on when you buy, build, or substantially improve your home. Also included in the definition is any debt you take on to refinance your old mortgage to the extent that it doesn't exceed the remaining principal portion of the acquisition debt on your home immediately before refinancing.

You may write off the interest on acquisition debt up to $1 million—or $500,000 if you're married and file separate returns.

Uncle Sam is less generous when it comes to writing off home equity indebtedness. The law defines home equity debt as a loan that's secured by your primary or secondary residence, but isn't used to buy, build, or substantially improve your property.

In short, this loan is secured by the equity in your house. In the case of home equity debt, you may write off the full amount as long as the debt doesn't top the lesser of the fair-market value of your house minus your total acquisition indebtedness or $100,000.

Also, if you bought a new home, refinanced your existing home, or took on additional mortgage debt before October 13, 1987, special rules apply.

You may still deduct in full the interest you pay on business loans—that is, money you borrow for business purposes.

Investment interest—as the term implies—is interest you pay on loans you have taken out to buy investments, including interest on a stock margin account.

Tip: You should know that the IRS makes you account for interest on so-called passive activities differently. We will define passive activity interest shortly. Keep in mind that the rules we explain below apply to nonpassive investments.

The rules say you may write off investment interest only from your investment income. If you make $3,000 from your investments and spend $2,000 of interest on a margin account, you may write off the entire $2,000, since that amount doesn't top your investment income.

If you're unable to deduct all your investment interest in one year, you may carry forward the excess and write it off in future years against your investment income.

In 1990, you may also write off 10 percent of the

investment interest in excess of investment income—up to 10 percent of $10,000. So, if you had $4,000 in earnings from your investment and racked up interest expense of $5,000, you could write off $4,000 against your investment income and an additional $100 (10 percent of $1,000). After 1990, you may deduct your interest only to the extent of your investment income.

There's an exception to this general rule. Interest on loans you take out to purchase tax-exempt securities isn't deductible.

Similarly, you may not write off interest on loans you use to buy single-premium life insurance or annuity contracts. Moreover, you may not deduct interest on loans taken out after 1986 from a 401(k) plan or a tax-sheltered annuity.

Passive activity interest, by contrast, is interest from passive activities. A *passive activity* is IRS jargon for a business that you don't "materially" participate in managing. A common example of a passive activity is a limited partnership.

The IRS says that you may deduct passive activity interest only from passive activity income. Just as with investment interest, you may carry forward any interest you're not able to deduct and use it to offset passive activity income in a future year.

However, unlike investment interest, you may write off any passive activity interest you hadn't been able to deduct when you sell the investment.

Finally, if you invest in rental property and actively participate in managing it, you may be able to deduct up to $25,000 in mortgage interest that tops your rental income.

But to qualify for this full write-off, your AGI must total less than $100,000. (You may collect a partial write-off if your AGI falls between $100,000 and $150,000.)

WHERE: You write off personal and mortgage interest on Schedule A of your Form 1040. Sole proprietors write off business interest on your Schedule C.

WHEN: You write off personal, business, and mortgage interest—within the limits allowed—in the year that you incur these expenses.

You deduct investment interest against your investment income. What if your investment interest exceeds your investment income? Then you may carry forward the excess and use it to offset investment income in future years. The same rule applies to passive activity interest.

Questions and Answers

What medical expenses aren't deductible?
The IRS doesn't allow you to write off the cost of life insurance; funeral, burial, or cremation expenses; health club dues; household cleaning help; nursing care for a baby who is healthy; or insurance that pays for ordinary living expenses should you get sick.

What isn't deductible as a miscellaneous expense?
You may not deduct campaign expenses; IRS penalties and fines; the cost of home insurance, rent, or repairs; funeral or burial expenses; life insurance, the cost of meals you eat when you work overtime; or personal legal expenses or living expenses.

Nor may you write off political contributions; the cost of self-improvement courses that are unrelated to your occupation; fines or penalties, such as parking tickets; or contributions you make voluntarily to an unemployment benefit fund.

What taxes aren't deductible?
Taxes on alcoholic beverages and cigarettes; fishing and hunting licenses; estate taxes; car inspection fees; federal gasoline taxes; fines; gift taxes; inheritance taxes; sales taxes; Social Security taxes; transfer taxes; and water, sewer, and other local service charges.

CHAPTER 23

TAX DEDUCTIONS FOR BUSINESSES

Uncle Sam knows that it costs money to operate a business—even a tiny one. So he allows you to deduct business expenses on your tax return.

What is deductible—and what isn't—when it comes to business expenses? In this chapter, we take a look—starting with automobile expenses.

Automobiles

WHO: If you own an automobile and drive it for business, you're entitled to claim a write-off for the cost of operating that car in your business.

WHAT: Did you know that it costs more today to buy a new car than it cost Christopher Columbus to equip and undertake three voyages to and from the New World?

That's why it makes sense to share the cost with Uncle Sam. When it comes to deducting car expenses, he gives you a choice. You may write off the actual business cost of operating the car, or you may claim a flat amount for each business mile you drive.

The decision is yours.

As far as the IRS is concerned, the *standard mileage rate* approximates the normal expense of operating a car. It takes into account the cost of gasoline, oil, repairs, licenses, insurance, and *depreciation*. It even increases with the rate of inflation.

Chances are that your actual costs of operating a car will add up to more than the standard mileage amount. So, in most cases, it pays to deduct actual expenses.

The standard mileage rate for 1989 was 25½ cents a mile for the first 15,000 miles of business travel and 11 cents a mile for mileage in excess of 15,000 miles. The 11 cents per mile also applied to cars that the IRS considers to be fully depreciated. For 1990 the milage rate for business use of a car is 26 cents a mile with no 15,000 mile limit.

If you opt to write off actual expenses, you may deduct only that portion of your expenses that's attributable to business use.

Say you use your car 60 percent of the time for business. That means you may write off 60 percent of the expenses you incur in operating your car.

What is deductible as a car expense? The list is extensive. It includes the cost of automobile club memberships, registration, and other licensing fees, gasoline, lubrication, and repairs, washing, car insurance, interest on a loan you take out to buy the car, and rent for a garage.

Tires with a *useful life* of less than one year are deductible in full in the year you buy them. However, tires that last longer than a year and are purchased separately from the car must be depreciated—that is, written off slowly over time.

You may also deduct parking fees and tools that you pay when you travel on business—and this rule holds true even if you opt for the standard milage deduction.

The cost of parking a car at or near your office, though, isn't deductible by you personally. However, your company may write this expense off—as long as it's organized as a corporation. Sole proprietors may not claim a write-off for parking.

You may also be able to claim depreciation—the break

the IRS gives you for the wear and tear on your business property—for the percentage of use that's business-related.

You should know, though, that recent IRS rules limit the ability of businesses to depreciate cars. The rules limit the amounts that can be written off each year based on two factors: the purchase price of the car (there's no faster write-off for Mercedes or Jaguars), and the percentage of miles the car is used for business (only cars used 50 percent or more in business can use accelerated depreciation methods).

IRS Publication 917, *Business Use of a Car*, is a must for people who are considering depreciating their cars for business.

Whichever write-off method you use—the flat mileage rate or actual expenses—the law generally requires you to maintain a log of your automobile mileage.

Keep a mileage log, and keep your records in clear, chronological order. Although you don't need to record your mileage every day, you should get in the habit of doing so on a weekly or biweekly basis. That way, you'll have an accurate account should you face an audit.

Are there any other rules you should know?

A few. For starters, commuting is *never* considered business use—even if you install a telephone and transact business while you're driving.

If you would like more information about writing off automobile expenses, ask the IRS to send you copies of these booklets: *Fuel Tax Credits and Refunds* (publication 378); *Travel, Entertainment, and Gift Expenses* (publication 463); and *Miscellaneous Deductions* (publication 529).

Also helpful are *Depreciation* (publication 534); *Business Expenses* (publication 535); *Basis of Assets* (publication 551); *Information for Business Taxpayers* (publication 583); and *Business Use of a Car* (publication 917).

You'll find *Travel, Entertainment, and Gift Expenses*

and *Business Use of a Car* particularly useful. They summarize what expenses are deductible.

WHERE: If you're a sole proprietor, write off your automobile expenses on Schedule C of your Form 1040. If you're a partner in a partnership, deduct them on Form 1065. If you're an owner of a corporation, write them off on Form 1120A (the short form) or Form 1120. If you're an employee, deduct these expenses on Form 2106 and Form 1040.

WHEN: You write off automobile expenses in the year you incur them.

Disability Insurance

WHO: If you're a key executive of a corporation, your corporation may deduct the cost of disability insurance for employees, including yourself.

However, sole proprietors and partners may not deduct the expense of these policies for themselves, although they may write off the cost of coverage for employees.

WHAT: A person who is between the ages of thirty-five and sixty-five is six times more likely to become disabled than die. So disability coverage for most people is vital.

You may provide disability insurance for yourself and your employees either under a self-funded plan or through a policy you purchase from an insurance carrier. To deduct the cost, you must inform workers that a disability plan is in place.

It's a good idea for key executives to buy disability insurance policies for themselves with their own money—not with funds drawn from the corporation.

Why? Payments you receive from a disability policy are taxable to you if the insurance premiums were paid by your corporation.

There's an income tax credit available for individuals with low to moderate incomes who become permanently and totally disabled.

But you don't have to pay taxes on disability payments

if you pay for the insurance policy premiums out of your own pocket.

WHERE: If your business is a sole proprietorship, write off disability insurance premiums on Schedule C of your Form 1040. If it's a partnership, claim these expenses on Form 1065. And if your business is a corporation, deduct premiums on Form 1120A (the short form) or Form 1120, or Form 1120S.

WHEN: Disability insurance premiums are deductible currently—that is, you may write them off in the year that you make them.

Gifts

WHO: Uncle Sam allows business owners to claim a deduction for business gifts—within certain limits, of course.

WHAT: The IRS doesn't care about the nature of the gift, as long as it's for a business purpose. However, you may deduct no more than $25 per person per year.

Say you buy a gold pen-and-pencil set for one of your top executives and pay $100 for it. You may deduct only $25 of the $100 you paid. (However, you may deduct the full $100 if you include that amount in the executive's gross income as compensation.)

One exception to the $25-per-person rule is advertising materials—pens, pencils, calendars, posters, notepads, matchbooks, etc. But to qualify for the exclusion, items must cost less than $4 each and be imprinted with either your name or your company's name.

Another exception to the $25 limitation are point-of-purchase sales aids that are handed out to retailers for use at their place of business. Common examples include metal display racks and signs that are given by book publishers to bookstore owners.

Also excluded from the $25 rule are noncash prizes passed out to employees in recognition of measurable accomplishments, such as safety and length of service.

IRS auditors scrutinize business gift deductions carefully, so you should maintain records that show:

- what you purchased;
- the price of the gift (the IRS requires you to have receipts for items that cost more than $25 even though your write-off is limited to $25);
- the date you bought the gift;
- the purpose of the gift (to recognize an employee's birthday, and so on);
- the name of the recipient;
- your relationship to the recipient (he or she could be an employee or even a business adviser).

After taking into account the exceptions noted above, the IRS will recharacterize a "gift" as compensation subject to income and FICA taxes if it's given to an employee because of services that employee performed. Similarly, if you give gifts to shareholders or business partners, you must show that the item is truly a gift and not disguising either a dividend or compensation.

You should know that different rules apply to gifts that are so-called *qualified plan awards*. Never heard of a qualified plan award?

It's an award of tangible personal property that's given under an ongoing program of an employer. The plan must be spelled out in writing, and employees must be notified of its existence. A handout explaining the program, for example, could be posted on a bulletin board or included in an employee handbook. You must give the award because of safety achievement or length of service.

Two other requirements: A qualified plan award program may not discriminate in favor of top executives or shareholders. And the average cost of all awards made during the year under the plan may not exceed $400. Single awards, however, may be as large as $1,600.

If you would like more information on business gifts,

ask the IRS to send you a copy of *Travel, Entertainment, and Gift Expenses* (publication 463).

WHERE: Sole proprietors write off business gifts on Schedule C of their Form 1040. Partnerships claim these expenses on Form 1065, while corporations deduct business gifts on Form 1120A (the short form), Form 1120, or Form 1120S.

WHEN: Claim a deduction for business gifts in the year that your purchase them—meaning the year that you pay for them or charge them to a charge or credit card.

Health Insurance

WHO: Corporations and partnerships may write off as ordinary and necessary business expenses any health insurance premiums they pay for employees. To claim the deduction, you must show that the health insurance benefits you provide meet the IRS's nondiscrimination rules.

Another set of rules applies to sole proprietors.

WHAT: When Congress adopted the 1986 Tax Reform Act, it did sole proprietors a favor. It voted to allow them to write off as a business expense 25 percent of their medical insurance policies for themselves, a spouse, and any dependents.

Previously, they couldn't deduct any of their health insurance costs as business expenses. The only conditions: you must not be covered by a spouse's health plan or by a plan sponsored by another employer. And the amount you write off may not exceed your earned income in your trade or business.

Uncle Sam provides a special line on page one of Form 1040 for writing off these insurance premiums. What about the remaining 75 percent of your insurance premiums? If you itemize, you may write off these amounts on your personal returns, if your premiums plus the cost of your other medical expenses top 7.5 percent of your adjusted gross income.

WHERE: If you do business as a sole proprietorship, Uncle Sam allows you to write off 25 percent of your health insurance premiums on your Form 1040 paid through September 30, 1990. He says you may deduct health insurance premiums you pay for employees on your Schedule C.

If you do business as a partnership, the partnership may claim your medical insurance premiums on Form 1065. If you're a corporation, the corporation may deduct health insurance premiums on Form 1120A (the short form), Form 1120, or Form 1120S.

WHEN: You write off the cost of health insurance in the year you incur it.

Home Office

WHO: When it comes to writing off home office expenses, the law is strict. You're entitled to a deduction only if you use your home office regularly and exclusively for business.

WHAT: Home offices—as you may have heard—are one of the thornier areas of the tax code, so make sure you abide by the letter of the law. Here are the conditions you must meet if you want to claim a deduction for your home office.

You may write off your home office only if it meets one of these three tests: It's your principal place of business; you use it regularly and in the normal course of your trade or business to meet with clients, patients, or customers; and its located in a separate building that's attached to your house.

Your home office also must be necessary to the pursuit of your trade or business, not simply for your personal convenience. However, the business doesn't have to be your primary business. You may have one office that's provided by your employer for one business, and you may use your home office for another business.

You must also use your home office exclusively for

business, although the space you write off doesn't have to be a separate room. You may use half your basement as an office and the other half as a workshop and still claim a deduction. But you may not use your home office as personal living quarters—a family room by night, for example, and a home office by day.

In any case, it's always a good idea to furnish your home office—even if it's half a room—as an office. Appropriate furnishings—a desk, filing cabinet, telephone, computer, and so on—demonstrate to the IRS that your home office is strictly for business.

How do you calculate your home office deduction? The first step, logically enough, is to decide what portion of your home is used for business.

If you have set aside one room in a five-room house, and the rooms are approximately the same size, the answer is one fifth. If the rooms differ in size, you must measure the square footage of your house, then figure what percentage of the total floor space the office occupies.

Once you make this calculation, simply multiply the percentage times your rental payments to get the amount you may write off.

Then multiply this same percentage times your other household expenses—heat, electricity, cleaning, telephone, and so on. Uncle Sam says that you may also write off a portion of the expenses when you maintain a home office.

What if you own your home? Then you're entitled to a depreciation deduction. Uncle Sam says you must use the straight-line method for writing off your property—that is, you must write off the same amount each year for 31.5 years.

You simply multiply the percentage of your house you use for business times the price you paid (less the price of the land, since you may not depreciate land).

Then you divide that amount by 31.5.

Next, figure out what portion of real estate taxes you

may write off by multiplying your yearly payments by the percentage you use your house for business.

Tip: You may deduct your home office expenses only up to the amount of net income you generate from it. Your net income? The IRS defines net income, in this instance, as gross income minus expenses—but not counting home office expenses.

Say that you sell $3,000 worth of cosmetics from your home, and you rack up $1,000 in expenses. You may deduct no more than $2,000 in home office costs—that's the difference between your gross income, $3,000, and your expenses, $1,000.

As we said, the IRS scrutinizes home office deductions carefully. Some people believe this deduction can even trigger an audit. Still, there's no reason *not* to write off a home office, as long as you can substantiate your deduction.

If you would like more information about writing off home office expenses, telephone or write your local IRS office and ask for a copy of *Business Use of Your Home* (publication 587).

You may also find these booklets of interest: *Miscellaneous Deductions* (publication 529) and *Depreciation* (publication 534).

WHERE: If you do business as a sole proprietorship, write off your home office expenses on Schedule C of your Form 1040. If you do business as a partnership, deduct these expenses on Form 1065. And if you do business as a corporation, write them off on Form 1120A (the short form) or Form 1120.

WHEN: Deduct home office expenses in the year you incur them. But you may carry forward expenses you don't write off to future tax years.

Life Insurance

WHO: When it comes to life insurance, the law is clear. Corporations may provide life insurance for key executives and employees and write off the costs. Sole proprietorships and partnerships, on the other hand, may deduct only the cost of life insurance policies that cover employees.

WHAT: Uncle Sam requires companies to report the cost of employer-paid life insurance as income to employees, unless the insurance is provided under a group-term plan.

But even under group-term life insurance plans, the benefit is tax-free only up to $50,000 of coverage. Any amount your company pays for additional coverage is compensation.

The cost of additional insurance isn't what the company actually pays, except in the case of certain highly paid employees. Rather, it's the amount based on an IRS table of *average* or *uniform* premiums. (Your financial or tax adviser will provide you with a copy.)

What else do you need to know?

Special rules apply to so-called key-person policies. These are policies that cover any officer, any employee, or other person with a financial interest in your company.

You may not deduct premiums for key-person insurance if the policy calls for the proceeds to benefit the company itself—by paying off some outstanding loans, for example.

If, on the other hand, you select a family member not connected to the company as beneficiary, the premiums are considered compensation and are deductible by the company but includible in the gross income of the employee.

In addition, if a bank requires you to take out a life insurance policy as a condition for obtaining a loan, you may not write off the premiums. This rule applies even if it's a business loan.

With split-dollar life insurance, you and your employee share the cost of an insurance policy on his or her life. For example, if the employee dies, you get an amount equal to the cash value of the policy. The remaining money goes to his or her beneficiaries.

Finally, to claim a deduction, you must show that the group-term life insurance benefit meets the government's nondiscrimination rules.

WHEN: Your company deducts the cost of life insurance premiums in the year it pays them.

WHERE: Sole proprietors write off insurance premiums on Schedule C of their Form 1040. Partnerships claim these expenses on Form 1065. Meanwhile, corporations deduct insurance premiums on their Form 1120A (the short form), Form 1120, or Form 1120S.

Travel and Entertainment

WHO: If you're a business owner and travel for business, you may write off the sums you spend for lodging and transportation. You may also write off 80 percent of the amounts you spend to entertain clients or to buy business meals.

WHAT: What are the rules governing travel and entertainment expenses? Let's take a look, starting with transportation expenses.

You may write off the cost of transportation—be it by car, cab, plane, or train—to and from a business destination, as long as you aren't commuting.

You may also deduct in full all the expenses involved in your away-from-home travel—hotel, business calls, and so forth—once you arrive at your destination, provided that the IRS wouldn't consider them to be lavish or extravagant.

The IRS has special rules for international trips that combine business and pleasure—a business trip to Paris, say, followed by a vacation on the Riviera.

For starters, Uncle Sam won't allow you to write off any expenses you have while you're on vacation. You may not be able to write off your entire air fare or other transportation expenses that combine business and pleasure. Here are the details.

If your trip outside the United States exceeds seven

consecutive days (excluding the departure day but including the return day), and your vacation adds up to more than 25 percent of the time you're outside the country, you're subject to the partial disallowance rule.

Under this rule, you calculate the portion of your trip that was for business. You multiply that percentage times your air fare and other transportation expenses.

Then you write off that amount.

You're exempt from the partial disallowance rule if the decision to take the trip isn't yours to make. For example, if your corporation's board of directors orders you to take a trip, you're off the hook as far as the partial disallowance rule is concerned. However, if the trip is a vacation and the company pays for it, its value may count as income to you.

What happens if you mix business with pleasure on your foreign trip? Uncle Sam says you may deduct transportation to your destination if you can prove the trip was *primarily* for business. If you cannot, you may not deduct any part of your transportation costs.

You may, however, write off any business expenses you incurred on the trip. If you do go on a business trip and take your spouse along, don't plan to write off his or her expenses unless you can prove a clear business purpose for your spouse's presence.

Now, on to entertainment and meals.

As you no doubt are well aware, when Congress adopted the Tax Reform Act of 1986, it took aim at business meals and entertainment deductions.

Today, these expenses are only 80 percent deductible. That is, you may write off only 80 cents of each dollar you spend on meals and entertainment—and this rule applies even to meals you eat on the road.

To deduct business meals (except those you eat while on a business trip), you must have discussed business during the meal. Similarly, if you take an employee to lunch or dinner to discuss business, you may write off 80 percent of the cost. To take a deduction for entertainment, you must also have had a clear business purpose in mind.

You should know, too, that you may collect a partial deduction for country club or social club dues used for business—as long as you use the facility at least 50 percent for business.

However, you get to write off only the percentage that was for business use. So, if you used the club 60 percent for business, feel free to deduct 60 percent of the dues.

Keep good records and take as many legitimate deductions as you possibly can for business meals, entertainment, and travel. To do otherwise would simply be foolhardy. However, if you cannot substantiate your expenses with good records, don't write them off.

What constitutes adequate documentation in the eyes of the IRS? You must have a record of the cost of the travel, meal, or entertainment; the date; the place; the business purpose; the general topic of business conversation; and the names and titles of the people you entertained. Remember, receipts for expenses over $25 are necessary.

WHERE: If you're a sole proprietor, write off travel and entertainment expenses on Schedule C of your Form 1040. If you're a partner in a partnership, deduct them on Form 1065. If you're an owner of a corporation, write them off on Form 1120A (the short form), Form 1120, or Form 1120S.

WHEN: You write off these expenses in the year you incur them.

Questions and Answers

I was driving my car on business when I was pulled over for speeding. May I deduct my speeding ticket as a business expense?

Sorry, but the rules say that fines for violating traffic and parking laws aren't deductible—no matter what the purpose of your trip.

I use my home office to manage my investments. May I claim a write-off?

Unfortunately, the rules won't allow you to take a deduction for a home office if you use the space solely to manage your investments—unless, of course, managing those investments is your primary occupation.

I operate a child-care center in my home. May I claim a deduction for the room where I operate the day care, even though we use it as a den too?

If you run a child-care business in your home, Uncle Sam gives you a break. You may write off part of your house, even though you don't use that portion exclusively for your business. Make sure your business is properly licensed, though, or you may lose the deduction.

I heard that I may not deduct travel and entertainment expenses that are lavish and extravagant. What does this rule mean?

Uncle Sam doesn't provide any guidelines on what he considers lavish or extravagant, but he does imply that he doesn't want you to live too high off the hog.

But there are no cases on record where the IRS has denied a deduction because the write-off exceeded a certain dollar amount or took place at a high-priced restaurant.

One rule of thumb: An expense is reasonable if it fits the needs and circumstances of a particular situation—and, sometimes, only caviar will do.

CHAPTER 24

WINNING TAX STRATEGIES

"I'm proud to be paying taxes in the United States," Arthur Godfrey once quipped. "The only thing is—I could be just as proud for half the money." So, it seems, could a lot of other people. But how do you pare down your tax liability? In this chapter, we take a look.

Defer Income

When it comes to tax planning, there's one often-repeated rule of thumb: Defer income. By following this tried-and-true prescription, you won't avoid taxation all together, but you'll at least postpone taxes on a portion of your earnings.

How, you ask, do you defer income? The easiest way—if you're self-employed—is to postpone billing clients or customers until the following tax year.

However, this tactic works only if you keep your books on the cash basis. If you use the cash method of accounting, you record income when you receive it; with accrual accounting, you record income as you earn it, regardless of when you collect the money.

If you're employed by someone other than yourself, one way to defer income is to ask your boss to postpone paying you your bonus until next year. (This is called *deferred compensation.*) For example, it may be just as easy for him or her to write you your check on January

5, 1990, as on December 31, 1989. This tactic works only if you ask your boss to defer the income *before* you earn it.

But take care that you don't get tripped up by the *constructive receipt* rules. These rules assume that you have received the income once the money is under your control, even if you haven't deposited a cent of it in the bank.

Say, for example, that a client writes a check to you on December 31, 1989, and delivers it to your home or office. You don't pick up the check until January 2, 1990. You still must report that amount as income in 1989. The reason is, you had constructive receipt of the money, since it was available to you on December 31.

A question our clients ask us frequently these days is: If tax rates remain the same from year to year, why defer income? The reason is simple enough. By deferring this income, you'll pay taxes on it later, not sooner. Meanwhile, the cash is in your pocket, not Uncle Sam's.

Tip: Deferring income isn't smart for everyone. Say, for example, that you expect a big increase in your income next year. If that extra income pushes you into a higher tax bracket, you may want to accelerate income. That way, you pay taxes on your earnings at your current lower rate.

Accelerate Deductions

Another often-quoted rule of thumb is to accelerate deductions. It's often easier to accelerate deductions than to defer income. That's because you control the money you pay out, but you don't necessarily control the money you take in.

Why accelerate deductions? When your deductions go up, your taxable income goes down, and when your taxable income declines, so does your tax bill.

One way to boost deductions is to pay all your outstanding bills by the end of the year. For example, if your bank keeps your property taxes in an escrow account, ask it to pay any city or municipal taxes that you owe before the year ends. This assumes you have sufficient funds in the account near year end, and that you know how much tax you owe.

You should pay before January 1 any estimated *state* taxes that are ordinarily due on January 15. The rules allow you to prepay estimated taxes, as long as the amount you pay is close to your final tax liability. If you pay too much, Uncle Sam may disallow the deduction on audit.

Another idea is to accelerate your charitable contributions. Why wait until the following year to donate to your favorite cause?

Clean our your closets in December—not January—and donate your old clothing to charity. That way, you're entitled to a deduction this year, not next.

Make any gift of appreciated property to a charity this year, not next. How does this tactic work? Say that you want to donate $1,000 to a favorite cause. Instead of writing a check for $1,000 to that charity, donate shares of stock that have appreciated in value.

Perhaps you bought fifty shares of Ace Automatic Corporation five years ago. You paid $500 for the stock, which is now valued at $1,000. If you donate the stock, you're generally entitled to a deduction of $1,000—the current market value of the stock—not $500.

Here's something else you may not know but should. You may claim a deduction for items you purchased in December even if you charge them to a credit card.

Practice Tax-Wise Investing

You may want to cash in on the benefits of tax deferral by putting money in a tax-favored vehicle, such as an annuity. Your earnings in the annuity accumulate tax-deferred until you withdraw them.

Tip: Here's a tip for mutual-fund investors. If you choose to redeem only a portion of your shares, specify to the mutual fund company and the IRS which ones you're selling and at what price they were purchased.

Why? Uncle Sam taxes you on your gain and, unless you have kept records, assumes that the shares you sell are the first shares you bought.

So it's smart—tax-wise, at least—to redeem your most expensive shares first. Just make sure you save all fund statements and redemption slips in case you're audited.

Claim Interest Deductions While They Last

The rules allow you to deduct 10 percent of your personal interest expenses—such as interest on credit cards and automobile loans—in 1990. The amount disappears entirely in 1991 and beyond.

So, if you have a lot of debt—for an automobile loan, for example—it probably makes sense to restructure it. How should you go about it?

The law allows you to deduct the interest on home equity loans up to $100,000. So why not borrow on your principal residence and pay off your credit card or auto loan debt? Then you may write off the interest on up to $100,000 of home equity debt.

Tip: Exercise caution when applying this strategy. You should make sure that you'll be able to comfortably pay off any home equity loan. After all, on many of these loans, interest is adjustable—and can rise precipitously as economic conditions change.

If you fail to make a payment on your car loan, you lose your automobile. Not a good situation, surely, but better than losing the roof over your head.

Shift Income to Your Children

In the old days, you could transfer assets to your child, and income from those assets would be taxed at his or her rate—which was usually much lower than your own. Nowadays, if your child is under fourteen, his or her nonwage earnings over $1,000 are taxed at the parents' rate.

But the law says that the first $500 of an under-fourteen-year-old child's earnings is tax-free. And the second $500 is taxed at his or her rate, which, in most cases, is only 15 percent. So it still makes sense for a younger child to collect at least $1,000 in annual earnings from investments.

And if your child is fourteen or over, you may certainly give him or her income-producing property. He or she will pay taxes on the earnings at his or her lower rate.

Remember that each parent—or any other person, for that matter—may give a child up to $10,000 a year, generally with no tax consequences on either side.

You should keep in mind, though, that once you make a gift to your child, that cash or property belongs to him or her. You have legally given up your right to it.

However, in most cases, you'll still be the custodian for the child. You may move the money from one investment to another, as long as you don't use it for your personal benefit and it remains available for your child's use. The money should be transferred to your child when he or she reaches legal age.

Consider Passive-Income Generators

Suppose in this current year you had a hefty amount of losses from your passive investments. (These investments, you recall, are those in which you don't actively participate in managing—a real estate limited partnership, for example.)

The rules say that you may offset these losses only with income from passive investments. This is where passive-income generators, or PIGs, enter the picture.

Ask your broker or financial planner about these investments. Their number has increased considerably since the new passive-income laws were formulated back in 1986.

Keep Tabs on Estimated and Withholding Taxes

The trick to paying estimated and withholding taxes is to not shell out more money than you should but to pay enough to avoid penalties.

Say you work for someone else. You, of course, had taxes withheld from your pay last year. You also received a $2,000 refund when you filed your Form 1040.

Lucky you. Or, perhaps, not so lucky.

You have, in fact, made a nice loan to Uncle Sam—all of it interest-free. That $2,000 could have been earning some extra cash for you. To rectify the situation in this current tax year, you should take another look at your W-4 form. Make sure you're taking all the personal allowances to which you're entitled.

What if you paid estimated tax? As you know, the total of your quarterly installments—plus any withholding—must equal the lesser of 90 percent of the current year's tax or 100 percent of the tax on your previous year's return.

It's safe to pay 100 percent of last year's taxes. But if you think you're going to owe less, don't hesitate to pony up 90 percent of what you'll owe in the current year.

If you would like more information about withholding and estimated tax payments, ask the IRS to send you a copy of its booklet, *Employment Taxes and Information Return Requirements* (publication 539).

Make Use of Any Carryforwards

The law allows you to carry forward some deductions—such as investment interest that tops investment income or passive losses—that you weren't able to write off in the current year. So, keep a careful accounting of these write-offs. That way you won't lose, by default, a perfectly legitimate deduction.

Make the Most of Your Retirement Contributions

Gone are the days when any working person could automatically contribute $2,000 to an IRA and deduct the entire amount. Nowadays, contributions are deductible only by people who either don't participate in a qualified retirement plan or, if they do participate in a qualified plan, their income falls below certain preset limits.

Say, for example, that you're single and participate in your company's retirement plan. You may deduct a contribution of $2,000 to an IRA only if your adjusted gross income (AGI) falls below $25,000. You're entitled to a partial deduction if your AGI is between $25,000 and $35,000.

Married people who filed jointly and participate in their company's retirement plan may deduct their contribution only if their combined AGI is less than $40,000 a year. They may claim a partial deduction if their combined AGI falls between $40,000 and $50,000 a year.

Our advice: If you can make a tax-deductible contribution to an IRA, do so. Likewise, sock away money in a 401(k) plan if you can.

With a 401(k), you contribute a portion of your earnings in a company-sponsored retirement plan, and the federal government excludes that amount (plus any interest, dividends, and capital gains that accumulate) from current taxation. (However, you still have to pay FICA or Social Security tax on your 401(k) contribution.)

What separates 401(k) plans from IRAs is the way the IRS treats the money that's contributed. If you qualify, dollars placed in an IRA are deductible on your tax return.

But funds that are set aside in a 401(k) plan are considered *deferred compensation*—that is, they aren't reported to the IRS as current income.

Say you earn $30,000 a year as a personnel director of a small company. You deposit 5 percent of your salary in a 401(k) plan, which means that you pay income taxes on wages of $28,500—your total income of $30,000 minus the $1,500 you contributed to the plan.

You should know that Uncle Sam caps your contributions to 401(k) plans at $7,627 for 1989. (This amount is adjusted annually for changes in the cost of living.)

What if your employer matches your contribution to a 401(k)? Another ceiling applies. Under the rules, the entire contribution—meaning your contributions added to your employer's together—may not top the lesser of $30,000 or 25 percent of your annual earnings.

If you're self-employed, we also recommend that you salt away as much as you can in a defined-contribution Keogh plan. The rules allow you to tuck away as much as 25 percent of your self-employment income—up to a maximum of $30,000—in one of these retirement accounts.

You may write off the entire amount you contribute to the plan, and your earnings accumulate tax-deferred until they are withdrawn, usually at retirement.

For more information on retirement plans, ask the IRS to send you copies of these booklets: *Tax Benefits for Older Americans* (publication 554); *Self-Employed Retirement Plans* (publication 560); and *U.S. Civil Service Retirement and Disability* (publication 721).

You may also find these booklets of use: *Tax-Sheltered Annuity Programs for Employees of Public Schools and Certain Tax-Exempt Organizations* (publication 571); *Pension and Annuity Income* (publication 575); and *Individual Retirement Arrangements* (publication 590).

All are free for the asking.

Stay on Top of Tax Law Changes

Some tax-law changes work to your advantage. But you can claim a deduction only if you know about it. So, follow the news when it comes to income taxes.

Watch for articles in newspapers and magazines. And speak to your financial adviser periodically. He or she will know the changes that may affect your tax situation. It doesn't take much time to stay informed—and the time you spend will result in tax savings to you.

Protect Your Deductions

When it comes to dealing with the IRS, you're far better off with good written records than with a sterling memory and an honest face.

Say you prepare a running diary or submit biweekly reports that indicate you made trips to a particular client's office. These records will be of far greater value during an IRS audit than your oral assurance that you visited the client at least once every two weeks.

The rule is, if you cannot substantiate a deduction, you aren't entitled to claim it. What if you ignore this rule and write off an expense for which you don't have adequate proof? Uncle Sam may—on audit—disallow the deduction.

You should, for example, jot down all your medical expenses—including doctors' bills, prescriptions costs, transportation to a medical facility, and parking once you arrive there. Then keep track of any reimbursements from your insurer.

The same rule holds true for all your potential deductions. Write down your expenses in a ledger throughout the year. Save your cancelled checks and other receipts. Believe us. Forewarned, as far as an audit is concerned, is forearmed.

The IRS accepts as proof: account books, diaries, and logs; documentary evidence, such as receipts and paid bills; trip sheets; and expense reports.

Another important rule: The IRS requires documentary evidence for all lodging expenses when you travel away from home on business and for all expenses of $25 or more.

You should know that the statute of limitations on keeping records varies from state to state. And state and federal regulations are often different.

To be on the safe side, some of our planners advise clients to double the federal statute of three years and keep their records for at least six years.

Tip: If you're a business owner and have net operating losses that you carry forward for many years, keep the records for the years until you have used up your entire loss. Until you have used up your loss, don't begin your six-year countdown for disposing of your records.

Many of our clients do a good job of documenting expenses, but they leave many deposits marked only "deposit," without identifying the source.

If you're one of these people and Uncle Sam calls you on the carpet, you may have to report the deposits as income even if they are loans.

One way to avoid this problem is to identify in your checkbook on your check register or check stub the source of each of your receipts.

Questions and Answers

I may not deduct my contribution to an IRA, because I participate in a pension plan at work. Should I make a nondeductible contribution?

Uncle Sam does allow you to make nondeductible contributions to an IRA, even if you do participate in another retirement plan and don't meet the income levels.

He even gives you a break: the interest and other earnings that accumulate on your deposit aren't taxed until they are withdrawn, usually at retirement.

The question, then, is, should you make a nondeductible IRA contribution? The answer depends on your situation.

IRA contributions are easy to make, especially to an existing account. Also, by using an IRA, you've earmarked those funds for retirement.

On the other hand, you may choose to contribute to a nonqualified annuity in lieu of nondeductible contributions to an IRA. The main benefit of this is that you can contribute much more than $2,000. In addition, you're not subject to the minimum distribution requirements at age 70½. Consult your financial advisor to see if nondeductable IRA contributions make sense for you.

I am joining a new company, and I plan to make contributions to its 401(k) plan. Who decides how to invest the money I deposit in the 401(k)?

The answer varies by employer. But most companies appoint an *investment manager*—typically, a financial services institution. And the investment manager allows you to choose investments from a preset menu of mutual funds, for example.

PART 7

YOUR RETIREMENT

- PLANNING FOR YOUR RETIREMENT
- PUTTING MONEY AWAY FOR RETIREMENT
- WHAT YOU NEED TO KNOW ABOUT SOCIAL SECURITY
- TAKING YOUR MONEY OUT

CHAPTER 25

PLANNING FOR YOUR RETIREMENT

How do *you* define retirement?

Webster's dictionary says it's "withdrawal from one's position or occupation." But you may think of it as "the chance to finally take all the trips, play all the golf, and cook all the gourmet meals I never had time for while I was working full time."

Whatever your definition, one fact is certain. Your happiness and comfort at this stage of life depends on what you do before you reach retirement age.

Retirement isn't something you just fall into—not if you expect to enjoy it. Your golden years require careful planning from the day you earn your first dollar.

You should know, too, that simply setting aside a lump sum each year in a retirement account isn't enough—although it's certainly a good start. As you grow older, your circumstances and needs, financial and otherwise, constantly change.

What seems like a good retirement plan at age thirty-five may be totally inappropriate at age fifty-five. That's because your tolerance for risk decreases as you grow older. Also, an investment vehicle that made sense ten years ago may have lost its appeal with the passage of new tax laws.

Some dictionaries define retirement as "the act of

falling back, retreating, or receding from a place or position."

Given the active lives that people enjoy for decades after their retirement, this second definition—we hope—misses the mark entirely.

With proper attention, retirement doesn't mean retreat of any kind, but rather an opportunity to move forward into new and rewarding activities—as long as you plan ahead.

In this chapter, we answer some questions you may have about retirement planning. So, roll up your sleeves and let's get started.

When should you begin planning for retirement?

Financial planners disagree on many subjects, but not this one. The time to begin planning for retirement is now, while there's still time.

Your retirement years may begin sooner than you think. Companies are downsizing and are luring employees into retirement with attractive benefits packages.

Also, there are more retirement years to plan for today than at any other time in our history. Improved medical technology means that more Americans are retiring healthier and are more active than ever before. Americans are also living much longer than was the case in the past.

Demographers tell us that the age group between sixty-five and seventy-four is more than eight times larger nowadays than it was in 1900. The age group between seventy-five and eighty-four is more than twelve times larger, and the group over age eighty-five is a remarkable twenty-two times larger.

Most of us can expect to live 25 percent to 30 percent of our entire life spans after retirement. Since most retirees no longer draw regular paychecks, planning properly becomes critical if these are to be truly golden years.

If you're young—in your twenties or early thirties, say—thinking about retirement is understandably difficult.

In these years it's common to concentrate on other financial issues, such as saving for a down payment on a house, buying furniture, or paying for a car.

By planning now, though, you can avoid having to accumulate enough money to retire in a hurry. And you should be able to accumulate a larger amount.

For example, if you invest $1,000 a year for twenty years at a compounded fixed-interest rate of 8 percent, your retirement total will add up to $45,760.

If, on the other hand, you start saving ten years earlier at the same interest rate—for a total of thirty years—you'll have socked away $113,000.

When should you retire?

This is a question everyone must answer for himself or herself. It involves knowing well enough to evaluate how you'll adjust to being away from your job.

Some people enjoy extra leisure time. Others miss the challenges of work and the social stimulation of the office. But you don't have to leave your regular job then do nothing but golf and travel for your remaining years. There are always in-between steps you may take.

Many people retire, then take up a second career—converting what was once a hobby into a profitable small business, for instance. Others assume a busy schedule of volunteer activities. Still others decide to take a part-time job.

Should you consider an early retirement offer?

Many big companies—and some small ones as well—are wooing longtime employees with early retirement packages. The idea behind these plans is simple: Companies want to cut costs by trimming high-level and highly paid personnel from their payrolls.

If you're offered this choice, should you take it? For most people, this decision is not an easy one to make.

After all, if you don't accept the offer, you may find yourself without a job six months or a year down the road. On the other hand, you have to calculate whether you and your family can live on the retirement package your company is offering.

How should you evaluate an early retirement offer? Most companies offer early retirement packages that include these four components:

- your regular pension reduced for your current age;
- a bonus that takes your earnings to the amount your pension would have been, or close to it (sometimes employers offer a bonus in the form of a lump payment, sometimes it's paid in annual installments);
- a bonus until age sixty-two to compensate for what Social Security would be;
- medical insurance.

You should know, too, that most plans don't offer employees what they would receive if they retired at the normal retirement age. Why?

Most companies calculate your benefits using a formula that's based on your earnings at retirement times the number of years you worked for the company.

Your first step in evaluating an early retirement offer, then, is to speak to the person in charge of employee benefits at your company.

Ask him or her what amount you can expect to receive each year after you retire. Figure out the difference between what you would collect if you retired early and the amount you would pocket if you stayed on the job.

Some companies—as an incentive to employees—pay part or all of this difference in the form of a bonus if you accept their offer to retire early.

Still, even with the extra money, your monthly retirement check may be considerably less than it would be otherwise. How do you make up for the difference?

One way is to pursue other career opportunities.

Your present employer might consider hiring you as a

consultant or as the manager of a special project. Or you might serve as a consultant to other companies.

Tip: Most financial planners recommend that you stay on the job as long as possible. The reason is straightforward: The value of a typical pension plan usually quadruples in the ten years between the ages of fifty-five and sixty-five.

If you have no choice but to retire early, you should at least know the amount of money on which you can rely. And by all means take advantage of any counseling or job placement programs your company may offer you free of charge.

How much money will you need when you retire?
Most financial planners estimate that a person needs as much as 80 percent of his or her regular income to live comfortably after retirement. But the exact amount you'll require will vary with your lifestyle and financial circumstances.

For example, it usually costs more to retire in a large city than a small town. And if you plan to travel, you need more money than someone who intends to stay home.

What if you plan to play golf or engage in some other sport? Then you count on racking up country club dues and equipment fees.

You may think your expenses will go down after you retire. "I won't spend as much on clothes," you think, "or transportation to or from work, or lunches out. Also, my mortgage will be paid off and my chidren will be out of college."

Yes, some of your expenses will plunge. But others will soar. Older people, as a rule, spend far more on medical care than their younger counterparts.

Moreover, no matter how modest your means, the chances are high that expenditures for hobbies and leisure pursuits will increase after you retire.

Activities you once sandwiched in during odd moments,

such as traveling, boating, gardening, golf, crafts, and gourmet cooking, may become mainstays in your daily life.

So, when you think of drawing up a retirement budget, you should allow a generous sum for these activities. Remember, the degree to which you enjoy retirement may depend upon having enough money to indulge your leisure passions.

To understand your financial needs for retirement, begin with where you stand today. Record your monthly income and expenses for several months. Then, based on your goals, compare these amounts with what you anticipate you'll need in the future.

Here's an example of how to calculate how much you'll need to maintain your current standard of living after you retire.

Say your current income adds up to $60,000. Of that amount $54,000 goes to pay your annual living expenses. Multiply 80 percent by $54,000. The result—$43,200—is the amount you'll need each year in today's dollars to maintain your lifestyle after retirement.

Let's say, too, that you plan to retire at age sixty-two, and your life expectancy is estimated to be seventy-eight. That means you would be retired for approximately sixteen years.

Multiply 16 times $43,200 to get $691,200—the least amount of money you'll need in today's dollars to finance your retirement and avoid outliving your resources. (You must take inflation into account, too. We'll explain how below.)

What steps can you take now to ensure that you won't exhaust your financial resources during retirement?

Most financial planners start by figuring out what you should expect to receive from all potential sources of retirement income. Add up the amounts you think you'll collect from Social Security, pension plans, IRAs, savings, investments, and, perhaps, some earnings.

Then see if there's a gap between what you'll need and what you expect to pocket. The difference is the amount you must accumulate before you retire.

When it comes to accumulating assets, we cannot make this point strongly enough: You should begin a saving and investment plan early. That way you can stash money away and build on these assets, while your potential for both earnings and savings is high.

You also save tax dollars *now* by starting early to save for retirement. How? If you salt away money in tax-deferred retirement vehicles, such as IRAs, Keoghs, and 401(k)s, your earnings on these retirement dollars aren't taxed until the money is withdrawn from your funds.

Then, your money may be taxed at a lower rate, because you may have shifted to a lower tax bracket. (We discuss these and other tax-deferred vehicles in the next chapter.)

As we noted, you must also consider inflation in your retirement planning. Say you expect inflation to run at a rate of 4 percent a year—a reasonable estimate.

To guarantee that your retirement income is adequate, increase those expenses that are vulnerable to inflation—food, clothing, travel, and so forth—by 4 percent a year.

You should also assess the true value of your company's pension plan. But don't make the mistake many people do of thinking that a pension plan from an employer is enough to take you comfortably through retirement. In 1986, for example, the average pension plan paid about $5,000 annually for someone who worked fifteen years at a salary of $30,000.

Ask the following questions about your company plan: Is it a defined-contribution or a defined-benefit plan? What is its investing schedule? Can you contribute to the plan? How much does the company contribute on your behalf?

Are benefits calculated from your final average pay or from your earnings throughout your career? How are the funds invested? Does the company publish investment reports? What's the earliest age at which you can retire?

What reductions are built in for early retirement? Are there increases for late retirement? Are your retirement benefits guaranteed for life once you retire?

Finally, ask about survivor and disability benefits. And find out whether your company continues to provide you with some benefits, such as health insurance.

How should you invest your money for retirement?
When you're in your twenties or thirties, you invest some or most of your retirement dollars for growth—in an aggressive growth or growth stock mutual fund, say.

But as you grow older and closer to retirement, you should invest your money more conservatively—for example, diverting these assets into income-producing investments.

CHAPTER 26

PUTTING MONEY AWAY FOR RETIREMENT

Where does your retirement income come from?

For most of us, it comes from three sources: your company pension plan, Social Security, and your personal retirement savings.

You can't do much about the first two—you either have a pension plan at work or you don't, and your Social Security income is established by the government.

Where you can make a difference is in the amount you set aside yourself for retirement. And one way to boost that amount is by using tax-favored retirement plans. With *qualified retirement plans*, you exclude the amounts you contribute, plus any earnings that accumulate, from current taxation.

Later in this chapter, we review tax-favored retirement plans, such as Individual Retirement Accounts, Keoghs, and 401(k)s. For example, we explain who may contribute to these plans and deduct their annual contributions and who may not.

Let's start, though, with a few words about annuities. Most annuities are non-qualified; they are retirement plans in which anyone can participate.

People who are looking for a convenient place to save for retirement, and are willing to invest their dollars for a period of time, should consider annuities. These annuities offer an excellent way to supplement any pension or

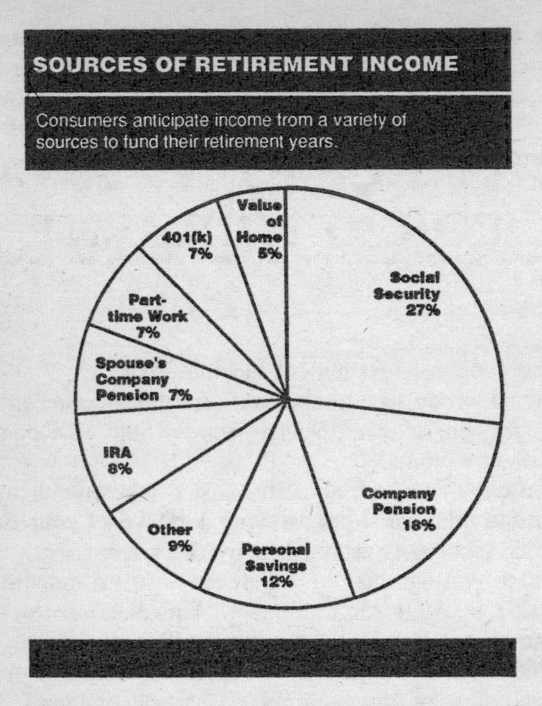

profit-sharing plan you may have. They are also not subject to the contribution limitations that apply to IRAs or similar tax-favored plans.

Annuities may make sense for you, as well, if you have changed jobs frequently, thus losing pension benefits, or if you have already contributed the maximum possible to your employer's retirement plan. They also make sense if you're self-employed but have paper losses, as far as your taxable income is concerned. In this case, you wouldn't be a candidate for a Keogh or Simplified Employee Pension Plan (SEP), but could contribute to a tax-deferred annuity. (We'll talk about SEPs later on in this chapter.)

Finally, since contributions you make to an annuity aren't limited to earned income, they may prove a good place to stash proceeds from an inheritance or insurance policy.

Keep in mind that these investment vehicles are appropriate for people who cannot afford to tie up their money for any length of time or for people looking for a place to park their cash temporarily.

Recent changes in the tax rules have eliminated or limited the tax benefits of many types of investments. However, an annuity continues to be a tax-deferred savings vehicle. In addition, these policies can pay you income for a specified amount of time—in most cases, from the date you retire until your death.

As we'll see, depending on the amount of risk with which you're comfortable, you can purchase annuities that provide either a fixed or a variable rate of return. You can also choose between options that guarantee a certain minimum number of payments or a refund of your investment, if you prefer.

Think of annuities as the opposite of traditional life insurance. Traditional life insurance policies promise to pay after you die; annuities, by contrast, promise to pay benefits while you're alive.

More than 12 million annuity policies are in place nationwide. Annuities come in a number of varieties, but there are two main types.

An *immediate annuity* is one that you purchase with a single lump-sum amount. It begins paying benefits within thirty to ninety days of purchase.

A *deferred annuity*, by contrast, provides income starting at a specified future date, usually at retirement. Or you can also take a lump-sum withdrawal, if you prefer. You, as the owner of the annuity, have the right to decide when and how you want to take the money out.

You can purchase both immediate and deferred annuities either as *fixed annuities* or *variable annuities*. That is, with both types you can collect either fixed or variable returns. (However, variable immediate annuities aren't very common.)

By the way, none of the annuities we have been discussing are the same as a *tax-sheltered annuity* (TSA), which is a typical pension vehicle for teachers and other employees of certain nonprofit organizations. These annuities operate more like 401(k)s—that is, contributions are deducted from your salary and are tax-deferred until you withdraw them.

When you purchase a deferred annuity, you may make a single lump-sum payment to the issuer or you may make payments over time—monthly, quarterly, semi-annually, or annually.

Your payments can be deposited in a fixed account or in variable accounts, or a combination. In a fixed account, your principal and earnings are guaranteed by the insurance company. You can often choose the length of time the interest rate is guaranteed, from one year to as long as ten years.

In a variable account, you can generally decide to allocate your money among several mutual funds, including stock, bond, and money-market funds. You can decide how much to put in each option, or there are funds that decide for you; they change the proportion from time to time, based on economic conditions. There are also variable annuities that invest their funds in real estate. (There's more information on variable annuities in the "Question and Answer" section at the end of this chapter.)

When you begin receiving benefit payments from your nonqualified annuity, then each payment you receive is considered partly a return of your principal and partly your earnings on that principal. Only the earnings portions are subject to income taxation—and at ordinary tax rates. **Caution:** if you receive payment before age fifty-nine and a half, the earnings may be subject to a 10 percent IRS penalty tax.

Among the annuity payment options that you, as an owner, may choose are:

- A *straight-* or *pure-life annuity*, which unlike a period certain plan, pays as long as the person lives, regardless of how much he or she contributed to the annuity. This guarantee by the life insurance company of lifelong income is one of the principal advantages of an annuity contract.
- A *period certain plan* that pays benefits for a specified number of years, whether or not the person who buys the policy lives to collect them. If a person dies before receiving the total amount guaranteed, the balance goes to a beneficiary. Benefits stop at the end of the specified period.

  A life and period certain plan is a popular combination of the above. Benefits will continue for as long as the person lives, but at least as long as the specified period certain.
- A *joint* and *last survivor annuity*, the most common of the annuities that cover more than one person. These annuities are written to guarantee a joint payment to a couple and to continue payment until the death of the surviving spouse.

In addition to paying out benefits at some time in the future, many deferred annuities allow you to partially surrender the contract before annuity payments begin. The IRS treats amounts you receive from a surrendered contract first as fully taxable income to the extent of income on the contract. Amounts you receive in excess of the income from the contract are treated as a return of your investment and aren't taxed.

The amount of the surrender included in taxable income will also be subject to a 10 percent IRS penalty on the earnings of the contract if you withdraw the money before age fifty-nine and a half. After that age, you'll pay income tax, but no penalty. The penalty also doesn't apply if you die or become disabled.

What factors should you consider—besides the payout—when shopping for an annuity? You should check to see whether your issuer requires annual minimum deposits (usually $300 to $1,000) to keep up your policy.

Also, find out the size of the penalty the issuer charges for early withdrawal of funds (such as the partial surrenders we discussed). It's usually 6 to 7 percent of the amount you take out prematurely and often grades down over a period of years.

Finally, make sure to scrutinize the financial stability of your issuer. In recent years, some annuity holders were burned when their issuer went bankrupt. However, due to state insurance department guarantee fund arrangements, most policy holders got their money back after considerable delay.

In any case, you should feel confident that the company that sells you an annuity will meet its obligations down the road, when your income comes due.

One way to check on the financial health of your annuity company is check its listing in *A. M. Best's Insurance Reports*, which is available in most libraries. Also your insurance agent or financial adviser should have a copy.

A. M. Best publishes information about the insurance industry. Each year, it evaluates the financial health of some 1,700 insurance carriers and assigns them one of seven grades—from A^{+} to "omitted," which is the equivalent of failing. Many financial planners say you should do business only with carriers that are rated A or A^{+}.

A. M. Best cannot tell you what policy to buy, but at least it can take some of the risk out of choosing the right company with which to do business.

The primary reason to invest in annuities is they can offer policy holders tax-deferred savings growth; plus once you decide to take money out, you can receive income for the rest of your life, whether you live for two days or for thirty years after annuitization. Also, unlike IRAs, there are no limits on the amount you can contribute, and there isn't a lot of paperwork to complete when you want to start receiving payments. Annuities also offer relative safety.

One disadvantage of deferred annuities is the surrender charge imposed by the issuer and the IRS's 10 percent penalty if you withdraw your money before age fifty-nine and a half.

Recent tax-law changes may require you to aggregate separate annuity contracts that you purchase within the same year for income tax purposes. This rule could cause a greater proportion of any amount you receive from a contract to be taxed as ordinary income.

Also, management fees may sometimes be high for variable contracts. Here are the reasons. If you die early, you get at least your premium amount back even if your account value is less than you put in. And you have the right to purchase a guaranteed benefit rate. So the company that issues the annuity is taking on some risk.

Annuities are available from a variety of insurance carriers and are sold by financial planners, banks, insurance agents, and stockbrokers.

If you decide to move from one insurance company to another—in order to combine contracts, say—the tax law provides a method for you to do so without realizing any taxable income. This type of switch is known as a 1035 exchange, and you should work closely with your insurance representative or financial adviser to make sure the exchange is accomplished according to the IRS rules.

Now, to our rundown of tax-deferred retirement plans.

Individual Retirement Accounts

WHO: Almost anyone may establish and make contributions to an individual retirement account (IRA) for him- or herself. There are only two requirements. You must be younger than age seventy and a half, and you must have some compensation—that's income from wages, salary, or self-employment, as well as alimony payments or commissions. (If you're over age seventy and one half, you may set up a "rollover" IRA by rolling over a retirement plan distribution.) However, as we will see, not everyone may *deduct* an IRA contribution from his or her taxable income.

WHAT: An IRA resembles other tax-deferred retirement plans in that the earnings on the money you put aside aren't taxed until you withdraw them. So your investment can compound tax-deferred until you take it out at retirement.

The annual limit on IRA contributions? It's $2,000 per year or 100 percent of your earned income, whichever is less. You may establish and make contributions to an IRA for a spouse who doesn't have compensation or who has only a very small amount of compensation. You must use separate accounts, but together you may contribute as much as $2,250 in any combination you like. You may split it evenly, for instance, by contributing $1,125 to each. You just cannot contribute more than $2,000 to any account in any one year.

But who is allowed to *deduct* IRA contributions?

Here are the rules:

Uncle Sam says that if neither you nor your spouse actively participate in an employer-sponsored retirement plan, such as a 401(k), pension plan, or a profit-sharing plan for any part of the year, you may make fully tax-deductible contributions to an IRA. If either you or your spouse actively participate in an employer-sponsored retirement plan, you may still be eligible to make fully deductible or partially deductible IRA contributions, depending on how much income you have and your filing status.

Sounds simple enough? Yes, but figuring your eligibility can be a little tricky.

First, there's the issue of defining "actively partici-

CAN YOU TAKE AN IRA DEDUCTION?

If you ARE covered by a Retirement Plan at work and your filing status is:				
If your AGI is At least	But Less Than	Single or Head of Household	Married Filing Jointly (even if your spouse is covered by a plan at work)** Qualifying Widow(er)	Married Filing Separately*
		Deduction	Deduction	Deduction
$0	10,000	Full	Full	Partial
10,000	25,001	Full	Full	No
25,001	35,000	Partial	Full	No
35,000	40,001	No	Full	No
40,001	50,000	No	Partial	No
50,000 or over		No	No	No

Maximum deduction. You can deduct IRA contributions up to the amount of the deduction (full or partial) you can take, or 100% of your taxable compensation, whichever is less.

$200 floor. The partial deduction has a $200 floor. For example, if your deduction would have been reduced to less than $200 (but not zero), you can deduct IRA contributions up to $200 or 100% of your taxable compensation, whichever is less. If the deduction is completely phased out (reduced to zero), no deduction is allowed.

*If you did not live with your spouse at any time during the year, your filing status is considered, for this purpose, as Single or Head of Household (therefore your IRA deduction is determined under that column).

**You are entitled to the full deduction only if you did not live with your spouse at any time during the year. If you did live with your spouse during the year, you are, for this purpose, treated as though you are covered by a retirement plan at work. (Therefore, your IRA deduction is determined under the similar column heading of that section of the chart.)

pate." What the IRS really means is whether you are *eligible* to participate in an employer-sponsored plan or whether a contribution has been made for you to the plan. If so, even if your eligibility covers only a portion of the year and you're not vested in the plan, you're deemed to be an active participant. As an active participant, unless your income falls below certain levels, you may not make a deductible IRA contribution. (You may make a non-deductible contribution, though, which we will discuss below.)

Furthermore, if you and your spouse file jointly and if even one of you is eligible for an employer-sponsored retirement plan, then neither of you may make a deductible IRA contribution if your adjusted gross income totals more than $50,000.

Let's take the simplest case first. Assume that neither you nor your working spouse is eligible for an employer-sponsored retirement plan. Each of you may make a tax-deductible IRA contribution of as much as $2,000 or 100 percent of your earned income, whichever is less.

What if your joint filing spouse doesn't work outside the home (or earned less than $250 during the year)? Both of you may still make tax-deductible IRA contributions—to the working spouse's regular IRA and to a so-called spousal IRA. Together, the contributions may not total more than $2,250. You may split them any way you like—$1,500 in yours and $750 in your spouse's, for instance—but you cannot contribute more than $2,000 to either IRA.

A spousal IRA is better than no IRA, of course, but would it not be nice if both of you could sock away a full $2,000, tax-deferred? Here's an idea if you're a business owner. Think about hiring your nonworking spouse.

If you do, it has to be legitimate, of course. You may not pay him or her more than the going market rate for the work performed. You'll also both have to pay Social Security tax on the wages earned.

On the other hand, a spousal IRA provides the opportunity for tax strategizing. If one of you is significantly older than the other, you can keep the funds invested in an IRA (and thus earning free of tax) longer by putting the bulk of the money in the younger spouse's account. If, on the other hand, you want to be able to get at your money sooner rather than later, make the larger contribution to the older spouse's retirement fund.

So far we have been talking about joint filing couples. What about separate filers? That's a little more complicated.

If both of you have earned income and neither of you is eligible for an employer-sponsored plan, then you may each make tax-deductible IRA contributions—the lesser of $2,000 or the full amount of your earned income.

If one of you has earned income and the other doesn't, the spouse with the earned income may make a deductible IRA contribution. The other may not. In other words, there's no spousal IRA if you file separately.

And finally, what if both of you have compensation but one of you—your spouse, say—is eligible for an employer-sponsored retirement plan? Both of you are then considered to actively participate and neither of you may make a deductible contribution if your separate income goes over the $10,000 limit.

There's one other situation in which IRA deductions may be only partially deductible. That's when taxpayers are covered by employer-sponsored retirement plans but don't earn over certain limits.

Married couples filing jointly may deduct the full amount of their IRA contribution(s) until their joint incomes reach $40,000. Single taxpayers may do the same until their incomes hit $25,000.

But at those respective limits, for people covered by company retirement plans, IRA deductibility begins to decline. It ends completely when income climbs $10,000—to $50,000 for married couples filing jointly and to $35,000 for individuals.

In those ranges—between $40,000 to $50,000 and between $25,000 to $35,000—IRA contributions are only partially deductible.

Married couples filing jointly subtract their joint adjusted gross incomes (AGIs) from $50,000 and divide the remainder by $10,000. The resulting percentage is the portion of their maximum permissible IRA contribution that's deductible. Single individuals use $35,000 instead of $50,000.

AGI, for this purpose, means your income, including the taxable portion of your Social Security income, before you subtract your IRA contribution but after you deduct any investment losses and any Keogh contributions.

Case in point: Let's run through another example. Sam and Sarah together earned $42,000 and file jointly. Sam is covered by his company's retirement plan. Their IRA contribution is only partially deductible.

They subtract $42,000 from $50,000 and then divide the remaining $8,000 by $10,000. Eighty percent of each spouse's maximum possible $2,000 IRA contribution is deductible. Assuming that both earned at least $2,000, each may contribute as much as $2,000 to an IRA, $1,600 of which will be deductible. But if Sam puts $2,000 into his IRA (and Sarah contributes nothing), he can deduct only $1,600, even though their joint IRA deductible limit is $3,200.

The minimum deductible contribution for anyone in the partial zone (up to $50,000 or $35,000, joint or individual) is $200. In other words, anyone who earns less than the maximum limits may deduct at least that contribution. Who qualifies for a deductible IRA? Basically, people who don't have an employer-sponsored or qualified retirement plan or people who earn less than the limits we discussed.

If your employer offers a retirement plan, you're eligible to participate and/or receive a contribution on your behalf, and you make more than $50,000 ($35,000 if you're single) and file jointly, you may not deduct an

IRA contribution. Keep in mind: You don't have to be eligible for a benefit from your employer's plan; you just have to be included in the group of employees covered by the contribution made to the plan to lose some or all of your IRA deductibility.

But even if you're an active participant in an employer-sponsored plan, if your income falls below certain levels you may still be able to deduct some or all of your IRA contribution.

You may administer your IRA yourself, so far as the law is concerned. And by "administer," we aren't talking about just making investment decisions, but about the tax reporting and other required paperwork.

On the other hand, you can avoid the bother by paying practically any financial institution a small annual fee (almost always less than $50) to act as your IRA trustee or custodian and to manage the account for you. The fee is deductible as part of your miscellaneous itemized deductions (subject to the 2 percent floor) if you pay it out of non-IRA funds.

The only real drawback to placing your IRA with a trustee institution is that the institution will probably limit the types of investments you can make with the money in your account. Opening your IRA with a bank, for instance, may mean that you cannot buy stocks for your account.

The solution to that problem is to have more than one IRA. With just two or three, managed by different types of institutions, you can probably extend your investment opportunities into practically any area of interest. Just remember, you'll pay a separate custodial or trustee fee to each institution.

Buying and selling investment assets within an IRA is no different from investing in a non-IRA account, except that you don't pay taxes on capital gains or get an offset for capital gains. Trading is done in the usual way, and you pay the usual brokerage fees, if any. Naturally, the more trades you make, the more fees you pay. However, you pay no taxes on any capital gains that result from these trades.

But, let's say you want to switch assets from one IRA account to another, or move the whole account from one trustee to another. Well, that's a little more difficult. Uncle Sam keeps his eye on these moves.

If you move assets from one IRA to another—this is called a *custodial transfer*—and you never take possession of the assets yourself, then Uncle Sam doesn't care. You may do that, so far as the government is concerned, as often as you like. Just direct one trustee or custodian to transfer the assets to the other.

But if you take possession of the assets at any time during the transfer—this is called a *rollover*—then the government does care. Why? Because IRA assets are supposed to be locked up by law until you reach retirement age at fifty-nine and a half. If you want to withdraw them before then, as you'll recall, you almost always must pay a 10 percent penalty on the amount withdrawn.

So, to keep you from trying to get around this restriction by moving your IRA, the law says you may take temporary custody of the assets in a specific IRA during a rollover only once in any twelve-month period. And, you may hold onto them for no more than fifty-nine days.

Let's say you took all the cash out of one IRA and held it for some period of time less than sixty days. Then you placed the cash in another IRA. That move is perfectly legal, and you don't owe any penalties or taxes. In effect, you have borrowed your own IRA funds for fifty-nine days. But for the next twelve months, you may not roll over any other assets from that first IRA.

If you have more than one IRA, you may "borrow" any or all of the assets in each, but no more than once in any twelve-month period per IRA and for no longer than fifty-nine days. Once you have rolled over even a portion of an IRA, you may not roll over any other part of that IRA for twelve months.

Borrowing, in the conventional sense of the word, from

your IRA is restricted by law. Just like early withdrawal, borrowing will cost you tax on the amount "borrowed" plus a 10 percent penalty. This restriction even applies to using IRA assets as collateral for a loan. Borrow against, as well as from, your IRA and you'll get hit with the 10 percent penalty in addition to ordinary income tax on the amount borrowed or pledged.

Finally, what if you want to borrow in the opposite direction? That is, what if you want to borrow money in order to make an IRA contribution? Is the interest on the loan deductible? It depends. If you use the money directly to make the investment, the interest counts as investment interest and is deductible subject to the investment interest expense limitation.

WHY: As we saw, the big catch with IRAs is that not everyone may make tax-deductible contributions to one. If you're not one of those, the money you place in your IRA has to be after-tax money. So why bother?

Because the interest and dividends that your IRA investments earn accumulate free of tax until you withdraw them at retirement. So, whether the tax laws allow you to deduct your annual contributions or not, an IRA is still a way of helping your retirement dollars grow faster than they would if they were subject to normal taxation.

Plus, some people like the idea of establishing a "forced" savings plan. By counting on making a certain contribution each year, they know that money is earmarked for their retirement nest egg.

WHY NOT: If you cannot deduct the contribution to your IRA, some people say, why contribute to one? The argument against making nondeductible IRA contributions? Just that: they aren't deductible, so you don't reduce your current taxes at all. Furthermore, once you have put money into an IRA, you cannot get it out again unless you die or become disabled (without paying the tax plus a 10 percent early withdrawal penalty) until you have reached age fifty-nine and a half.

When you pay the tax at that age (without the penalty), you may be in a lower tax bracket. An alternative to an IRA would be a tax-deferred annuity, which offers the benefits of tax deferral without the reporting requirements. It also allows you to invest more than the $2,000 IRA limit. (We covered annuities earlier in this chapter.)

Maybe you don't want to keep your capital tied up that long just for the sake of tax-deferred earnings. You can get the same federal tax break without locking up your cash by investing in tax-free municipal bonds or in mutual funds that themselves invest in these securities.

Of course the return on munis may not be as high as you would earn on other investments. Moreover, you do risk losing some of the value of your investment if you choose to liquidate your position after a drop in market value. Still, it's an alternative to consider.

On the other hand, you would also lose value inside your IRA if the investment vehicle you chose was stocks and bonds and you had to take a distribution. So the timing issue is a wash from this point of view.

WHERE: When it comes to defining where you should put your IRA investment, it's easier to first say where you shouldn't. You shouldn't invest IRA funds in securities, such as municipal bonds and municipal bond funds, that are already tax-free. You don't gain any tax advantage that way. Not only that, you'll pay tax on your investment and its earnings when you take them out.

Otherwise, any investment that makes sense for you—given your tolerance for risk and your financial goals—is an appropriate IRA investment. Remember that the securities in your IRA are just a part of your total investment portfolio.

It can make just as much sense for one individual to invest IRA funds in high-risk growth stocks as for another to buy nothing but high-grade corporate bonds with IRA dollars.

The law does contain a few prohibitions. You may not

use IRA funds to buy assets from yourself or to purchase stock in a company that you already own.

Also, you may not invest your IRA funds in art objects, antiques, stamps, or other so-called collectibles. As for gold and silver coins, the only ones allowed by law for IRA inclusion are the gold and silver Eagles minted by the U.S. Treasury. Finally, you may not invest your IRA assets in life insurance.

WHEN: You can make a current year's annual IRA contribution any time after January 1. But you must deposit money in your account no later than April 15 of the next year—the date your tax return is due. You get no extensions for making your contribution—even if you obtain an extension for filing your taxes.

Keogh Plans

WHO: If you have self-employment income, you may be able to make a tax-deductible Keogh contribution.

WHAT: Keogh plans come in two basic flavors; one is called a defined-benefit plan, the other, a defined-contribution plan. Then there are two main variations of the defined-contribution plan: profit-sharing plans and money-purchase plans.

With defined-contribution plans, the law sets limits on the size of your annual Keogh contribution. With profit-sharing plans, the limit is 15 percent of your net self-employment income. With money-purchase plans, you may contribute up to 25 percent of your net income or $30,000 from self-employment.

Why are we emphasizing "net" self-employment income? Because the rule can be confusing. What the IRS means is that you figure the percentage after you have deducted the amount of the contribution. Here's an example that should make this point clear.

Let's say that you earned $23,000 net of all expenses other than the Keogh contribution by consulting outside of your regular job. You contribute $3,000 to your profit-sharing Keogh. Is that the maximum 15 percent contribution the law allows? Indeed it is.

Subtract the $3,000 contribution from your $23,000 gross self-employment income. What you have left is $20,000, your self-employment income net of the Keogh contribution, and $3,000 is exactly 15 percent of this net amount.

The calculations for money-purchase plans work the same way, the only difference being that you may sock away as much as 25 percent of your net self-employment income.

Actually, now that you understand what the rule is, there's an easier way to apply it. Just figure that you may set aside 13.043 percent of your gross self-employment income into a profit-sharing Keogh or as much as 20 percent into a money-purchase Keogh. This shortcut makes the calculation a lot easier and yields the same results. We will use this technique in our examples to follow.

As a practical matter, the difference between a profit-sharing and a money-purchase plan is this: The money-purchase plan lets you make a larger annual Keogh contribution (as much as 20 percent), but it requires you to contribute the same percentage of your net self-employment income every year—whether you want to or not.

With a profit-sharing plan, in contrast, your maximum annual contribution is smaller (13.043 percent), but you may contribute that amount, less, or nothing at all as you wish, as long as you make what the IRS calls "substantial and reoccurring" contributions over several years.

Tip: There's a neat little trick you can use to give you the benefits of both kinds of Keoghs—the greater contribution of the money-purchase type and the flexibility of the profit-sharing type.

Open two Keoghs, one a money-purchase and the other a profit-sharing plan. Set up your money-purchase plan so that you agree to contribute 8 percent of your annual net self-employment income.

When you combine this amount with the 12 percent that you may contribute to your profit-sharing plan, you have created a very flexible program. With this arrangement you have allowed yourself the privilege of putting away a full 20 percent of your self-employment income—as much as you could if you had only a money-purchase plan. But you're obligated only to contribute the smaller amount—8 percent.

While the defined-contribution Keogh puts limits on what goes into your retirement account, a defined-benefit plan, the other kind of Keogh, allows you to contribute whatever is necessary to achieve the retirement benefit you want. What's limited by law isn't so much the contribution, but the annual retirement benefit.

In 1989 it may not exceed the lesser of $98,064 (a figure that's adjusted for inflation annually) or 100 percent of your average annual earnings during the three consecutive years in which your earnings were the highest.

Once you have determined the benefit you want to achieve, you have to hire an actuary to figure out the contribution required to fund that benefit. This figure will change annually, depending upon the actual and projected performance of the investments in your defined-benefit Keogh account. However, you should be prepared to make substantial contributions each year.

Don't try to figure the contribution yourself. To begin with, the IRS won't permit it. In any case, it's a difficult calculation.

By the way, there are limits that apply to your contribution to a defined-benefit plan. For one, it may not be greater than your net self-employment income for the year.

So, which type of Keogh—defined-contribution or defined-benefit—is the better retirement plan for you? Of course, it depends on your circumstances.

In general, younger people should stick with defined-contribution plans. The other sort are much more difficult to administer, and the fees associated with defined-benefit plans are considerably higher.

But, as you get older, there comes a point at which a defined-benefit plan is a better deal. How is that? Well, it lets you put away more each year than you could with a defined-contribution plan.

(You should know, however, that you cannot just change from a profit-sharing plan that you have maintained for many years to a defined-benefit plan, because you're now older. The defined-benefit plan would be restricted, based on the amount you had historically contributed to the profit-sharing plan. The actual calculation is very complex.)

Many of the rules regarding Keogh investments, management, and administration are the same as those governing IRAs.

You may manage the Keogh yourself, subject to the tax code, or you may hire a Keogh trustee or custodian—usually a financial institution—to manage it for you. All the same advantages and disadvantages that we discussed in the section above on IRA managers apply here as well.

As for borrowing from or against your Keogh—don't do it.

WHY: A Keogh is an excellent way for people with self-employment income to sock away funds for retirement and gain a tax deferral at the same time. Except in the circumstance we describe below, it makes sense to fund your Keogh to the maximum possible.

WHY NOT: Here's one disadvantage to Keoghs. If you have employees, you must also cover them in your Keogh plan. Also, a Keogh is just like any other qualified pension plan in limiting your use of an IRA. But that's the only hitch. You may make the maximum allowed deductible contributions to a Keogh and still participate in other, non-IRA, pension plans sponsored by your employer (provided you're not the majority owner of that company).

Sometimes, for some people, a Keogh isn't a very good deal. They would be better off with an IRA. Let's say you earned $5,000 in net self-employment income. The largest Keogh contribution you could make probably would be $1,000—20 percent of $5,000. But, if you're eligible to make tax-deductible IRA contributions, you could put away $2,000. This is because IRA contributions can be as great as 100 percent of earned income up to a limit of $2,000.

So, as long as your self-employment income is less than $10,000, an IRA might be better for you than a Keogh. Of course, if you're not eligible to deduct your IRA contribution, you should probably stick with the Keogh.

WHERE: The same investment restrictions—and more—that apply to IRAs apply to Keoghs. If you do invest Keogh dollars into a prohibited investment asset—Oriental carpets, for instance—the IRS treats the amount of that investment as an early withdrawal, and you pay the 10 percent penalty.

Almost any investment that makes economic sense is a good Keogh investment. As with IRAs, though, you don't want to buy tax-free securities for your Keogh account. Not only would this strategy gain you nothing, but you eventually pay tax (when you withdraw the funds at retirement) on what should have been tax-free income. Also, unlike IRA, you may use life insurance as a Keogh investment, subject to certain restrictions.

You may make noncash Keogh contributions—stocks, mutual funds, and so forth. But the rules here are complex. Don't attempt this type of contribution without professional advice, and the best advice may be not to attempt it at all.

WHEN: Make sure that you set up your Keogh by the end of your fiscal year, usually December 31 of the year in which you want to make your first contribution. The law says that you must. But you don't have to make the actual contribution until the tax-filing date for that year, or, if you get one, until the date of your filing extension.

You must make contributions to defined-benefit plans quarterly.

Employer-Sponsored Retirement Plans

WHO: By definition, you have to work for someone else to participate in one of these plans. And, of course, your employer has to offer a plan.

WHAT: Except for 401(k) plans, which we discuss next, qualified retirement plans sponsored by employers don't offer you—the employee—many choices. Basically, you get the plan that comes with the job.

Of course, that doesn't mean that employer-sponsored plans aren't a good deal. They are. After all, your employer is making the contribution for you. Employer-sponsored retirement plans come in the same two varieties: defined-contribution plans and defined-benefit plans.

With a defined-contribution plan, your employer contributes a certain amount each year (as specified in the plan) on your behalf. With a defined-benefit plan, the plan defines the amount you receive each year after you retire.

WHY: Uncle Sam doesn't tax either the contributions made on your behalf or the earnings that accumulate until you receive them from your retirement account. You pay no tax until you receive a distribution from your retirement plan.

WHY NOT: There's no good reason not to participate in an employer-sponsored plan. In fact, you usually have no choice.

WHERE: Employees rarely have too much choice about how their retirement funds are invested and who manages those investments in a typical employer-sponsored plan. The company may set up a plan to give employees the right to choose from three to five investment options.

WHEN: Generally, your employer makes an annual contribution for each eligible year. You're vested in the plan—that is, you're entitled at retirement or termination of employment to collect what has been set aside for you—after five years of continuous employment with the company.

401(k) Plans

WHO: You're eligible to participate in a 401(k) plan if your company has adopted one, and you meet the plan's eligibility requirements.

WHAT: 401(k) plans, whose name comes from a section of the tax code, is really a hybrid type of retirement plan. This is because your company sponsors it, but you and your employer can make contributions to it on your behalf.

With a 401(k) plan, you choose to make contributions up to the limit allowed by law and by the plan. Your salary is reduced by the amount of these contributions. In general, you may contribute as much as 15 percent of your annual salary up to a maximum of $7,627 in 1989, an amount that's annually adjusted for inflation. Your plan, however, may set lower limits.

As we saw, your employer may contribute, too, as either a matching contribution or as a profit-sharing type contribution. (In fact, your employer may contribute even if you don't.) Between the two of you, the total contribution may not exceed $30,000 annually, or 25 percent of your salary. (This amount is reduced if your employer also has other plans in which you participate.)

WHY: 401(k)s are among the best deals around for building up retirement income relatively painlessly. Your contribution reduces your wages for federal income tax each pay period. Of course, the amount that goes into your 401(k) isn't taxed currently by the federal government. You don't pay income taxes until you withdraw your money, usually upon retirement.

WHY NOT: If you have the chance to participate in a 401(k) plan, take advantage of it—to the maximum possible. It's a painless and effective way to save for your retirement years. The sole objection some people have to investing money in a 401(k): they aren't comfortable with locking up their money until age fifty-nine and a half. However, most plans allow you to borrow against your investment for such "emergencies" as purchasing a principal residence.

WHERE: Your plan document states whether participants may direct the investments in their account. If they can, employees may choose from a list of investments provided by the plan administrator, which is usually the company. How the funds in your company-sponsored 401(k) are invested is up to the individual who administers the plan for the company. He or she will work with an investment management firm. Some plans offer you a choice of investment types—growth-oriented or fixed-income, for instance. Others offer you specific mutual funds from which to choose. If you have a choice, you should make your selection according to the same criteria you would use for any other type of retirement investment.

Simplified Employee Pension Plans

WHO: You can open a Simplified Employee Pension plan—called a SEP, or SEP-IRA if you're self-employed, or your employer can open one for you if you're eligible.

WHAT: Like 401(k)s, SEPs are another hybrid plan. They work on many of the same principles as IRAs, except your employer also makes contributions to the plan. The contribution limits are the same as for any profit-sharing plan.

That is, the business or employer for which you work may contribute as much as 15 percent of your salary or $30,000, whichever is less, to a SEP. Whatever amount it contributes, it may deduct that amount from its taxes, and the contribution isn't taxed as income to you.

You may also make tax-deductible contributions yourself to a SEP-IRA. The annual limit? Fifteen percent of your pay up to a maximum of $7,627. This limit becomes 15 percent of your net self-employment income if you're self-employed.

WHY: In a SEP, earnings accumulate untaxed, just as in an IRA, until you begin to withdraw them at retirement. Contributions to a SEP are excluded from an employee's income, and are deductible by the employer.

WHY NOT: If you're self-employed and have employees, it might make more sense for you to contribute to a Keogh plan. Here's why.

The initial eligibility requirement for employees may be more stringent for SEPs than it is for Keoghs. However, after the employee meets these requirements, all employees with more than about $300 in earnings would have to receive a contribution. Also, a Keogh plan can have a vesting schedule.

WHERE: SEPs are just like IRAs. So you may invest your money anywhere you can invest IRA funds.

WHEN: You or your employer must make your SEP contribution by the tax-filing due date for the company.

Questions and Answers

I'm considering purchasing a fixed annuity. How is the money paid out?

A fixed annuity is—as the name suggests—an annuity that pays you a specified amount based upon a fixed rate of return on the money you deposit.

You choose when to receive your regular payments—monthly, say, or quarterly, or even annually. The decision is yours.

These annuities are for the safety-conscious investor, since you receive guaranteed principal and interest. This type of annuity invests in fixed-rate instruments.

I'm considering purchasing a variable annuity. How is the money paid out?

A variable-dollar annuity pays you a fluctuating amount based upon the investment performance of an underlying pool of assets. In this sense, it operates similarly to an equity or bond mutual fund.

With a variable annuity, you can decide in what kind of underlying assets the plan is to be invested—in stocks, for example, or bonds, or mutual funds that are offered by the insurance company. The issuing company may also offer investments in money-market, real estate, precious metals, and junk bond funds.

You decide how to invest—and you may transfer between options without getting hit by a tax.

Your income from the plan fluctuates with the earnings on the underlying investments. If the investment is in stocks and the market declines, so, too, will your annuity income. This investment risk is borne by you, the policy holder, not by the insurance company or financial institution that issues the annuity. For this reason, this vehicle might be more suitable for younger people.

Tip: You should know that a variable annuity is riskier than a fixed annuity, because your return isn't guaranteed. (There are, however, combination annuities which are, in effect, variable annuities that also provide a fixed guaranteed option.)

CHAPTER 27

WHAT YOU NEED TO KNOW ABOUT SOCIAL SECURITY

When calculating your post-retirement income, you shouldn't forget the obvious. The obvious? Your Social Security benefits. Almost everyone is eligible for them, and while they won't support a jet-set lifestyle, they are far from negligible.

How far from negligible?

In this chapter, we will show you—in question-and-answer form—how to make sure that you're eligible and how to double-check your eligibility and account balance with the Social Security Administration. We will also show you how to calculate your benefits and what effect post-retirement earnings have on benefit levels.

One point before we begin. Despite the alarms of years past, the Social Security system is considered in good shape these days. If you're entitled to collect these benefits—and most of us are or will be—you need not fear that the government coffers will be empty when your turn arrives.

Your Social Security Benefits

What kind of benefits does the Social Security system provide?

The Social Security system provides four types of benefits. These are: medical insurance, or Medicare, which begins at age sixty-five; disability benefits that you can collect if you're unable to work for a prolonged period of time (your spouse and children can also collect payments); survivor's benefits for a spouse, minor children, and dependent elderly parents of a covered worker; and retirement benefits for workers and for spouses and dependent children of retirees.

When did Social Security begin?
Social Security was enacted into law with the Social Security Act of 1935.

Who is covered by the Social Security system?
Most employees who work in private industry and members of the United States armed services are covered by Social Security. So are most self-employed people.

Federal employees who were hired after December 31, 1983, are covered by a new three-tier retirement system that includes Social Security as one of its components. Members of Congress who were elected after that date are also covered under the new system.

How is Social Security funded?
The Social Security system is funded by a combination of employer and employee contributions. For 1990 and beyond, a company is required by law to pay 7.65 percent of an employee's earnings into Social Security; you as an employee are required to match that contribution. The government, however, puts a lid on the amount of annual earnings that are subject to Social Security tax.

In 1989, that ceiling came to $48,000; in 1990 the ceiling is scheduled to be $51,300. And the ceiling is recalculated every year.

In 1990, if you're self-employed, you will pay a self-employment tax of 15.30 percent on your net income from self-employment. However, you'll also be eligible for a deduction that equals one half of your self-employment tax liability. So, if you're in the 28 percent tax bracket, your self-employment tax will come to 13.16 percent ([72 percent of 7.65 percent] + 7.65 percent).

The Social Security tax is known as FICA, which stands for the Federal Insurance Contributions Act.

The tax you pay as a self-employed individual is known, appropriately enough, as a *self-employment tax*.

Whatever they are called, however, they are both taxes that go toward funding Social Security benefits.

When may you start collecting Social Security retirement benefits?

You're entitled to full benefits if you retire at your "retirement age"—that is, age sixty-five for people retiring today (see the discussion below). You can collect reduced benefits if you apply at age sixty-two.

Here's how the system works. Your benefits are reduced by about 0.5 percent for every month before your retirement age that you begin receiving them.

However, the reverse is true as well. If you wait to collect benefits until after your retirement age, the amount you'll collect increases. The benefits go up for each month after you turn sixty-five and before age seventy that you postpone your benefits.

You should know, however, that in 1983 the law was changed. The age at which workers can collect full benefits was altered to sixty-seven. This change won't take effect all at once. If you were born before 1938, you won't be affected by it at all.

Say, however, you were born between 1938 and 1942. In this case, you'll have to wait an extra two months for each year after 1937 to collect full benefits. So, if you were born in 1940, you'll have to wait until age sixty-five and six months. If you were born between 1943 and 1954, you'll have to wait until you reach age sixty-six to collect full benefits.

If you were born in 1960 or later, you'll have to be sixty-seven years old before you can collect in full.

How do you become eligible for Social Security retirement benefits?

The federal government has a complicated "quarters of coverage" system that determines when you'll be eligible for most benefits under Social Security.

But here's the bottom line. If you have credit for ten years of work, you're guaranteed full coverage, no matter if you never work another moment.

(If you're age sixty-two in 1989 and want to receive benefits, you need to have worked only nine and a half years; in 1990, you need to have worked only nine and three-quarters years.)

What factors determine how much Social Security income you will collect?

Uncle Sam determines your benefits by your average earnings compared to the maximum earnings covered during your working lifetime and the average earnings for all workers during that period. The formula is very complex, but the bottom line is that the more money you put into the system, the more you can take out. Your benefits aren't limited by how wealthy you may be. As long as you qualify and your earned income remains below certain limits ($9,360 for persons age sixty-five through sixty-nine in 1990), you collect full benefits.

Also, if you and your spouse are both eligible, you'll receive benefits independently of one another. (A working spouse with very low earnings may collect more in the form of spousal benefits.) However, a spouse who doesn't work outside the home will receive one half of your benefits as long as you live or 100 percent of your benefits after you die. A surviving spouse will collect survivor benefits if he or she is age sixty or older.

Even in the best of circumstances, Social Security income doesn't begin to cover all your retirement needs—it doesn't even come close. So it's critical that you think

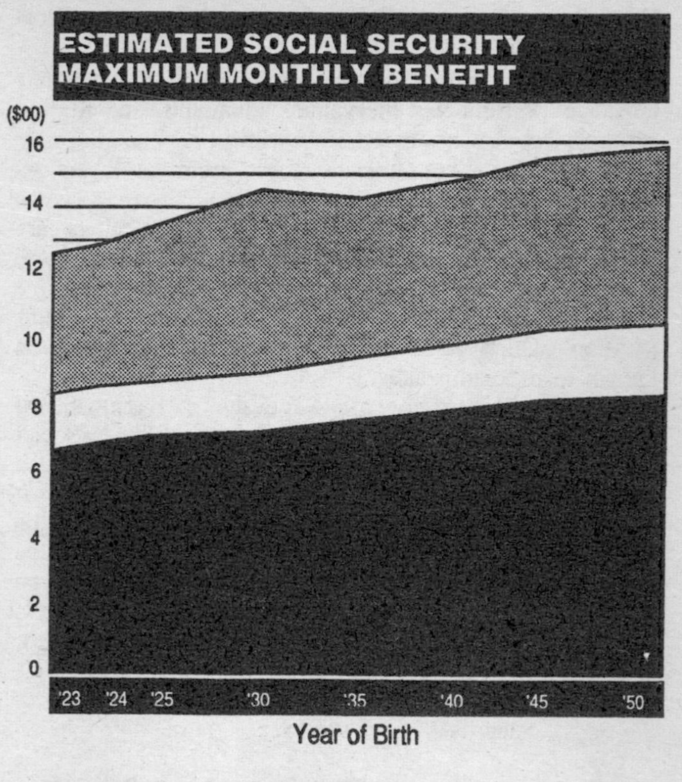

of it only as a supplement to your other retirement income.

Accurately predicting future Social Security benefits is difficult, since they depend on your exact earnings and changes in the economy. The chart above assumes your wages keep pace with national averages.

How can you make sure your earnings record is correct?
The Social Security Administration, which is headquartered in Baltimore, Maryland, maintains records of earnings for every individual with a Social Security number. It gets these earnings reports from employers or, if you're self-employed, from the IRS.

It's a good idea to check that your earnings are accurate. We suggest you do it once every three years, so you'll have plenty of time to correct any errors. We don't want to be alarmist, but the Social Security Administration, which is an enormous bureaucracy, has been known to make mistakes.

You should ask for a "Request for Earnings and Benefit Estimate Statement" from your local Social Security office. Or call 1-800-234-5772 (you can also obtain a free copy of the booklet *Social Security: How It Works for You* by calling the same number). Fill out the form the office will send you, and within two to three weeks, you should receive a response. The statement you get back shows your Social Security earnings history, tells you how much you have paid in Social Security taxes, estimates your future Social Security benefits in today's dollars, and provides some general information about how the Social Security system works.

Are Social Security payments indexed to inflation?
Yes, they are.

How often do you receive payments?
You can count on receiving a check every month after you retire. The government tries to mail the checks so they arrive by the third day of the month.

How do you begin collecting benefits?
You file an application for benefits with the office of the Social Security Administration that's nearest your home. You should apply two or three months before you expect

to begin collecting. That way, you won't have to undergo an unnecessary delay.

Also, you must prove your age. So make sure to bring with you a copy of your birth certificate or a hospital birth record. The administration will also accept a baptismal certificate.

Will you pay tax on your Social Security benefits? Unfortunately, if your "modified adjusted gross income" exceeds a certain amount—$32,000 for a married couple filing jointly and $25,000 for a single filer—you may have to include up to half your Social Security income in your taxable income.

Here's how it works.

Essentially, if your adjusted gross income (AGI) plus half your Social Security benefits tops $32,000 for a married couple filing jointly and $25,000 for a single filer, part of your benefit payments becomes taxable. Also, any tax-exempt interest you may earn is added to your AGI for this purpose.

The taxable part comes to either one half of your benefits or one half of the difference between the total calculated above and the ceiling amount we mentioned above—whichever is less. Here's an example.

Say you're married and your AGI before adding in your Social Security benefits comes to $50,000. (You have no tax-exempt income.) One half of your Social Security benefits equals $5,000. So your income for the taxability test comes to $55,000.

This amount is more than the $32,000 ceiling, so you must pay taxes on some of your benefits. How much?

We subtract the ceiling amount—$32,000—from your taxability test income of $55,000 and get $23,000. One half the difference is $11,500. Half your benefits—$5,000—is less than half of that difference, or $11,500. So you must pay taxes at your regular rates on the $5,000.

Do you lose your Social Security benefits if you work? Unfortunately, in 1990 you can lose all or part of your monthly benefits if you're older than age sixty-four but under age seventy and your earnings are more than $9,360. You can also lose some of your benefits if you're under age sixty-five for the whole year and your earnings top $6,840 in 1990.

How much do you lose?

It depends on the amount you earn over these ceilings. In 1990, Uncle Sam subtracts $1 of benefits for each $3 in earnings above these limits. But the first year you become eligible for benefits, the government also applies a monthly test.

If, in 1990, you retire at age sixty-five, you're entitled to collect full benefits for any month in which you earn less than $780. It doesn't matter what your total earnings are for the year.

If you retire between sixty-two and sixty-four, you lose no benefits in any month during this first year that your monthly earnings don't top $570.

CHAPTER 28

TAKING YOUR MONEY OUT

So far, we have looked at the ways in which you may accumulate a nest egg for retirement. And we have examined the types of plans, including Social Security, that help you build up funds for these later years.

You need to know one more basic fact about your retirement income: how to take assets *out* of your plans. You'll see that there are some hard-and-fast rules you must follow. But you have some choices, too.

In this chapter, we take a look at the most common questions and answers individuals have about withdrawing money from their retirement plans.

What options do you have when it comes to withdrawing your money from a retirement plan?
Individual plan documents stipulate how distributions may be made from the plan. You may take your money out at retirement as defined in the plan or even, perhaps, before retirement. In most plans, you may also choose whether to take your money out in one lump sum or spread your withdrawals over time. All of these choices involve consequences, which we will discuss below.

Is it necessary to see an accountant or other financial adviser before taking out your retirement money?
This is one area where it nearly always makes sense to do so. The rules governing withdrawals can get quite

complicated. And mistakes you may make could follow you, literally, for the rest of your life.

Are there any general differences among the types of plans when it comes to withdrawing money?

Yes, there are. The rules are different for each type of plan. For example, usually a pension plan may not make a distribution to an employee who hasn't left the company. But a profit-sharing plan may be able to, depending on the actual terms of the plan document.

Is there any rule against taking too much money out of a plan?

Unfortunately, there is. As a general rule, you must pay a 15 percent penalty tax on the excess if, in one calendar year, you receive as income one or more distribution of more than $150,000 from all your retirement plans. The rule applies to the total you receive from all of the following: IRAs, qualified retirement plans, and tax-sheltered annuities. It doesn't matter if you're over fifty-nine and one half or under that age.

Also, you pay the same IRS penalty tax on the excess if you take a lump-sum distribution and use the special tax calculation for lump-sum distributions that top $750,000.

What are the advantages and disadvantages of taking your retirement plan savings in one lump sum?

The advantage is you get your money all at once. Depending on your employment status, age, income, and financial obligations, you can then pay taxes on your payout and use the money to buy mutual-fund shares, say, or municipal bonds to boost your retirement income.

The disadvantage, of course, is that you also must pay taxes all at once on that lump sum. When it comes to an IRA or a SEP, amounts withdrawn during a tax year are subject to ordinary income taxes.

Uncle Sam gives you a break with qualified plans,

however. You may be able to use five-year averaging—or, in certain circumstances, ten-year averaging—which means you may pay less federal income tax.

Here's how five-year averaging works. You pay your tax in one year. But the tax is calculated as if you had received your money over a period of five years. And this means the tax is often less.

You should know, however, that you may use special averaging only once in your lifetime.

And the law says you may not use averaging until you receive a lump-sum distribution after age fifty-nine and a half. (However, if you had already reached age fifty by January 1, 1986, you're exempt—or "grandfathered" from this rule.)

So, if you receive your money before you reach this age, you should consider rolling it over into an IRA or annuity or another qualified retirement plan. If you don't, you will not only pay tax but also fork over a 10 percent penalty tax for early withdrawal, unless you meet a specific exception to the penalty tax.

Uncle Sam also makes your ability to use five-year averaging dependent on a number of other conditions. Among these: you must have actively participated in the plan for five full years before the tax year you take your distribution, and you must receive your distribution from all plans of the same type from the same employer within a single tax year. Also, you have to receive the distribution due to death, disability (if you're self-employed), retirement, or termination of service (unless you're self-employed).

The five-year averaging rules weren't enacted until the Tax Reform Act of 1986. So, if you were born on or before January 1, 1936, you may use either five- or ten-year averaging. (However, if you take the ten-year option, you must use tax rates that were in effect in 1986.)

Usually, using averaging will pay off, unless your retirement fund is more than $450,000 (for five-year averaging) or more than $473,700 (for ten-year averaging).

If you're eligible for both five- and ten-year averaging, you must run the numbers to see which method would be more advantageous.

What is the other option you can take?

If you don't take a lump-sum distribution, you may take out your money over time. Known as an annuity, this option pays out the money in your employer-sponsored pension plan over your lifetime. Two common types of annuities are a joint and survivor annuity and a life annuity. The former pays benefits until both the employee and his or her spouse or other beneficiary die; the latter pays benefits only while the employee is alive.

In many plans, you can also receive periodic payments at a rate or amount you select that isn't designed to continue payments through your entire life.

In any case, all *deductible* contributions you made to the plan and all earnings are fully taxable when you receive your annuity payment. (This rule, of course, doesn't apply to nondeductible contributions.) Your plan administrator will tell you your exclusion ratio—that is, the ratio of your nondeductible contributions to the total value of your plan benefit.

You then multiply your annual annuity payment by this ratio to see how much of your payout is tax-free.

What about making early withdrawals?

As a general rule, if you withdraw money from your retirement fund early—usually before you reach age fifty-nine and a half—you'll pay, in addition to taxes, a hefty 10 percent early withdrawal penalty tax. This situation might crop up, for example, when you leave one company for another.

How do you avoid this penalty tax?

One way is to roll over the taxable portion of your lump-sum distribution into an IRA, a Keogh, or another qualified retirement plan within sixty days from the time you receive it. Also, if you die, your spouse must roll over a distribution from your retirement plan to an IRA within sixty days of receipt in order to avoid current taxes.

You can also partially avoid a IRS penalty tax if you use your distribution to pay for deductible medical expenses that total more than 7.5 percent of your adjusted gross income. No penalty is due on the amount in excess of the 7.5 percent calculation. (This exception doesn't apply to distributions from an IRA or SEP, however.)

Nor will you pay the penalty tax if you receive your benefits in the form of an annuity that's spread out over your life or the joint lives of yourself and your designated beneficiary. To qualify, you must receive payments at least annually, and they must be about equal in size. Also, these benefits must continue for at least five years or until age fifty-nine and a half, whichever is longer.

Four other situations exempt you from paying the penalty tax: you retire after you reach age fifty-five, and the plan allows for distributions (this rule doesn't apply to IRAs); you received distributions from an Employee Stock Ownership Plan (ESOP) before January 1, 1990; you receive distributions after you become disabled; or your beneficiary receives distributions after you die.

Do you have to begin making withdrawals at some point?

Yes. You must begin taking minimum required annual payouts from an employer-sponsored pension plan, IRA, and tax sheltered annuity (TSA) no later than April 1 following the year you reach age seventy and a half. This rule applies even if you retire after that age. Each year after the year you turned age $70\frac{1}{2}$, you're required to take a distribution by December 31.

If you don't begin taking distributions—or enough in distributions—by that age, you must pay a 50 percent nondeductible penalty tax on the difference between the amount you're required to take and the amount you actually receive.

(The amount you're required to take each year is based on specific formulas and tables that estimate life expectancies.)

How does the Retirement Equity Act affect me?

Congress adopted this act in 1984 to address the concerns of spouses, ex-spouses, and survivors of spouses. According to this law, an employer must automatically offer survivor benefits to the spouse of any employee who dies with vested benefits in the employer's pension plan.

If you die before you retire, your spouse receives your vested interest in the plan in the form of an annuity. He or she receives the first payment in the year you would have reached retirement age had you lived.

Also, the act mandates that employees must secure their spouses' approval in writing and notarized before they can opt out of these survivor benefits. In the past, an employee could cancel his or her spouse's survivor benefits without the spouse knowing a thing about it.

The act also reduced the age at which employers must allow eligible employees to participate in their pension plans. Eligible workers must be included in a plan as soon as they reach age twenty-one and have completed a year of service. Further, an employer must begin counting an employee's years of service for vesting purposes—that is, the right to receive further benefits in the future from a plan—after the age of eighteen.

Say a participating employee leaves a company, then returns. The act mandates that the employee must receive credit for the first years he or she worked. This rule doesn't apply, however, if the "break in service" is five years or is more than the number of years the employee first worked for the company, whichever is greater.

New parents may take a year of leave without this time counting as a break in service.

Finally, because of the act's provisions, courts now

have the authority to distribute part of an employee's pension to a former spouse as part of a divorce settlement.

May you borrow money from your pension plan?
Under some circumstances, you may borrow from your 401(k). However it depends on the rules of your plan.

If you do borrow, you must repay the loan within five years. If you don't, Uncle Sam considers the money a distribution. The only time this rule doesn't apply is when you buy a principal residence. Also, you must make your repayments of both principal and interest in equal installments and at least quarterly.

You should know that the law imposes a ceiling on how much you may borrow. Usually the ceiling is one half your interest in the plan. Under no circumstances, however, may you borrow more than $50,000.

How should you invest a lump-sum distribution from your employer's pension plan?
Naturally, you want to keep intact this nest egg that may have been accumulating over a lifetime. However, many people find themselves wrestling alone with the sudden responsibility of managing more money than they have ever seen in their lives.

Uncle Sam's rollover deadlines heighten the pressure to find places to invest lump-sum distributions that individuals may receive when they terminate employment. As you know, once you receive your check, you have only sixty days to decide whether to roll over your money into an IRA or do something else with it. This time pressure often makes people react emotionally and invest without really thinking through the consequences.

Information overload can also cause a problem for new retirees. After all, looking at dozens of prospectuses from many different companies is confusing and frustrating. At that point the urge to make a move—sometimes any move—can be overwhelming.

There are a number of options available, such as rolling some or all of the money into an IRA or paying tax on the entire distribution and investing the balance in a selection of investments that meets your retirement needs.

By rolling over the taxable portion of a lump-sum distribution into an IRA, you avoid paying any current tax on the amount rolled over. And you get flexibility as well. You can use an IRA rollover to, in effect, create your own personal retirement plan. Also, at a later time you could roll over the IRA to another qualified plan, if no other money has been commingled with the rollover IRA.

As you know, you must make minimum required withdrawals for each year once you reach age seventy and one half. These withdrawals are generally based on your life expectancy. Your first withdrawal can be delayed until April 1 of the year following the year you reach age seventy and one half, but this may then require you to take two years' worth of withdrawals in that year.

A financial planner and your tax advisor, of course, can help you figure out which alternative meets your objectives, needs, and tolerance for risk.

The important point to understand here—as with all investments—is that there's no free lunch. Playing it safe, for example, usually brings lower returns; and obtaining current income often comes at the expense of capital growth.

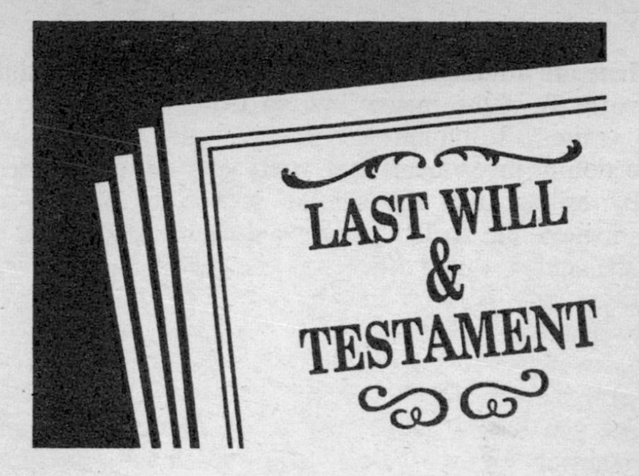

PART 8

YOUR ESTATE PLAN

- WHAT YOU NEED TO KNOW ABOUT ESTATE PLANNING

CHAPTER 29

WHAT YOU NEED TO KNOW ABOUT ESTATE PLANNING

People make thousands of plans for life, but sometimes none for death. Unfortunately, family and friends may pay the price for those who die without an estate plan.

For example, people who die without a will lose the opportunity to transfer their belongings and other assets to their intended beneficiaries. A longtime companion, say, might end up with nothing at all or far less than the deceased intended.

Worse yet, a poorly planned estate means added frustration and anguish for already distraught family members and friends.

A good estate plan will transfer your belongings and other assets efficiently to your beneficiaries. Insurance, wills, gifts, and trusts may all come into play.

A good place to start is with a *will*, which is the cornerstone of any estate plan. And that's where we start in this chapter.

Why do you need a will?

One way to drive home the importance of making a will is by examining how your estate would be divided if you died *intestate*—that is, without one.

A court in your home state would appoint someone to

divide your assets. In most cases, that person would be your surviving spouse. But should your spouse die before you, a court usually gives one of the children the authority to divide your property.

Fine, you say; but wait a minute. Your current spouse may not be fair to your children from a previous marriage. Also, trying to get two or more children to agree on managing an estate can lead to trouble—as anyone who has dealt with this delicate situation knows.

Even worse is the case where there's no relative to assume the responsibility of dividing your estate. In this instance, a court would appoint a public administrator, who would add your estate to the hundreds of others already under his or her management.

Then he or she would set about dividing your estate among your known living relatives. Your closest friends and associates would get nothing.

Worse still, if you leave behind a child under the age of eighteen, a court would appoint a legal guardian—and not necessarily someone of whom you would have approved.

Clearly, a will is vital.

Not only does it make sure that your children are cared for and assets are distributed to the right people, it speeds settlement and helps keep administrative costs low. Additional expenses that sometimes result from not having a will often stem from the extra steps that are needed to settle the estate without the benefit of directions in a will.

What does a will do?

A will divides your assets among your intended *beneficiaries*. Most wills contain two types of bequests—*specific* and *general*.

What is the difference between them?

With a specific bequest, you describe a particular item and name its intended recipient. You want to leave a certain necklace to your niece. So you describe the item—

"an eighteen-inch strand of pearls"—and list its recipient—"my niece, Rachel."

Or you want to leave $5,000 to a cousin, or stock worth about $25,000 to help see a grandchild through college. You might write in your will: "I leave to my cousin, John Edwards, $5,000 from my savings account (number 113-452-117) at the First National Bank of Smalltown." Similarly, "I leave my granddaughter, Molly, my 500 shares of Growth Corporation, Inc."

Specific bequests are—as the name implies—specific. And they always come first in a will. What about specific bequests of items with little monetary but great sentimental value? You may not want to include these in your will.

Instead, consider leaving your instructions for these items with one trusted person—a spouse, perhaps, or a sibling or good friend.

In a separate letter, spell out exactly who gets what. In most states, this letter is *nonbinding*, which means that your designated caretaker isn't legally bound to follow your instructions, although presumably the person you have chosen will carry out your wishes. But, in some states, such a letter is binding. (Your financial adviser will know the rules in your state.)

What writing these instructions separately does is save you the time and expense of revising your will each time you want to add or subtract a sentimental item.

Of course any changes you make in the distribution of major assets, such as money or property or valuable possessions, should be officially recorded in your will.

Now, on to general bequests.

General bequests don't spell out the source of the funds that you're giving away. You write: "I leave to my cousin, John Edwards, $5,000"; not: "I leave to my cousin, John Edwards, $5,000 from my savings account (number 113-452-117) at the First National Bank of Smalltown."

With general bequests, it's up your *executor*—the

person responsible for settling the affairs of the estate—to decide how bequests will be met. For example, he or she may decide not to withdraw money from your savings account to meet a bequest but sell some stock instead.

Once you subtract your specific and general bequests from your estate, what is left is known as your *residual estate*. Frequently, people make lists of bequests to friends and relatives, then specify that the residual estate be divided among their spouse and children.

Since all specific and general bequests—as well as taxes and debts—are paid out first, it's important to know the total value of your estate. Otherwise, those people nearest and dearest to you may end up getting shortchanged.

Something else you should know: gifts to charity may take the form of either specific or general bequests. You should list the amount of your donation and the recipient.

Some people choose to leave their favorite charity a gift of something other than cash—a plot of land, say, or shares of stock. You may want to, too.

Besides dividing your assets, your will should spell out who would get custody of your children in the event of your death. It should also name an executor, which is another decision that sometimes can lead to disputes and problems.

Parents of children under age eighteen should name a guardian in their will who will be responsible for the children's welfare.

It's important that you discuss the issue with whomever you appoint guardian. That person—or persons—must be aware of the responsibilities involved.

What if you're uncertain whom to appoint as guardian? You may designate a person in your will to make that decision in the event of your death.

The question of guardianship often changes as your children grow older. If you're the parents of small children, and your own parents are relatively young, they may be your first choice for guardians. But, at some point, your parents may become too old to shoulder that responsibility. That's the time to change your will and name someone else, such as a sibling or close friend.

There's one legal point to remember.

You may *not* choose a guardian for your child if the child's other natural parent is still alive. It doesn't matter that you're divorced or have full custody of the child. Courts always recognize the rights of a natural parent in guardianship cases.

When making out your will, state that the guardian of your child isn't required to file a bond, which in some states can come to $1,000 or more.

Naming an executor is almost as important as naming a guardian. An executor is responsible for managing your estate, distributing the assets as ordered in your will, filing your estate tax return, and, if necessary, making investment decisions.

You may name two executors if you like, or you may name your children's guardian as executor. The number isn't important. What is important is that you choose a person—or an institution—that you can trust to act wisely on your behalf.

Executors are often spouses, relatives, or close friends. If your estate is large, you may want to consider naming an attorney, or even a bank or trust company to act as executor. Or you may want to name both a bank and a relative as co-executors. That way, you make sure that the estate is looked after by a professional hand as well as a trusted personal one.

Executors are paid fees that are determined by individual state laws. They typically run from between 1 and 3 percent of the gross estate.

In some states, the fees double if you name two executors and triple if you name three. You may want to find out the rules of your state before you decide to name multiple executors.

What else do you need to know about wills?

You should know that wills come in three varieties: *witnessed wills*, *holographic wills*, and *statutory wills*. Witnessed wills—which are accepted in all fifty states—may be handwritten or typed, but they must be witnessed by two or three people, depending on local laws.

Most states accept a will that's witnessed by two people, but Connecticut, Georgia, Maine, New Hampshire, South Carolina, and Vermont require three witnesses.

A holographic, or handwritten will, must be dated, written, and signed in your handwriting only. It may not include any typed or printed material.

Holographic wills are accepted by only seventeen states: Arkansas, California, Iowa, Kentucky, Louisiana, Mississippi, Montana, Nevada, North Carolina, North Dakota, South Dakota, Tennessee, Texas, Utah, Virginia, West Virginia, and Wyoming.

A handful of states accept statutory wills. These wills are simply preprinted forms with instructions on how to fill them out.

They are available from your local bar association and also at many office supply stores. These wills are intended for people with modest and uncomplicated estates.

If your estate is moderate or large or at all complicated, it's wise to seek the help of a lawyer in drawing up your will.

If you do enlist the aid of an attorney—and we recommend that you do—you should provide him or her with all your vital statistics, including your full name, address, telephone numbers, Social Security number, and the same for your spouse, children, and other people in your will.

Also, he or she will need to know your complete marital history—the dates of former marriages, the names of your former spouses, children from these marriages, and so on—in order to see to it that there are no claims to your estate from those people.

You may want to ask your attorney to keep the original

draft of your will in his or her office. And you should keep a copy in a safe place that's known to your executor—or executors, if there's more than one. If you have a safe-deposit box, keep another copy there. The idea is that when you die, you don't want to make it difficult for the necessary people to find your will.

Most wills begin with an opening paragraph that identifies you, the *testator*, by name and lists your address. Also included is a sentence stating that you're knowingly making your last will and revoking all prior wills in your name.

The next paragraph usually directs your executor to pay your burial expenses, debts, and taxes. These bills are always paid ahead of your bequests.

You should know that unless you specify from which account you want your debts and taxes paid, they will automatically be charged, on a pro rata basis, against all bequests. That means that each of your heirs will shoulder a portion of those charges.

What about estate taxes?

In the two centuries since Benjamin Franklin pressed a quill against parchment, nothing has been certain in this country but death and taxes—usually higher taxes.

But, in recent years, many taxes—including those levied against the gifts we make and receive and the estates we leave and inherit—have decreased.

The tax law now allows almost all of us to keep more of what we inherit and what we receive as gifts. The methods that make this possible are varied. The principal method, however, is the *unified credit*. And that's where we start.

The unified credit applies to everyone. And it usually amounts to an exemption from gift and estate taxes for estates valued at $600,000 or less.

How does the credit work? Let's take a look. The unified credit is a device created to replace separate taxes levied on gifts and estates.

Simply stated, the value of gifts made during your lifetime—over and above the tax-free limit, which we get to shortly—is added to the total value of your estate when you die. The estate also considers gift taxes paid, if any. It's your executor's job to pay federal and state income, estate and inheritance taxes, and make all disbursements to beneficiaries named in your will.

An estate tax bill is computed, and if the bill is more than the unified credit—your heirs owe a tax on the excess. The unified credit now equals the previously untaxed amount of taxes that would be due on a $600,000 estate, which means that estates valued at $600,000 or less may be inherited federal-estate-tax-free.

You should remember that this credit is offset, first, by taxable lifetime gifts. Whatever part of the credit is left over can then be used to offset taxable inherited property. Here's a simplified example. In 1989, the credit is $192,800, and this means that $600,000 of otherwise estate taxable property can be deducted from an estate as an exemption.

So, if a widower, during his lifetime, gave his children $75,000 above the allowable amount of tax-free gifts, the children could later inherit $525,000 (a $600,000 estate minus $75,000 in gifts) free of further taxation.

The benefits of graduated rates and the unified credit are phased out for transfers in excess of $10 million. Ask your tax consultant about current gift and estate tax rate schedules.

Now, on to the unlimited marital deduction. The government allows you to leave your entire estate to your spouse, and no matter how large it is, the beneficiary—that is, your husband or wife—pays no federal estate taxes on it.

This rule doesn't mean that the IRS loses. On the contrary, it still will collect its due, but only after the death of the second marriage partner.

Deciding whether to capture the full advantage of the

unlimited marital deduction is an individual issue. And that's how it should be addressed.

Tax-wise at least, whether or not you should pass large amounts to a spouse under the unlimited marital deduction will depend on the following: The advantage of eliminating the estate tax on the property when the first spouse dies, with this tax to be paid at the time of the second spouse's death, versus the disadvantage of raising the second spouse's estate into a higher tax bracket at the time of his or her death.

What the unlimited marital deduction does, then, is postpone estate taxes during the life of the surviving spouse.

Warning: You should know that three major assets—IRAs, pension or profit-sharing plans, and annuities—have income tax consequences upon your death. The amount socked away in these plans will be taxed eventually, although your spouse does have deferral opportunities.

What else is involved in estate planning?

In addition to drawing up a will, estate planning involves taking a look at investments and assets to make sure that they are properly placed.

A common mistake is not leaving enough readily available money in an estate to pay the inheritance or estate taxes that survivors often face.

For example, a person may have a large amount of his or her estate tied up in the family home. Faced with sizable inheritance taxes, survivors may be forced to sell the house to obtain the cash necessary to pay the estate tax bill.

You can avoid this trap by gradually converting stocks, bonds, and property into cash investments as you grow older. You can also buy a life insurance policy that pays cash directly to a named beneficiary, then leave instructions on how this money is to be used.

Another potentially costly mistake involves people with estates valued at more than $600,000. As long as money passes from one spouse to the surviving spouse, the survivor pays no federal estate taxes—regardless of the size of the estate.

But when the surviving spouse dies, other heirs face paying a federal estate tax on the amount that exceeds $600,000.

One way you can avoid large tax bills is by setting up a *trust*, which is an arrangement for a third party (often a bank) to control assets for another person's benefit until a specified time.

Trusts can be used to transfer just about any asset to whomever you wish, with whatever restrictions you want to impose. In addition, some trusts can be used to reduce taxes, both currently and upon your death.

Among their advantages: they allow the transfer of assets without the money being subject to probate expenses; they can reduce or eliminate federal estate taxes and in many cases reduce your current income tax liability; and they allow money to pass to your heirs gradually or in installments instead of in one lump sum.

They also offer professional management of money, which can keep a spendthrift from blowing all his or her money in short order.

You've covered a lot of territory since picking up your copy of this book. You've been educated about your current financial situation, insurance protection products, accumulating wealth, doing income taxes, preserving wealth, and planning for retirement.

As we pointed out in the beginning of the book, there's still much more to know about the world of finance—volumes in fact, too unwieldy to include in one publication. But if you've read and digested all or part of this guide to financial planning, you're well on the way to being in control of your financial future.

We encourage you to take the next step by putting together your own financial plan. It's the only way we know of to make your financial dreams come true. Good luck!

INDEX